Britain's competitiveness

Britain's competitiveness

The Management of the Vehicle Components Industry

Christopher Carr

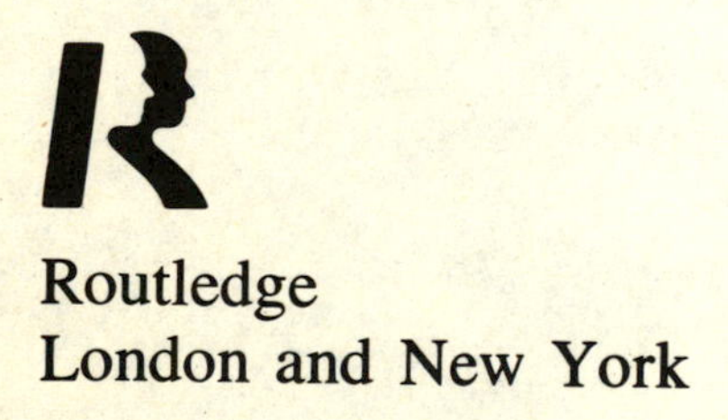

Routledge
London and New York

First published 1990
by Routledge
11 New Fetter Lane, London EC4P 4EE

Simultaneously published in the USA and Canada
by Routledge
a division of Routledge, Chapman and Hall, Inc.
29 West 35th Street, New York, NY 10001

Printed and bound in Great Britain by
Biddles Ltd, Guildford and King's Lynn

British Library Cataloguing in Publication Data

Carr, Christopher
Britain's Competitiveness: the Management
of the UK Components Industry
1. Great Britain. Industries. Competitiveness
I. Title
338.6: 048.0941

ISBN 0-415-00409-8

Contents

Figures and Tables

Figures

Tables

Foreword

The roots of this book date back fourteen years, to a decision on completion of my final economics examinations at Cambridge to continue my professional training as an engineer and to return to industry. Having worked in industry, studying economics kindled an interest in the issue of why British industry seemed to be failing to compete, and more importantly in what could be done about it. Yet once kindled this interest was scarcely quenched by studying economics.

Indeed the sheer generality of many theoretical approaches often seemed to preclude sufficient attention to many specific issues arising out of the unique contextual circumstances of British production. There were of course many instances of more practical approaches, such as my tutor C F Pratten's work in the field of international productivity comparisons, but somehow what was regarded as mainstream economics appeared to have sidestepped the issue of industrial competitiveness, an issue seemingly so central to Britain's needs: it was as if some impasse had been reached.

Whilst continuing to develop my academic interests, I therefore determined to make use of my early training by returning to industry as an engineer so as to see the problem from a participant's viewpoint. My early training, much of it supervised by Cambridge, involved visiting or working with about one hundred factories throughout the

UK and elsewhere in Europe and permitted a broad perspective. For the next five years I continued to work with GKN. For about half this time I was a development engineer on 'product and process development' in the area of forgings (one of the cases discussed in this book); for the other half as a project engineer on international projects, including GKN's project to establish, in liaison with German operations, manufacturing facilities for constant velocity joints in the USA. Only then, when I had attained qualifications as a Chartered Mechanical Engineer, in management studies, and in ICMA professional accountancy examinations, did I feel properly equipped to begin this study, a study of Britain's competitiveness, focused onto an important sector where my past experience can be of most use.

Although focused, this is not however yet another narrow study, of interest only to those closely concerned. The sector chosen is quite deliberately complex and large enough to be economically significant in itself; whilst yet being amenable to an examination of the specific competitor companies and countries. The case approach adopted is envisaged as providing a bridge between those studies of Britain's competitiveness which because of their generality are necessarily over-aggregated, and many case studies which tend to be too narrow to link back to any more general picture.

Research findings are bound to be influenced by the disciplinary approach of the researcher. Thus it is natural for an economist looking at the problem of the UK's declining industrial competitiveness to seek in this phenomenon lessons for economic policy. Similarly a marketing expert will seek lessons in terms of how British firms can improve their approaches to marketing. Indeed in reviewing contributions to this issue it is clear that every discipline (including those with engineering backgrounds such as my own) sees the issue primarily as one of its subject area. Methodologically such stances are particularly attractive, since in taking a single discipline approach it is possible to establish more rigorous tests of hypotheses. Yet from a policy perspective competitiveness is a multidimensional issue and a balanced multidisciplinary approach is essential, though this in practice precludes more quantitative methods.

The difference in perspective offered by this approach may be illustrated by a military analogy. Modern business competition is, in fact, very much like warfare. Doubtless, whether winning or losing, staff despatched to the front line would see highlighted lessons for particular functions. It would be possible to write treatises on how logistics for example could be improved, of general interest to anyone interested in that subject. However, a policy perspective attempts to take a commander's broad viewpoint. First, he wants some feel (through a balanced report with some quantitative back-up where appropriate) as to how the war is going. Are we winning or losing? How serious is the situation? Even establishing this may be no mean task. More importantly however, what are the key problems and therefore key requirements if the situation is to be improved? This is the perspective attempted here. Of course the commander may also wish to draw on those more specialist staff functions which seem likely to be of critical significance, but that entails a different perspective.

Unlike war though, decisions affecting business competitiveness are not made by any single commander but reflect decisions and choices made by many parties. The competitive situation of the automotive components sector is affected by choices made by the wider community (including government) which can considerably affect the climate for business, decisions by UK vehicle assemblers, and decisions within the component companies themselves from top level 'strategic decisions' right through to choices adopted on the shop floor by employees and labour unions. After studying the situation I have come to the view that each of these parties, in isolation, is quite helpless to deal with what appears to be a dangerous erosion of the country's competitiveness in this sector. Accordingly, this study simply attempts to describe the actual situation and underlying issues as accurately as possible. The target audience therefore is all these parties involved; it is hoped to contribute both to debate and ultimately to securing a more united response, without which it seems likely the UK will continue to decline.

Finally it has been most encouraging that the ESRC

sponsored workshop involving many industrial participants, 'SSRC Initiative on the Competitiveness and Regeneration of British Industry' (Russell Hotel, London, 17 October 1983), appears to have endorsed many of the specifications drawn up for this study. This called for research focusing on business sectors exposed to international competition, focused onto specific companies and specific competitor countries in particular Germany, Japan and the USA, and finally onto issues of particular concern to management. The emphasis in the business policy approach adopted is on how effective thinking on issues relating to business strategy can be improved.

Acknowledgements

I should like to thank all those organisations who have assisted in this study for their time and help. To reduce problems of confidentiality these are not listed. I am also particularly grateful to the Science Department at the British Embassy in Japan for organising my research programme in Japan.

I should like to thank the ESRC for funding my earlier doctoral study and the substantial overseas travel that this entailed, and Professor B.T Houlden at Warwick University for supervising this period of my research.

In compiling this book I should like to thank Mrs Elspeth Andrew in the Staff Office of the School of Management at Bath University and staff at the Computer Department, particularly Miles Osborne and Andrew Hunter.

Notes and Abbreviations

OE(M): original equipment (manufacturer(s))
AM: aftermarket

The main focus in this study has been on the OE situation, but a fairly broad perspective has been adopted recognising that OE and aftermarkets are highly interrelated. Similarly the term 'vehicle' generally refers to cars, but suppliers were also encouraged to discuss the commercial vehicle situation where appropriate, and many anyway did not distinguish the two activities.

In just a few cases, company names have been disguised. Thus UKF1 refers to a UK forging company, JF1, USF1 and GF1 to Japanese, US and German forging companies respectively. Subsequent numbers, as in UKF2 for example, denote further forging companies of the same nationality. UKS1 similarly refers to a UK silencer company, but there are no other products for which this has been necessary.

1
Britain's Competitiveness: Background to the Issue

The Historical Situation

The issue of British competitiveness today is deeply rooted historically. By the middle of the nineteenth century, Britain's major business sectors were the most internationally competitive the world has ever known: 'over 40% of the entire world output of traded manufactured goods [were] produced within the country' (Mathias, 1969, p. 250). Even this figure grossly understates Britain's domination of higher value-added business sectors at that time. 85% of visible exports were in the form of finished goods, whereas 92% (by volume) of imports represented raw materials. Britain was producing approximately two thirds of the world's coal, half its iron, five sevenths of its steel, two thirds of its hardware and about half of commercial cotton cloth (Kennedy, 1981, p20).

The history of Britain's subsequent decline is well documented. As the rest of the world began to develop, such a lead was of course to prove unsustainable. As industrial development took off elsewhere, Britain's growth in industrial production slowed - from 4% p.a. during 1820 - 1840, to 3% p.a. during 1840 - 1870 and just over 1.5% p.a. during 1875 - 1894, far less than its chief rivals. In the newer more important industries, such as steel, chemicals, machine tools and electrical goods, Britain quite rapidly lost what early lead it possessed. Also it was pushed back out of European and North American markets as other governments, with less vested interest (at that time) in free trade, developed their emerging industries behind protective tariff barriers.

German steel output, only half that of Britain in 1870,

was twice its size by 1910. However, alarm over the competitive situation felt in this and many other industrial sectors was to have little impact on those formulating policy. Other business sectors, many closer to government, held opposite interests. Businesses in the service sector, particularly those in the City but also industries such as shipping and shipbuilding, held opposite interests because of their involvement in the expanding activities of overseas rivals. Kennedy (1981, p.25) also argues that those involved in policy formulation 'did not usually concern themselves in any intimate way with economic trends, and frequently manifested an aristocratic scorn for business men'.

Indeed, as even countries well behind have since outpaced Britain, no adequate response to overseas competition appears to have been forthcoming at any point in Britain's subsequent history.' Britain's trade performance has steadily declined from 1900 to the present day (previously summarised in *Barclays Review*, 1983). Not only has Britain's share of world trade fallen, but import penetration has accelerated in recent years to the point where, for the first time this century, Britain is now running a deficit on trade in manufactured goods (previously examined comprehensively in the House of Lords Select Committee Report on Overseas Trade, 1985).

Britain's Post-War International Trade Situation

Britain is highly dependent on international trade, most of this being trade in manufactured goods. With the coming of North Sea Oil, manufactured goods have fallen only slightly as a percentage of all exports, from 80% in 1955 to 75% in 1980. As a percentage of all imports, manufactured goods have risen sharply over the same period, from 23% to 64%

Like other advanced countries', Britain's dependence on international trade has been growing. At the same time the trade position in the important manufacturing sector has deteriorated alarmingly as rising import penetration has rapidly outstripped the growth in exports, as shown in Table 1.1.

Table 1.1: Trade in manufactured goods 1955 - 1986

	1955	1965	1975	1980	1986
Imports/home demand %	8	11	22	26	34
Exports/mfr sales %	19	18	27	27	29

Source: Williams, Williams and Thomas (1983, pp.138-9). Figures for 1980 and 1986 from Annual Abstract CSO 1988 Table 12.2

A number of forces of course influence an economy's overall trade balance, and will anyway tend to keep the total position in equilibrium in the long run. However, since the trade balance has been a problem constraining the economy in the past, such trends if allowed to continue could pose serious problems in the future, particularly after North Sea Oil ceases to make such a positive impact.

More significant is the evidence of a decline in Britain's share of world exports of manufactures, in comparison to performances of other advanced competitor countries, as shown in Table 1.2. This point is less subject to qualification from international trade arguments.

Table 1.2: Division of world manufacturing exports %

Country	1955	1965	1970	1975	1980	1985
UK	20	14	11	9	10	8
Germany	15	19	20	20	20	19
France	9	9	9	10	10	9
Italy	3	7	7	7	8	8
USA	24	20	18	18	17	17
Japan	5	9	12	14	15	20

Source: Williams, Williams and Thomas (1983, pp. 116-7)
CSO Annual Abstract 1987 Table 12.2

UK manufacturing has been losing ground to other major competitor countries, particularly Japan and mainland Europe. After 1970 Japan continued to move ahead, but these figures suggest the situation otherwise began to stabilise. Britain, inevitably, fell back somewhat from its very strong position in the aftermath of the War and this factor may explain the decline also in the US position. Yet the extent to which decline persisted is disturbing, and the reversal of the UK and West German position suggests the problem was not merely one of an inability to sustain an unrealistically high share.

Concern over the issue of Britain's 'de-industrialisation' has given rise to much discussion (see particularly Blackaby, 1979). Although some have argued that manufacturing decline may be mitigated by the rise in services, Brown and Sheriff's paper showed that decline taking place in the main manufacturing business sectors did not merely reflect a switch to services, since as Table 1.3 indicates services have also displayed some decline in competitiveness, if slightly less sharp.

Table 1.3: Britain's share of trade in other sectors

	1955	1960	1965	1970	1975
Mfr'd goods %	20	16	14	11	9
Invisibles %	25	21	18	16	13
Services %	26	22	17	17	16

Source: Brown and Sheriff (in Blackaby, 1979)

Along with Singh (1977), Brown and Sheriff also argue that the UK economy is heavily dependent on manufacturing, since the net balance of payments contribution from services is relatively small.

Comparative Output Performance

I consider output levels and long-term sustained growth in output as significant indicators of competitive performance. From a general economic point of view Britain's level of output per capita has been lower than many rival countries, especially the USA as is shown in Figure 1.1.

Figure 1.1: GDP per capita $

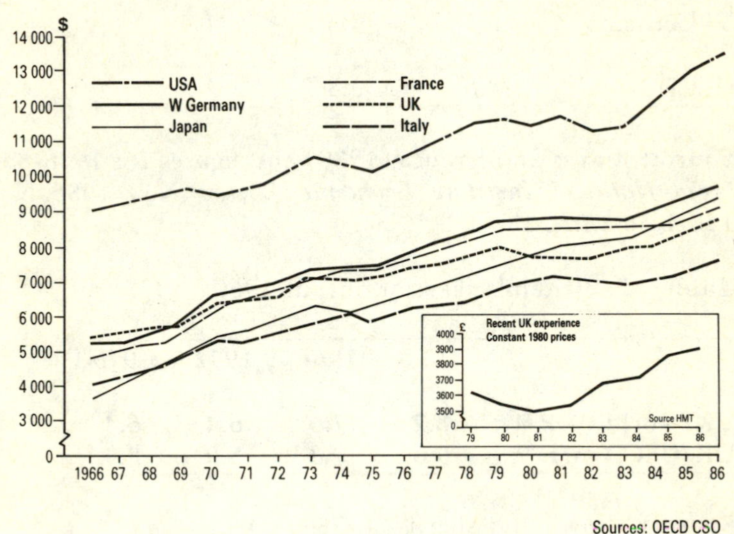

Exchange rate conversions - average rates for year given.

Source: British Industrial Performance & International Competitiveness over Recent Years, NEDO (1987a)

Table 1.4 shows Britain's economic growth has been consistently lower than competitor countries, though the gap has narrowed in recent years particularly as against the rest of Europe, partly because of more depressed conditions everywhere.
In consequence, Britain's share in world output has been gradually falling, but the decline of its share in manufacturing output has been particularly serious as indicated in Table 1.5.

Table 1.4: Average annual growth rates of GDP (%)

Country	1957-67	1967-78	1978-85
UK	3.1	2.3	1.4
USA	4.1	3.0	2.2
Japan	10.4	7.2	4.7
France	5.6	4.4	1.5
W Germany	5.5	3.8	1.7
OECD	4.8	3.8	2.3

Source: Caves and Krause (1980) and figures for 1978-85 from *National Institute Economic Review* Nov 1986 No 118 4/86 Table 18

Table 1.5: Britain's share of output 1960 - 1975

	1960	1966	1972	1975
UK/world GDP %	8.2	7.6	6.4	6.4
UK/OECD mfr %	9.6	7.3	5.9	5.8

Source: Brown and Sheriff (1978)

In recent years, as Table 1.6 demonstrates, Britain's manufacturing output has fallen even further behind.

Profitability and Investment

Sustained business growth depends upon profitability, which appears to have been lower in the case of UK manufacturing than for rival countries.

Given the UK's relatively high levels of inflation and its consequently high cost of finance, such levels of profitability seem unsatisfactory and may have contributed to the poor investment record indicated in Table 1.8.

Table 1.6: Manufacturing output growth 1970 - 1985

	1970	1973	1975	1979	1981	1983	1985
USA	100	122	109	144	142	140	161
Japan	100	128	109	145	160	164	190
EEC							
exc UK	100	115	108	128	125		
of which:							
Germany	100	113	103	122	119	117	126
France	100	122	114	136	125	127	128
Italy	100	114	107	131	136	127	134
UK	100	111	102	106	91	94	101

Source: Begg and Rhodes (1982) and figures for 1983 and 1985 from OECD cited in *Financial Times* 30 March 1987

Table 1.7: Net rates of return in manufacturing

Average per period	UK	USA	W Germany
1960-71	13	30	23
1972-75	8	21	16
1976-79	6	22	17
1980-84	6	11	13

Net return is defined as net operating surplus as % of net capital stock of fixed assets (excluding land).

Source: Begg and Rhodes (1982) and figures for 1980-84 from OECD National Accounts Vol II 1972-1984

Table 1.8: Investment per head in manufacturing (ECU)

UK	Belgium	Holland	Italy	France	Germany
72	86	96	64	106	155

Source: Begg and Rhodes (1982) Figures from *Eurostat Review*, 1970-79

The issue of the UK's low economic growth has been widely discussed at the broader economic level (for example Beckerman, 1979), but there is recognition that competitive problems have been deep rooted and require analysis at the more micro-level.

Productivity

One reason underlying poor performance appears to be Britain's relatively poor productivity. Labour productivity has improved, as is shown in Table 1.9, but not as much as elsewhere.

Table 1.9: Growth in output/person/hour in manufacturing 1976-1985, % p.a.

UK	France	Germany	Italy	USA	Japan
2.8	4.0	3.1	3.4	3.5	4.5

Source: *National Institute Economic Review* No. 118 4/86

In relative terms there has been a substantial productivity gap and this has yet to be bridged, as shown in Table 1.10.

Table 1.10: Relative output/person/hour in manufacturing

	1973	1980	1984	1986
UK	100	100	100	100
France	160	193	179	184
Germany	190	255	232	178
Italy	154	173	156	155
USA	287	273	262	267
Japan	144	196	177	176

Source: NIESR: 1973 figures quoted in *Financial Times* 30 November 1987, 1980-86 figures quoted in *Financial Times* 28 May 1987

Table 1.11 shows that capital productivity is also well below that achieved by overseas rivals.

Table 1.11: Relative capital productivity

UK	France	Germany	USA	Japan
100	170	190	207	208

Source: 'Whose really most productive?', *Sunday Times* 29 March 1987 p.73

Cost Levels

Relative cost levels depend both on productivity differentials and on relative wage rates, which in turn depend on two factors: first, any changes in relative rates of inflation expressed in terms of domestic currencies, and second any changes in exchange rates. Figure 1.2 shows trend changes in UK wage costs compared with overseas rivals after making both adjustments. (Statistics from different countries are on different bases, so Figure 1.2 does not purport to show absolute wage differentials at any particular point in time, but trend changes which are of more significance are reflected fairly accurately.)

Up until 1979 UK earnings rates had been falling consistently compared with most rivals, offsetting a relatively poor productivity performance and keeping relative cost levels reasonably in line. In 1980 an unprecedented rise in the inflation adjusted exchange rate meant that UK earnings rates rose substantially in relative terms, exposing the effects of poor productivity and undermining cost competitiveness. Since then the inflation adjusted exchange rate has fallen back and the cost position has improved substantially in relation to most countries.

Table 1.12 gives a more accurate picture of absolute wage differentials and shows unit labour costs after allowing for productivity differentials in 1980 after the substantial rise in the inflation-adjusted exchange rate in 1980, and more recently in 1986.

Figure 1.2: Earnings trends in UK compared with overseas

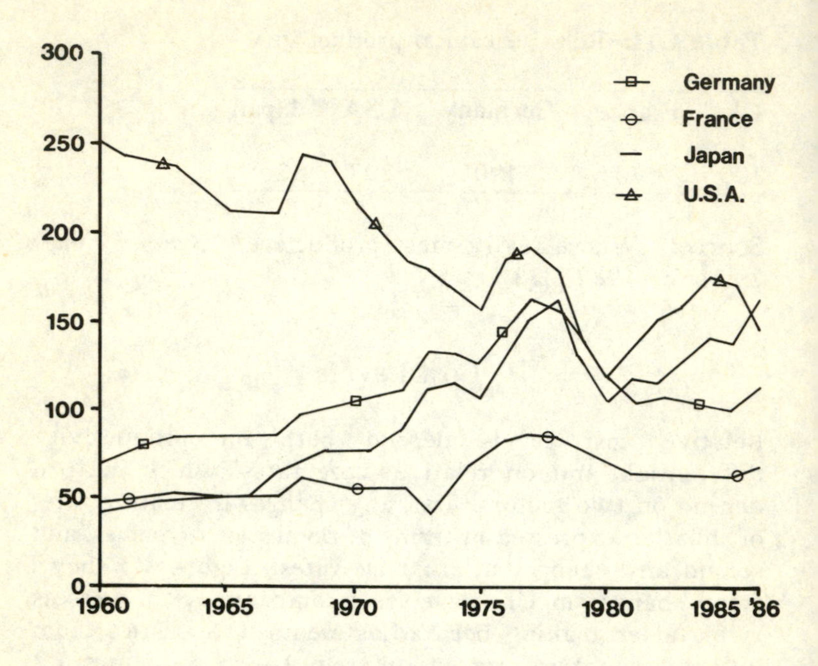

Source: UN Monthly Bulletin of Statistics for earnings rates indices and CSO for average yearly exchange rates

Table 1.12: Hourly and unit labour costs (UK=100)

	Total hourly labour costs		Unit labour costs	
	1980	1986	1980	1986
UK	100	100	100	100
France	80	129	63	66
Germany	165	173	65	97
Italy	108	127	62	82
USA	126	161	46	60
Japan	80	129	41	73

Source: NIESR, quoted in *Financial Times* 28 May 1987

Industry Sectors

Tables 1.13 A and B suggest that competitive decline among major manufacturing sectors has been widespread, but has been a particular problem in engineering industries (electrical, mechanical, instruments, and vehicles) and also textiles, leather goods, clothing and footwear.

Table 1.13A: UK import penetration %

Year	1970	1980	1986
Chemicals	15	20	27
Metal mfr.s	16	29	36
Mech' eng'	14	19	25
Instr' eng'	23	33	40
Elec' eng'	14	23	33
Vehicles	7	28	41
Metal goods	5	10	14
Textiles	12	26	36
Leather gds	16	31	36
Clothing etc	11	25	31
Food, drink	18	14	17
Timber, furn	26	26	30
Paper, print'	18	17	19
Office m/c.	52	52	56

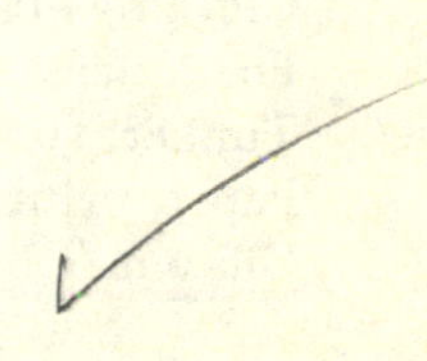

Import penetration is defined as imports (c.i.f.) / home demand + exports. Sectors as defined by SIC codes.

Source: Barclays Review, November 1983 (based on Business Monitors) and CSO Annual Abstracts (Table 12.2)

Literature giving more detailed attention to particular sectors often suggests the decline is far more serious than is revealed in such aggregated statistics: examples include motorcycles (Boston Consulting Group, 1975), portable power tools and typewriters (Prais, 1981), textiles (Toyne, Arpan, Ricks, Shimp and Barnett, 1984), telecommunications (NEDO, 1978). Other examples of sectors which have virtually collapsed include cameras, cash registers, colour televisions dishwashers, busses, shipbuilding, and more recently trucks, bicycles and helicopters also seem close to the brink. Together such industries represent a major proportion of the country's manufacturing infrastructure.

Table 1.13B: UK export sales ratios %

Year	1970	1980	1986
Chemicals	21	31	35
Metal mfr.s	13	15	25
Mech' eng'	29	36	32
Instr' eng'	32	37	29
Elec' eng'	19	27	28
Vehicles	30	28	20
Metal goods	12	13	11
Textiles	17	22	19
Leather gds	20	22	23
Clothing etc.	10	14	13
Food, drink	3	9	9
Timber, furn	2	5	4
Paper, print	6	9	9
Office m/c.	47	45	44

Export / sales are defined as exports (f.o.b.) / manf' sales + imports

Source: Barclays Review, November 1983 (based on Business Monitors) and CSO Annual Abstracts (Table 12.2)

Analysis directed at specific UK industry sectors, such as Boston Consulting Group (1975) in the case of motorcycles, seems to get closer to the heart of Britain's problems of competitiveness than more broadly based economic studies. As more recent studies of global industry competition have increased in sophistication (e.g. Toyne, Arpan, Ricks, Shimp and Barnett, 1984), so have the opportunities for understanding competitive issues facing manufacturers in various countries. This study extends and develops this sort of approach, specifically to examine the issue of Britain's competitiveness, and to establish what can be done.

Clarification of the Issue

One problem in facing up to the issue of competitiveness is that the term has been abused to mean almost anything: so much so in fact, that some politicians have even been able to claim credit for virtually solving the critical problem of competitiveness, a proposition which does not easily reconcile with the facts so far presented. Clarification of the issue of competitiveness requires some definition or concept which recognises the problem both at the economic level and also at the business level.

Competitiveness broadly refers to the ability of a business, group of businesses or indeed a country's economy as a whole, to sustain future growth. At the level of the firm, competitiveness may be defined by a business's sustainable growth rate relative to actual or likely competitors. This same definition can also be extended to a group of businesses such as a business sector in a given country, or indeed to the group of business sectors in a country comprising its economy, in which case the issue is one of economic growth relative to that of rival countries.

At all levels the concept of sustainability is important, because it is this that rules out superficial analysis and forces deeper examination of fundamental factors underlying the strength or weakness of an economy or of a particular business. In either area, it is not difficult to obtain a temporary boost to performance. Demand policy can stimulate faster economic growth in the short-term, and this incidentally can improve the immediate prospects even of businesses or whole business sectors facing underlying competitive problems. Similarly a company in a weak position can even succeed in increasing market share for a short while. The problem in all these cases however reduces to sustainability. If the underlying position is weak, a business will ultimately have to concede further growth as weaknesses show up in areas such as finance and, at a higher level, economic growth will inevitably suffer as soon as bottlenecks of one type or another begin to make themselves felt.

In the long-term of course, the effect of competitiveness shows up in the growth of living standards (or real wage levels) that is sustainable, either for those working in a business or more generally in relation to the living standards available to people or workers in a given country. Again the key word is sustainable: it may not be difficult to obtain a temporary boost to living standards by pillaging the investment or ploughback on which competitiveness depends. This creates a paradox. Undue increases in immediate living standards will almost certainly undermine competitiveness; yet we should not lose sight of the whole objective of improved competitiveness which is to increase not reduce living standards and real wage levels in the longer-term. Such confusion can be avoided if we distinguish carefully between short-term and longer-term issues. Competitiveness in this longer-term sense seems closer to the challenge presented here, if Britain is finally to grapple with its most fundamental problems, problems that have been ongoing for a century or so.

Yet, it also seems that the issue presented by competitiveness can pose problems that can rapidly become highly acute: it is more than merely a matter of gently slipping behind rivals. What makes this so is that the intensity of competition generally appears to advance relentlessly in the longer-term, though short-term cyclical effects may sometimes result in some temporary amelioration.

At sector level there is already concern that in some cases falling behind rivals has already become an issue of survival: as competitive conditions intensify it is of course those who are marginally less competitive who are the first to go. Finally, at the level of the firm the dangers of falling behind rivals in terms of relative growth (loss of market share) have been widely recognised, since at some point the cost position usually becomes untenable because of the 'experience' effect (Hedley, 1976). In discussing the cases of corporate collapse Argenti (1976b) argues that the problem often 'steals up unawares', with intensifying competition finally making its mark either in an unanticipated price war or in the next business downturn.

A similar threat faces Britain at the broader economic

level. So far Britain's relative decline has been associated with generally rising living standards. The same level of relative performance, if continued in conditions of increasingly intense international competition, risks declining living standards at some point, an altogether less comfortable phenomenon and one that could threaten the social fabric.

The degree of seriousness with which policy makers in Britain regard the issue of competitiveness in the face of other policy trade-offs, will of course depend on views on particular issues, such as whether North Sea Oil can be counted on to provide acceptable living standards in the long-term, if the competitive position of major business sectors is not safeguarded. It is even possible that limited trade-offs might be necessary against other desirable economic targets such as controlling inflation, though of course policies with major inflationary consequences would almost certainly be unsustainable and hence counterproductive.

It is important to maintain a sense of direction and a proper perspective of what is happening in the real economy, rather than pursuing merely the symbols of economic management. In the context of a century of almost continuous competitive decline, problems such as inflation and the balance of payments (though by no means trivial) have always come and gone. There is a danger of policy makers becoming obsessed with merely the symptoms of a more deep-rooted disease, which (though understandably less tractable in terms of more familiar policy instruments) may nevertheless continue unabated.

Yet ultimately the problem does not merely lie with policy makers. It is also up to people more generally to decide how seriously to take the problem of competitiveness. It is they who stand to suffer lower living standards or unemployment, and it is they who will feel the effects if other desirable policy targets have to be temporarily sacrificed in order to tackle the problem. Nevertheless appropriate choices, just as appropriate decisions, call for greater understanding. The principles behind competitiveness can be understood by anyone and, as the next chapter attempts to show, without the need for jargon.

2
Achieving Competitiveness: Fundamental Principles

Traditionally competitiveness was discussed mainly in terms of economics. Economic factors can contribute substantially through producing a more favourable business environment. Yet any benefit will be wasted if critical issues at a company level remain unresolved and internationalisation, in particular, has increased the importance of also paying commensurate attention to the question of how competitiveness can be improved at this level.

This is so for two reasons. First, the economic environment is increasingly determined at an international level: the scope for influencing this at a purely national level has become more marginal as world economies become more interdependent. Second, as most of the major wealth-creating business sectors have become more concentrated internationally, countries such as Britain have found themselves squeezed out in sector after sector, not only because of poor economic choices but also because of inadequate strategies and policies in a relatively small number of companies. Merely tampering with macro-economic choices can not offset the effect of the resultant loss of so large a proportion of the country's wealth creating capability.

Achieving competitiveness calls for a systems approach. No one would dream of trying to design a world class racing bicycle by having one team working on the framework and another working on the wheels as if they were isolated problems; yet the policies which affect the competitiveness of British businesses are influenced by two relatively isolated groups whose perspectives are difficult to reconcile - economists with an understanding of the framework of the economy, and business orientated people with an understanding of the wheels of industry.

Improving competitiveness calls for an approach which effectively integrates the relevant principles from the fields of both economics and of business, particularly with respect to the emerging field of business strategy, and the main principles to be discussed in this chapter are summarised in Figure 2.1.

Figure 2.1: Principles for achieving competitiveness

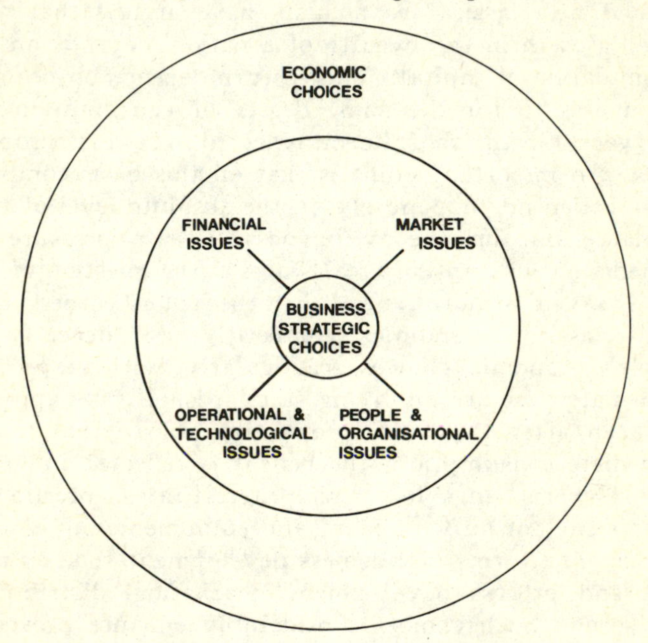

Economic Principles

Classical Economics

The complexity of modern economics has tended to eclipse the principles through which people can if they wish improve competitiveness. There is an alternative to continuing decline which is not some act of God, but in part at least an act of choice.

Some of the most powerful economic principles for improving competitiveness were already laid down in classical economics. We should not lose sight of these essentially simple principles, in reviewing more recent ideas; nor should we forget that Britain's pre-eminent international competitive position at the end of the last century was associated not with the complex array of economic policy instruments available today, but with an adherence to essentially lassez faire economic principles advocated by classical economists.

Adam Smith in his 'Wealth of Nations' and later classical and neo-classical economists have argued that sustained growth in the 'wealth of a nation' depends on the accumulation of capital. This in turn depends on people's willingness to forsake some degree of consumption (or real wages) in the short-term, reflected in savings propensities. An important point is that on this basis competitiveness depends not merely on the absolute level of performance but on the willingness to ease pressure on immediate consumption (real wages): the question of the penny saved' is more crucial than the 'pound earned'.

In classical economics competitiveness depends on people's economic choices, particularly with respect to immediate pressure on living standards. If, as happened in Japan after the War, people are prepared to forego immediate consumption, the benefit is reflected in lower costs, higher savings, lower real interest rates, encouraging investment not only in plant and equipment, but also in less tangible forms of business development such as product and process development, marketing, distribution and so on. Such choices considerably enhance prospects for sustained growth.

A problem for many countries is that people and their representatives tend to be myopic as to the effect of immediate choices on future growth in living standards - a problem exacerbated as political representatives seek to outbid each other in terms of what they can offer to the electorate. Divisions may also undermine any common effort to safeguard the future.

If pressure on immediate living standards (real wage levels) becomes too high classical economics suggests the result will be reduced 'voluntary unemployment', accompanied by lower output and thus reduced competitiveness. People's preferences may push up real wage levels. Transmitted via the price mechanism increased competition will squeeze out marginal business projects (even conceivably whole business sectors), thus raising the marginal product of remaining labour until it matches the new real wage level. Marginal employees are rendered uncompetitive in the labour market and so become unemployed. Thus unemployment, although in itself a serious problem, is really only an extreme manifestation of a lack of commitment in people's economic choices to competitiveness.

Prospects for future growth will also be undermined if economic choices contribute to a decline in the balance of international trade. This is particularly evident when such choices lead directly or indirectly to an unduly high exchange rate, but the underlying problem may again be one of real wage pressure.

Evidence on UK import and export elasticities (Dornbusch and Fischer, 1980) does not contradict international trade arguments that after allowing for some initial adverse impact due to the 'J' curve, a falling exchange rate would make British business sectors more internationally competitive, other things being equal. However the crucial problem, which has led to some disillusionment at the Bank of England, with respect to exchange rate policy, is that wage demands in recent years have taken into account the inflationary impact of devaluation, so as to negate any improvement in the relative cost position within a few years. If so, the underlying problem may again be undue pressure on real wage levels: once again the effect will be to price out marginal business activities, particularly in sectors highly exposed to international trade.

Thus whilst reduced pressure on immediate real wage levels enhances competitiveness, undue pressure on the other hand not only damages competitiveness, but will also tend to lead to increased unemployment and a deterioration in the international trade position.

However, government's most constructive role (apart from urging people to moderate real wage demands) is viewed as one of non-intervention. According to this argument, government should not create distortions by attempting to support businesses or business sectors advancing their particular vested interests. Many organisations would naturally seek conditions which by reducing competition offer the possibility of easy profits. As well as creating allocative distortions, this would merely lead to greater complacency, damaging future prospects. The same argument would also apply to the question of protection from international competition. Indeed, government should if necessary take active steps to prevent any such group (including trade unions) seriously jeopardising the effective functioning of the market mechanism.

Vigorous competition is important. Accumulation of capital has been high in many communist countries as a result of central planning, yet in stifling competition such bureaucratic and monopolistic systems have produced relatively poor results; Japan's success on the other hand reflects vigorous internal competition as well as a willingness to save and invest.

Keynes

Keynes' 'General Theory', whilst in large part accepting the classical 'equilibrium' model and its assumptions, nevertheless demonstrated that rigidities, in the way in which economic systems actually operate in the real world, could result in disequilibrium phenomena not allowed for in classical theory: because of this there is a case in certain circumstances for a degree of more pragmatic intervention by government, so as to sustain the level of aggregate demand.

In the absence of such intervention 'involuntary unemployment' could arise (accompanied of course by marginal business activities unnecessarily being rendered uncompetitive), without accurately reflecting people's true preferences in terms of the trade-off they wished to make between real wages and the prevention of unemployment.

> Men are involuntarily unemployed if, in the event of a small rise in the price of wage-goods

> relatively to the money-wage, both the aggregate supply of labour willing to work for the current money-wage and the aggregate demand for it at that wage would be greater than the existing volume of employment.
> Keynes (1936)

It will be noticed that if in fact real wage demands were not flexible, unemployment could not be described as 'involuntary' and there would be no case for government intervening to restore aggregate demand. In the context of the 1930s, with price levels in fact falling, Keynes did not believe wage bargaining reflected pressure by labour for any general level of real wages but felt that it was a process directed merely at protecting relative real wage differentials.

> In other words, the struggle about money-wages primarily affects the distribution of the aggregate real wage between different labour groups and not its average amount per unit of employment, which as we shall see depends on a different set of forces. The effect of combination on the part of a group of workers is to protect their relative real wage. The general level of real wages depends on the other forces of the economic system.
> (Keynes, 1936, p.14)

Keynes clarified how his policies would affect the level of real wages if they were to be successful. As output increased (as a result of demand policies) Keynes agreed with the classical assumption that this would result in a decline in the marginal productivity of labour, and since he too maintained the assumption that this was equated to the real wage it followed that the real wage would also fall. Indeed he stressed that demand policies were precisely the mechanism by which labour could be assisted to achieve the reduction in the real wage necessary to restore full employment equilibrium, in the context of difficulties in the wage bargaining process such as differentials and the consequent stickiness of money wages.

> So long, indeed, as this proposition holds, any means of increasing employment must lead at the same time to a diminution of the marginal product of labour and hence of the rate of wages measured in terms of this product.
> (Keynes, 1936, pp.17,18)

Keynes was aware that any attempt by government to use demand policy to deal with 'voluntary unemployment' (i.e. where the general level of real wages was genuinely inflexible), would be inappropriate and merely lead to inflationary problems.

In summary, according to Keynes governments could and should intervene, through the use of demand policy, to prevent unnecessary unemployment (or marginal business activities being unnecessarily made uncompetitive), but *only* so far as people were genuinely prepared to relax demands on the *general* level of real wages. In such circumstances, Japan's more pragmatic demand policies in recent years appear to have helped in maintaining output growth and employment, but have not given rise to inflation.

Keynesians and the Monetarist Backlash

Macro-economic policies reflecting Keynes' ideas were used fairly successfully by many countries to stimulate growth and employment until about the 1960s. Inevitably however, governments increasingly succumbed to the temptation of using demand policies less sensitively than Keynes envisaged to maintain full employment, even beyond the point where people were really prepared to accept a fall in the general level of real wages.

Sustained full employment after the War naturally led employees and unions to the feeling that the traditional trade-off between wage demands and unemployment (expressed in the Phillips curve relationship, which even many economists were coming to doubt) no longer applied. Increasingly wage targets came to be set in real, and not merely in monetary, terms as people became more aware of the retail price index. But the apparent success in employment terms of Keynesian policies came at the price of increased inflation. The problem arose that the initial benefit of Keynesian demand policies seemed to come through effectively frustrating people's attempts to gain higher real wages. Although money wages were successfully increased, so long as government sustained adequate monetary demand, companies restored acceptable profit margins by increasing price levels. Since the result was merely to frustrate underlying demands with respect to real wage increases, this contributed to a vicious circle of spiraling inflation.

Demand policies, as Keynes would have anticipated, became gradually less effective, since real wage flexibility was no longer the case. From an immediate policy viewpoint the problem was that an increasing proportion of any injection of aggregate demand was becoming dissipated in price rather than output increases, plus the fact that at some level inflation had anyway to be brought under control.

The inevitable neo-classical backlash, urging an end to Keynesian policies, was supported by research into the longer-term implications of governments increasing the money supply (most notably by Milton Friedman). The adoption of monetarism by Britain and some other countries in 1979 was essentially, a return to the more extreme classical position of non-intervention. Keynes' own arguments, having been tarnished by the same accusation of inflation, which no doubt applied to later so called Keynesian policies, were then ignored. The new emphasis on securing more stable longer-term conditions was in itself potentially beneficial to competitiveness, yet it also caused two immediate problems.

First, the shift away from a broadly expansionary stance in fiscal policy had an immediate deflationary effect, reinforcing the impact of the world downturn following the oil price hike in 1979. Such a shift was particularly marked in Britain but also occurred to a lesser extent in other countries and was reflected, for example, in priorities established at the 1979 summit conference of the major industrial nations. Demand for goods rapidly contracted, following a path similar to the step-down multiplier process described by Keynes and this was accentuated by destocking. Second, employees were slow to anticipate the effect of monetary policy on price levels, company profit margins, and on the real value of wage increases sought, and they were anyway frequently reluctant to acknowledge the trade-off between real wage increases and unemployment. Profits plunged and falling investment reduced demand for goods still further.

Marginal business activities were hit hard, particularly in Britain, and this led to a rise in unemployment even more severe than elsewhere. Britain's internationally exposed sectors were particularly affected because, in such circumstances the emphasis on monetary policy simultaneously led to a rise in real interest rates, and contributed to an unprecedented rise in the exchange rate.

The debate between post-War Keynesians and monetarists advocating a return to classical economics is clearly still highly contentious, but on balance both extremes appear to have something to learn from each other. The over-use of demand policy, beyond the point envisaged by Keynes himself, where labour is really prepared to relax pressure on the general level of real wages, has often encountered problems such as inflation and may have been counterproductive in some cases (e.g. France's experience in the early 1980s). Yet the processes described by Keynes are still very much in evidence, and where there is greater real wage flexibility such as in the USA, demand policies do appear to play a part in reviving business conditions conducive to growth.

The American experience would seem to confirm the views economists such as Layard (1986) that more can be done to revive demand levels and employment. However the danger in expecting too much from government is that this encourages people to forget that the major contribution must come from their own genuine willingness to reduce pressure on immediate consumption. So far such a message has been politically unsellable. Unions have tended to prefer to blame successive Conservative governments for unemployment, rather than accepting any trade-off in the living standards of members actually in work. Neither do any of the major political parties wish to face up to such an unpopular trade-off. In the 1987 election all, whilst professing to make unemployment the main priority, nevertheless emphasised their own offerings in terms of further immediate consumption, either in the form of additional public services or private consumption through the promise of further cuts in personal taxation.

Without consensus on the need to moderate demands on immediate consumption (in whatever form) some of Layard's newer ideas, such as tax incentives aimed at reducing the inflationary consequences of stimulatory demand policies, would probably prove unworkable. Yet if a greater degree of consensus were forthcoming, demand policy by government could well play some limited role.

To produce conditions conducive to growth and competitiveness, government needs to be sensitive to context. If wages and working practices are inflexible and inflation is high, government may have little choice but to adopt more conservative demand policies which at least contribute to restoring lower inflation. Ultimately this offers the benefit of more stable conditions, but care should be taken to avoid sudden policy shifts which may exacerbate a downward spiral in the level of demand for goods. In the right conditions, demand policy by government probably can play some limited role just as it has in America; but the primary responsibility for restoring competitiveness lies with people themselves, in their willingness to forego if necessary more immediate improvements in living standards.

The Role of Industrial Policy

Several economists, concerned with Britain's competitive needs, have attacked both classical and Keynes' theoretical models as artificial and have argued for more pragmatic intervention.

Frank Hahn, a leading theorist, warns that many assumptions within even modern, more sophisticated 'equilibrium' models of the economy are inappropriate to the real world of policy making. He warns that 'the vulgarisations of most text-books of economics are both scientifically and politically harmful' (Blackaby, 1979, p.140). Keynes' assumptions are subject to the same reservations.

Indeed having reviewed 'The British Economic Crisis', Smith (1984, p.183) concludes the main problem is that too much reliance on economic policies based on such over-general theoretical approaches has distracted policy makers' attention from other real and urgent problems:

> But policy interventions of that type seem to offer little in the face of the problems outlined in the first section of this book. These problems are specific ones concerning manufacturing performance, and the R & D, investment, engineering and education inputs to that performance. Keynesian policies of demand management are aimed elsewhere; they are pitched at an abstract level which brackets out the specific problems of industrial organisation which face Britain.

For this reason it is necessary to explore such problems directly, without relying on policy panaceas derived from the highly abstract preoccupations of theoretical economics. It is not that theoretical economics is not important, not a worthwhile and necessary activity. It is simply that it is time for politicians and others to stop thinking that it can offer simple answers. The government should be guided by 'more realistic assessments of our future prospects, and the mechanisms that have made them so bleak' (Smith, 1984, p.200) and should be prepared to take direct action at the more specific industrial level; it could also afford to be more pragmatic in terms of more general economic policy.

An example of this approach is Japanese industrial policy, where a number of successes have hinged on specifically rejecting general economic arguments adhered to in the West. Smith (1984, p.220) cites Mr Y. Ojima, Vice-Minister for International Trade and Industry, as stating that it was

> decided to establish in Japan industries which require intensive employment of capital and technology, industries that in consideration of comparative costs of production should be the most inappropriate for Japan, industries such as steel,

> oil refinery, petrochemicals, automobiles, aircraft, industrial machinery of all sorts, and electronics including electronic computers. From a short-run static viewpoint, encouragement of such industries would seem to conflict with economic rationalism. But from a long-range viewpoint, these are precisely the industries where ... demand is high, technological progress is rapid, and labour productivity rises fast.

The Japanese have not in fact ignored the major economic principles (already discussed) conducive to competitiveness, but they have recognised the danger in taking theoretical economic models too far. The Achilles Heel of course is the lack of any long-range vision of where the economy is going. Keynes' classic dictum, that 'in the long run we are all dead', is scarcely satisfactory if the longer-term issue of declining competitiveness is really to be addressed. Policy advisors in Britain seem to have been obsessed with relatively short-term disequilibrium problems, such as inflation, the balance of payments and unemployment, whilst neglecting the underlying long-term problems experienced by business sectors suffering competitive decline. Japan's sense of direction on the other hand reflects an over-riding priority to the long run growth and competitiveness of critical business sectors. Britain should not overlook the major economic principles so far discussed, but it may need to recover a similar sense of longer-term direction.

Broader Economic and Social Issues

To understand why such relatively straightforward principles so essential to competitiveness have not been put into practice, we must recognise the way in which, again and again, British attitudes and institutions have led to the profitability and competitiveness of businesses being sacrificed on the alter of other goals.

Many economists examining decline have found evidence of this broader problem (Glyn and Harrison, 1980; Eatwell, 1982; Williams, Williams and Thomas, 1983;

and Pollard, 1982). Pollard notes the generalist background and affinity of those in many institutions such as the Treasury, which predispose them towards general policy measures: indeed he sees them as almost addicted to the more 'symbolic' goals of economic management. Attitudes of many involved in the political decision-making process, he argues, are inherently geared to the short-term and still reflect a contempt for what is happening in specific business sectors. The contempt for what is happening at the level of production also extends he feels to unions, who having lost confidence in their company's ability to win future business are ambivalent about ensuring companies keep ahead in terms of production developments aimed at maximising efficiency.

The linkage of British economic decline and 'generalist' attitudes has been noted by Wiener (1981) as an almost cultural phenomenon, deeply rooted in history and in the educational system. Moreover Dahrendorf (1982) links Britain's poor economic performance to the traditional cultural virtue of tolerance. Alas, it seems that tolerance extends equally to a rather complacent acceptance of allowing the competitiveness of businesses to become eroded. Certainly a cursory inspection of Britain's history suggests that the country has not always been exactly tolerant of its more committed leaders, until situations have actually reached crisis point, from Clive of India to Churchill. It might appear that the other face of 'tolerance' is a certain contempt for 'commitment', that is until crises finally jolt the British people into responsiveness.

Britain's lack of commitment to the rapid development of its business sectors also of course reflects the greater priority afforded to other goals doubtless laudable in themselves. Crucial investment has been crowded out by consumption, partly through real wage levels being too high and partly through resources going into public services which have only at best an indirect effect on assisting business competitiveness. The government sector has been used to soak up unemployment. Choices in particular policy areas, such as housing subsidies and mortgage tax relief, non-repayable student grants, the welfare state generally, have had a significant effect. All this has been reflected in the cost and availability of funding for productive investment.

The argument is broadly summed up in Bacon and Eltis (1978): the productive sector of the economy (defined essentially as businesses in the free market sector of the economy) is seen as having been critically weakened by a premature dissipation of resources into other activities, the public sector in particular. It is of course a question not merely of whether the UK diverts more resources than other rivals such as Germany into housing, education or the public sector, but of timing; for premature moves in this direction may have damaged the competitiveness of our business sectors so that they are now too weak to support the weight of other activities which they are required to bear.

Yet these issues may be summarised as further manifestations of a lack of sensitivity to the position faced by Britain's business sectors, in the face of other policy priorities. The car industry provides a well documented example of the damage wrought through changes in taxation and hire purchase conditions and through dispersion policies, as governments have subordinated the industry in pursuit of other objectives (Dunnet, 1980). The additional 10% tax levy imposed on the industry has still not been removed.

In such a light, many of the chronic economic problems which have dogged progress in the UK, such as balance of payments problems leading to stop-go policies and to some extent inflation, and with which economic advisors have become so preoccupied, may in this light be seen merely as symptoms of a more fundamental problem - the problem that Britain has not been prepared to make the trade-offs that would have allowed its business sectors sufficient resources to ensure a competitive future. As has been discussed unemployment is also a related phenomenon. Britain's top priority must now therefore be to divert resources back to business to rebuild competitiveness.

Business Principles

Competitiveness, though it can be assisted by better economic choices, ultimately depends on appropriate company policies. The main principles for ensuring companies remain competitive are again fairly straightforward, despite the apparent sophistication of more recent techniques such as financial and portfolio analysis.

Entrepreneurial Approaches

At an early stage in the development of business, strategic decisions were typically taken by an owner-manager or entrepreneur, just as in many small businesses today. Few formalised analytical techniques were involved: the entrepreneur relied heavily on initiative and decisiveness, supported by experience, judgement and perhaps some creative vision.

Ohmae (1982) argues that the success of many large Japanese corporations, such as Sony and Honda, is due not to the application of complex analytical techniques or strategic decision-making processes, but to the type of creative flair and total competitive commitment characteristic of entrepreneurial approaches. He cites the boldness and commitment of leaders such as Konosuke Matsushita and Soichiro Honda in the execution of their plans regardless of minor shifts in circumstances; by contrast, he argues, the detailed sophisticated planning characteristic of bureaucratic organisations makes 'about as much sense as rearranging the deck-chairs on the Titanic' (Ohmae, 1982, p.82). Furthermore, he continues, 'all of today's industry leaders, without exception, began by bold deployment of strategies based on KFS' (that is to say by concentrating on a few simple, key success factors).

Successful entrepreneurs such as Amstrad's Allan Sugar frequently exhibit decisive market entry strategies, respond quickly to opportunities, and subsequently retain a clear notion of their business's intended basis of competitive advantage - characteristics also highlighted in a recent study examining why Japanese companies have done relatively better even when operating in Britain (Doyle, Saunders and Wong, 1985, pp.10 and 18). Just as is true in a military context, successful business strategies need not be elaborate, but they must be cogent and sufficiently focused to overwhelm the competition at the crucial points of contact (Quinn, 1980).

Decisive competitive commitment is also manifest in being prepared to accept risks where necessary, as Ohmae (1982, p.49) argues:

> The strategist must have the courage to gamble and accept the risks involved. This gamble - the strategic decision - is the narrow gate through which a company must pass if it is to win superiority in the demanding field of competitive business, particularly in head-on competition.

Having committed himself to early investments, the entrepreneur is keenly aware that withholding crucial future investment risks competitors getting ahead, which could render valueless all sunk costs and create the risk of bankruptcy, a stark fact not always fully appreciated by timid accountants. Continued competitive commitment is in the long run the only source of profit, and the only way to survive.

Many larger corporations today have been revitalised by simple steps to ensure directors' personal interests are a little more in line with those of committed entrepreneurs, with their own money at stake.

Entrepreneurs rarely make the mistake of downplaying the strategic importance of more specific contextual issues, which is an inherent danger with all analytical concepts and techniques of general application, if over-sold or employed naively. In advocating business education, Andrews (1971) advances his first chapter 'The Importance of Being General', yet fails to balance his argument by reminding readers that effective strategy thinking can rarely afford to stop at the general level or it is likely to be superficial. For this reason, hard-nosed bank managers who have to assess small business entrepreneurial ventures are rarely impressed (despite the common conception) merely by fancy financial figuring, and in practice place much greater emphasis on finding out whether the detailed logic has been really thought through. This point is perhaps particularly poignant in a British context, since the problem of declining British competitiveness has been partly linked to a generalist bias in British culture, and particularly in the culture of managers (Wiener, 1981; Terry, 1979; Mant, 1979; Hampden-Turner, 1983).

The willingness to pay commensurate attention to more specific and detailed issues also leads to a fuller appreciation of the strategic contribution made by people working on more specific tasks, for example in the production area. By contrast Andrews' defence of a more generalist approach is in danger of encouraging elitism and contempt for technical details or mere functional specialists, a criticism sometimes levelled at inexperienced business school graduates:

> The generalist above all cannot allow himself to be intimidated by the language, demeanor, and organisational insensitivity of his highly educated subordinates ... The successful generalist survives and succeeds in a specialised world by virtue of his management skills rather than his technical knowledge.
> (Andrews, 1971, pp.20-21)

The point is of practical importance in strategy implementation. Germany's better performance in toolmaking, for example, has been attributed to relationships between German managers and functional staff/employees being more 'continuous and contiguous', leading to greater employee commitment and fewer industrial relations problems (NEDO, 1981). Again recent literature suggests such simple principles as 'management by walking about' are a distinctive feature of highly successful corporations (Peters and Waterman, 1984; Goldsmith and Clutterbuck, 1984).

In implementing strategic change, it would be naive to ignore organisational issues such as corporate culture, but neither should such problems be used as an excuse for endless procrastination. The entrepreneur's response is leadership. He is aided by a simple, communicable sense of direction, often lacking in bureaucratic organisations, and by a sensitivity to issues and people based on intimate involvement: a simple principle that has survived the test of time (Barnard, 1972; Follett, 1973; Prior, 1977).

With leadership, commitment demonstrated at the top will permeate an organisation, creating that strength in depth so evident in Japan, and releasing that extra 10% of effort within people's individual discretion. Such commitment can make a nonsense of gloomy financial projections. When the chips are down most people like entrepreneurs themselves, are prepared to work longer hours and if necessary for less pay, to ensure organisational survival. For competitiveness is not merely a theoretical problem in optimisation: people's livelihoods and often lifelong efforts are involved.

The entrepreneurial sense of direction and determination which originally created an organisation's competitive position, can if maintained do much to preserve it.

Financial Analysis

Techniques of financial analysis have now become central to the strategic decision-making process, partly because of increasing organisational size and complexity, and partly because of increased pressure to perform financially from the City and from the threat of take-over, particularly in the context of more difficult trading conditions (Horngren, 1984, p.18 and *Business Week* 15 August 1984, p.84). Inadequate attention to the financial situation, both to profitability and also cash flow, may in the extreme result in collapse and competitiveness can scarcely be assured without continued financial viability in the short-term!

Financial techniques enable management to anticipate and control any areas which might otherwise become an unacceptable drain on either profits or cash flow. In this way competent management can generally preempt the more extreme situation of corporate collapse and more specialised indicators such as Z and A scores can also be helpful (Argenti, 1976b). A related and more common problem in today's more competitive conditions, is that of retaining competitiveness in less extreme situations, where it is nevertheless necessary to turn around performance rapidly to avoid collapse (Slatter, 1984; Bibeault, 1981). Turnaround measures generally involve greater attention to traditional accounting issues, retrenchment and rational-isation, and decisively re-focusing a company's strategy and market position.

Apart from these fairly extreme circumstances, financial analysis reminds us that sustainable growth can only be achieved if care is taken to maintain a business in balance. Expansion or diversification has constantly to be balanced against the need for retrenchment and rationalisation, for without some 'pruning' financial, managerial and other resources will become overstretched, weakening the competitive position and the foundations of further growth. Financial analysis assists an organisation to evaluate its 'portfolio' of activities (whether products or entire divisions) to ensure profitability (or cash flow) is adequate to justify future inclusion.

Specifically any business area which cannot achieve a long-term return on capital employed above the real cost of finance (now much higher) must be reviewed, or the effect will be to curtail the organisation's overall sustainable growth rate. Current cost accounting has emerged to ensure those really concerned to maintain their competitive position in the longer-term are fully aware of additional provisions needed to allow for the effects of inflation (it is less relevant for businesses which may ultimately wish to withdraw from activities concerned).

No one concerned with ensuring competitiveness can ignore such financial issues, but it must also be remembered that financial analysis is only the starting point in assessing an organisation's strategic situation: Buchele (1962) enumerates several limitations. An overemphasis on financial considerations can be dangerous and may have contributed to declining competitiveness in the case of some US industries (Hayes and Garvin, 1982; Hayes and Abernathy, 1980). In Britain the case of Norton-Villiers-Triumph is often cited as a case of over-cautious financial policies resulting in a situation of competitive retreat and ultimately collapse (Boston Consulting Group, 1975).

Superficial use of financial techniques could encourage complacent organisations, unwilling to tackle specific problems (for example manning levels in production), to recover financial control through premature retrenchment or rationalisation. Financial crises may be put off for many years, and profitability can probably be sustained at reasonable if not exciting levels; but the real cost, in insulating management from their more specific problems, is paid through retreat in the marketplace, so that competitiveness suffers accordingly. Costs associated with retrenchment are inherently difficult to handle when making financial appraisals and rarely receive adequate attention.

In conditions of unemployment, it may also be possible, if unpleasant, to restore financial performance in marginal areas and projects, if people can be persuaded to reduce pressure on real wage levels - this of course changes the basis of all financial appraisals. Recent American experience suggests that given greater commitment by management and employees, real wage flexibility can play an important role in restoring competitiveness.

Used effectively financial systems lay the foundations of sustainable growth, and can hence contribute to an organisation's competitiveness, a well documented example being the case of Norcos (see Channon, 1971); unduly relied upon however, they can encourage management to postpone adjustments necessary in other important respects, thereby providing a dangerous crutch.

Marketing and Competitive Strategy

Increasing competition, in the context of efficient financial markets and the changing structure of British business, had led to greater recognition of the importance of financial analysis in strategic decisions; but further intensification of competition, in the context of a rising proportion of discretionary spending following the Second World War, highlighted the danger of emphasising financial considerations to the detriment of other potential strategic issues such as marketing. Organisations could no longer assume customers would buy their products just because they were the lowest cost producers, as Ford had found to its cost some years earlier when its market position was overtaken by General Motors.

Levitt's influential article 'Marketing Myopia' (1965) evidences many organisations whose competitiveness has declined as a result of failing to respond adequately to changing customer needs; in the long run profits, we are reminded, ensue only by doing so. To do so more effectively organisations should track their target market segments closely and orientate their operations accordingly. Product portfolios being offered can be evaluated against 'product life cycles', so as to respond to areas of growing customer demand rather than becoming trapped in 'mature' or 'declining' market segments whose prospects are inevitably limited.

Adherence to this 'marketing concept' involves a product rather than cost centred organisational philosophy, with each centre the responsibility of a product manager. His prime task is to coordinate the various functional areas to ensure the best final 'mix' from the viewpoint of satisfying the target customer's needs effectively. An armoury of marketing weapons, such as the key four 'p's of price, place (distribution), promotion and packaging, have been researched and developed to assist in the battle for markets. Yet what is essential is to be organisationally committed to the task of responding adequately to changes in the external market place, and there is indeed evidence of British organisations being less marketing orientated than, for example, their Japanese counterparts (Doyle, Saunders and Wong, 1985).

Amstrad exemplifies how British companies can succeed by such means. Their chief executive Allan Sugar has moved swiftly into fast-growing markets (car radio aerials, hi-fi, and personal computers), and he has also carefully timed his exits so as to avoid being overdependent as growth tails off. Each time, innovation has been focused on ways to offer the customer exactly what he wants, usually through cost-effective integral product offerings such as complete hi-fi systems. Organisationally the company is market-driven, in stark contrast to the technological orientation of Sinclair Electronics which has ultimately proved less successful in business terms.

Naive over-eagerness to switch into faster-growing market segments is however dangerous, since competition inevitably intensifies later in the product life cycle. This, and the likelihood of scale economies and experience effects, often makes it important to achieve a reasonably dominant market share position at an early stage.

Boston Consulting Group's (BCG) research on the experience curve suggests that unit costs tend to fall by a set proportion, roughly between 20% and 30% depending on the industry, every time accumulated production doubles. Accumulated production experience is directly proportional to market share, which consequently becomes an issue of strategic importance: in the long run high share companies ought to dominate business sectors since their costs ought to fall faster than competitors' (Boston Consulting Group, 1968, 1975; Hedley, 1977). There are provisos of course, such as the need for careful business definition. Benefits do not derive automatically from experience, but require considerable organisational commitment. Product innovation can discount the benefit of experience gained on earlier products.

Such analysis has been particularly useful in highlighting key competitive issues in technology-driven industries such as electronic calculators, and the importance of these ideas was perhaps illustrated by the domination of this market in the USA by Texas Instruments, a major proponent of this approach. The power of the concept was enhanced through organisational changes and new control systems, so that competitive commitment could be harnessed throughout the organisation - indeed it is a good example of how strategy analysis can transform corporate culture. The bankruptcy of its rival Bowman, once number two in the US calculator industry, as Texas Instruments slashed prices whilst ruthlessly exploiting experience benefits, was a dramatic illustration of the strategic importance of such issues.

The Boston Consulting Group's somewhat fragile statistical evidence as to the advantages of market share more generally is corroborated by figures published by PIMS (Schoeffler, Buzzell and Heany, 1974) which suggest return on investment for companies with relative market shares over 80% average three times that for companies with market shares under 20%.

Portfolio approaches and PIMS

Since market growth and market share both represent potentially important strategic issues, BCG's 'portfolio approach' goes on to classify business units by their position along both these dimensions. 49% of US Fortune 500 corporations are now estimated to employ some type of portfolio matrix approach in their strategic planning (Haspeslaugh,1982). High market share, high market growth businesses at one extreme are particularly attractive. They are also demanding in terms of cash and diversified companies therefore need to consider their overall business portfolios, since it may be worth diverting funds from other activities with lesser long-term attractions. Again evidence from the PIMS company performance database provides general support for these assertions.

Such ideas are, however, scarcely foolproof, as exemplified by Texas Instruments' more recent problems in the cases of digital watches, telecommunications, and minicomputers - problems attributed by Uttal (1982) directly to this very approach. Researchers utilising the same database have demonstrated that there are numerous exceptional situations where low share companies do extremely well, particularly where attention is given to carefully constructed competitive strategies (Woo and Cooper, 1982). Newton (1983) cites industries where low share companies have consistently outperformed high share companies over many years: Rugby Portland Cement for instance achieved twice the return achieved by the two UK market leaders over many years whilst at the same time building market share. Likewise Porter (1980) evidences a number of industries in the USA where the market leaders are considerably less profitable than the followers.

Even basic ideas such as product or industry life cycles' are still contentious. Van Rossum (1984), for example, argues: 'The glaring fallacy is the underlying assumption that death is inevitable, that the cycle is ultimately determined by predestination'. Recent evidence for example demonstrates that the former classification of the motor industry as 'mature' was misleading and overpessimistic from the viewpoint of smaller companies such as Austin Rover (Altshuler, Anderson, Jones, Roos and Womack, 1984; Jones, 1981; Chew, 1984). Hall (1980) also evidenced the success of many low share companies in eight 'mature' US industries.

There is also another quirk in the BCG's earlier findings which has not been much enlarged on since. Boston Consulting Group (1975) deals at some length with the problem of exchange rate movements whose impact they found could be even greater than that of experience curves. Thus although Japanese motorcycles displayed typical experience curves with costs calculated in yen, the same curves expressed in dollars were actually slightly upward sloping, rather than downward as would normally be expected. BCG therefore recognise that where international competition is being considered it is necessary to adjust for exchange rate trends. This is in fact merely a special case of a more general proviso already noted: that any differences between competitors in real wage levels, and any trend differences, significantly affect competitiveness even where experience effects are important.

Of a number of variants, Shell's Directional Policy Matrix explicitly deals with shortcomings due to equating 'market attractiveness' with simply 'growth', and equating 'strength of competitive position' with merely 'market share' (Coate, 1983). Yet additional sophistication and realism is gained only through a large number of fairly subjective evaluations. Answers to similar questions can be further refined using PIMS's increasingly powerful database which models 37 key determinants of strategic performance; but its advocates are correct in warning that their results should be treated as 'directional indicators' and not as a substitute for managerial judgements - a point which applies to all analytical techniques.

Companies must be sensitive to potential strategic issues such as market orientation generally and also more specifically market growth and market share. Yet given such qualifications, they must also be extremely wary about allowing notions such as market growth or market share (or both) to undermine their competitive commitment to existing business activities. This has led some British corporations into prematurely cutting back on investment particularly in low share, low market growth business activities ('dogs') and into divestment for unrealistically low prices; Hillsdown Holdings for example has done well from buying up such 'dog' companies cheaply and reviving profitability through a more determined managerial approach. Companies should therefore look very long and hard at the specifics of their own competitive situation before contemplating any decision which would undermine commitment to existing activities: ideas that are true more often than not may well prove to be quite wrong in their specific situation!

Porter's approach

Free markets will in theory lead to intensification in competition (exacerbated by new entrants) and eventually destroy any possibility of profitability (beyond the cost of capital, with some allowance for risk), unless companies can achieve defensible niches offering potential for some degree of monopoly. Porter (1980) utilises principles from the economic theory of imperfect competition, to draw up ground rules so that companies can manage this situation and direct themselves to areas of less-intense competition.

> The intensity of competition in an industry is neither a matter of coincidence nor bad luck. Rather, competition in an industry is rooted in its underlying economic situation and goes well beyond the behaviour of current competitors.
> (Porter, 1980)

Porter distinguishes three main 'generic' competitive strategies: overall cost leadership (e.g. Henry Ford's original method of dominating the car industry), differentiation (eg Mercedes relying on more distinctive products and marketing and thereby avoiding head-on competition from lower cost producers), or finally focusing on narrow segments of the market (e.g. by specialising to meet the needs of a particular group of customers). Successful companies, he argues, follow consistently any of these three approaches but avoid being 'caught in the middle'.

Strategies must also be coherent in the context of an industry's competitive dynamics, and Porter details the factors behind five major sources of competition - the threats from substitute products or new entrants into the industry, from increasing customer power on the one hand or from the increasing power of one's own suppliers on the other, and finally internal rivalry among existing competitors. This approach is also applied to a number of generic situations such as declining industries (see also Harrigan, 1980), global competition, fragmented industries and so on. The collapse of Prelude's low-cost volume-orientated strategy in the US lobster fishing industry provides an example of the dangers of ignoring factors such as low entry and high exit barriers, poor scale advantages etc which lead to an inherently fragmented pattern of competition.

These issues cannot be ignored, but Porter's framework does have some limitations. Many of Porter's strategic guidelines make use of matrix portfolio approaches already discussed and as such are subject to many of the same reservations. Porter (1980) ignores the issue of real wages not being the same for all competitors. This is particularly important in the context of global competition in which he takes a particular interest. The whole basis of international trade theory in economics, the concept of comparative advantage (see for example Ohlin, 1933) is that over long periods of time real exchange rates in competitive countries will move to offset competitive advantages achieved by one country over another. It is well recognised that considerable productivity differentials exist between countries offset by real wage adjustments. By discounting such factors Porter's position here seems inconsistent with international trade theory. BCG's international work does, as has been discussed, recognise the need to allow for varying exchange rates. Porter's approach may therefore risk underplaying the role that real wage variations can play in sustaining competitiveness.

More fundamentally, economic models of imperfect competition explicitly assume that all competitors are equally efficient and that factors of production are given for any operation. This may be a useful assumption in the explanation of the behaviour of some markets, but it is a poor assumption in understanding the situation between many competitors. The existence of considerable residual productivity differentials between companies and countries, even after allowing for type of equipment, scale etc. is well documented (Pratten, 1976a, b; Central Policy Review Staff, 1975). Even small improvements here or in other areas of efficiency make an enormous impact on residual profit margins and ROCE. Leibenstein (1966) demonstrated moreover not only the importance of such efficiency differentials in comparison to gains possible through allocative efficiency (Porter's arguments lie in the latter area of economic theory), but he also demonstrated the importance of changes in X-efficiency in determining competitive behaviour among companies.

Porter may well feel that in the long run efficiency differentials against both actual and potential competitors are less important from the viewpoint of strategy than the gains from achieving a position of less-intense competition, but this thesis is not fully supported. Moreover in the long-term even a reasonable degree of monopoly power may well prove unsustainable as its existence sets up many countervailing forces. It should also be noted that the increasing power of product and process changes continually undermine any gains through monopoly power.

Many of Porter's themes are essentially exploitational. The key strategic issues on which he focuses attention are how a company can achieve less-intense competition, rather than the key issues it needs to face in order to improve its own performance and effectiveness relative to that of competitors. In the long-term this approach is likely to prove extremely dangerous. First, particularly in markets characterised by longer-term business relationships such as industrial markets, it is well established that prices are considerably influenced by the notion of the fair price (Bailey and Farmer, 1981), which limits exploitational possibilities. In the case of automotive component suppliers, Ford for example have sophisticated procedures for undermining attempts by any supplier to increase their degree of monopoly/exploitation.

Second, the intensity of competition is relentlessly increasing. Any company that achieves some temporary cushioning against competition is likely to adapt accordingly with overheads and inefficiency tending to increase (see Leibenstein, 1966), and many gains will be eroded by additional wage settlements (others can play the power game too). Ultimately competition will anyway intensify. Probably in the next severe downturn, price levels will fall towards minimum cost levels. In this situation any companies which have not maintained maximum pressure on cost reduction may later find their advantageous bargaining position with respect to customers has anyway become eroded. Any company that is relying on a marginally better bargaining position may well find that it becomes 'locked in' to a more cushy 'high cost' position. Others showing greater commitment to increasing internal efficiency and effectiveness may prove leaner, fitter and more adaptable in the face of the next wave of intense competition. This may prove of far greater benefit than any small gains possible through bargaining power.

The contribution of Porter's ideas, which are richly supported by examples, lies in sensitising those concerned with strategy to the need to find a coherent niche in the longer-term; companies may otherwise become indecisive and merely reactive in the face of immediate competitive pressures. The danger with any such general approach to competitive strategy is however that it risks underplaying the importance of more mundane contextual issues such as production/operations and changing technology.

Production and Technology

Levitt (1965) argues that many US railroad companies failed because, instead of defining themselves in terms of customer needs for transportation, they placed too much emphasis on distinctive operational characteristics, ie of operating railways. Yet this inherent tendency in the marketing approach, to define the business in terms of products or services, can also prove dangerous. An organisation might well have far more resources and competitive advantages vested in operational assets and skills than on the marketing side, where the potential synergy could well be very low, particularly for business sectors such as automotive components manufacture.

Recent research has highlighted this danger of downplaying the strategic importance of manufacturing considerations (Skinner, 1978, 1985; Hill, 1983; Hayes and Wheelwright, 1985). Further endorsement has come from research suggesting that manufacturing policy has been a distinguishing feature of the Japanese approach to strategy, and one that has underpinned their competitive success in industries such as automobiles. Abernathy, Clark and Kantrow (1981) conclude:

> Managers must recognise they have entered a period of competition that requires of them a technology-driven strategy, a mastery of efficient production, and an unprecedented capacity for workforce management.

Also noteworthy is a broader vision: that if the wider issue of industrial competitiveness is to be addressed then policy makers at the macro level as well as at the level of the firm must appreciate the key importance of such issues:

> Managing change successfully proved difficult because policy makers in business and government, trained in an old economic calculus, have found it hard to see the new competitive realities for what they are - or to identify the best terms in which to analyse them.
> Policy makers fail to understand that the old rules of thumb and worn assumptions no longer hold... As a result, decision makers who continue to act as if nothing has happened are, at best, ineffective and, at worst, inadvertent agents of economic disaster.

Depending on an organisation's particular strategic context, even quite mundane matters may emerge as being of key importance to continued competitiveness: for example in one industry Garvin (1983) traced the key reasons for Japan's success against US competitors to manufacturing policies resulting in better levels of quality.

Where this is the case it may prove essential to move to the more production orientated type of organisation, notable in companies such as Honda, and to deal with issues such as power, status, remuneration, training and organisational arrangements. In Britain, there has been considerable concern about production becoming a 'Cinderella function' in the face of increasingly powerful staff functions such as accountancy and marketing. There is also evidence suggesting that British management is particularly weak in the area of manufacturing policy, by comparison with rivals such as Germany (Hutton and Lawrence, 1978, 1979).

There is a similar danger (particularly pertinent to component manufacturers) of downplaying the potential strategic to associated operational areas such as procurement (Bailey and Farmer, 1981); but the problem applies to the 'mundane' issue of technology more generally. The key role played by technology in determining competitive success has been evidenced in a number of industries (Pavitt, 1980). The impact of Pilkington's float glass process in 1958 on the pattern of competition is an example of this. Lorenz (1986) highlights the importance of design. Yet despite an excellent record in terms of fundamental research and inventions, Britain again appears weak in comparison with Germany, in terms of more basic engineering (Hutton and Lawrence, 1981).

None of this is to deny the importance of financial and marketing principles already discussed; but strategic thinking risks becoming dangerously superficial if more detailed operational and technological issues are not properly addressed.

People and Organisation

The evolution of businesses into complex multiproduct organisations has itself raised issues of strategic importance (Chandler, 1962; Channon, 1973; Rumelt, 1974; Dyas and Thanheiser, 1976).

The promise of faster corporate growth and risk reduction presented by diversification does not always survive the test of time. Where companies become overstretched even core activities may be put at risk, financial performance suffers, and radical cut backs may be required before growth can be resumed. On average diversification probably does offer slightly enhanced growth prospects at the corporate level, though the impact on profitability is more ambiguous (Newbould and Luffmann, 1978).

In practice however, most diversification occurs through merger or acquisition. Competitiveness is not enhanced merely by corporations re-shuffling their assets and activities; what matters here is whether industrial re-organisation really creates additional value added through some sort of 'synergy', and it is therefore important to distinguish any resultant improvement in constituent businesses' overall organic growth. On average mergers and acquisitions result in little, if any, overall improvement in financial performance, and any net benefit is frequently absorbed by substantial premiums paid to the shareholders of organisations acquired (Singh, 1972; Kitching, 1967).

Such moves are only likely to lead to a genuine performance improvement if they are part of a well planned, coherent strategy, effectively implemented (Ansoff, 1968; Rumelt, 1974). Formal planning does appear to help (Ansoff, 1972; Stuart Jones, 1982), but managerial problems are such that more obvious benefits through some form of relatedness are not in themselves any guarantee of success (Hogarty, 1970). Successful implementation often depends on Chief Executives becoming personally involved and committed, and the role of individuals able to undertake the role of 'change-masters' in such sensitive human situations is both important and extremely difficult (Mace and Montgomery, 1969).

Managing increased diversity successfully has often required changes in formal organisational structure: for example, businesses in many countries have generally had to move towards divisional forms of organisation (Chandler, 1962; Channon, 1973; Dyas and Thanheiser, 1976; Rumelt, 1974). Formal organisational changes may also be required as businesses become more internationally orientated (Brooke and Remmers, 1977).

The strategic significance of such visible changes may be slightly overstated. The term 'strategy' is used by such writers almost as a misnomer for a particular strategy, diversification, despite acknowledgement in the most recent study on 'strategy and structure' that by far the majority of companies examined over the last decade had undergone no diversification at all (Luffman and Reed, 1984). Whilst Europe remained awe-struck in the 1960's in the face of 'the American Challenge' it was natural to focus on US companies' sophisticated systems for managing highly developed and complex corporations. Since then, conditions have become less conducive to growth and diversity. The competitive challenge from the USA has waned, whilst the newer managerial challenge presented by Japan appears to have little to do with diversification, acquisitions or with more formalised managerial control systems so popular in the USA.

Here subtler, less visible, organisational issues seem to be involved. Their investigation requires more in-depth investigation at a company level (see for example Pettigrew, 1985), even though from a purely academic stance this necessitates some loss of generality. The real success of Japanese companies is the way in which they have secured commitment to change throughout the entire organisation, from top to bottom (Saunders, 1984). This broader issue has of course been of central concern since the inception of literature on management (Burns and Stalker, 1966), though its importance has increased as modern organisations have become larger and more diverse.

Continued competitiveness demands that internal policies be continuously and appropriately adapted in the face of increasingly rapid, external environmental change, and this is scarcely going to happen if organisational processes are deficient. Such processes are important both in the formulation and implementation of strategic change (Miles and Snow, 1978; Johnson and Scholes, 1984; Johnson, 1987).

Competitiveness ultimately stems from a system's performance along so many dimensions, that the final reason for differences in company performance is merely the accumulation of slightly better performance in a host of specific areas, rather than any single 'big issue'. Performance then hinges on whether management can tap that extra element of personal commitment, which individuals hold within their own discretion, no matter what formal carrots or sticks are applied; management in successful companies, such as Marks and Spencer in Britain, do not generally neglect the subtler 'human side of business', cultural issues, nor adages such as the importance of 'management by walking about' (Peters and Waterman, 1984). An organisation's greatest asset is its people, and the ultimate test of good organisation is whether management can tap and develop (through appropriate training throughout the organisation) such an asset to the full. This in turn demands both leadership and a genuine and close, long-term relationship of trust between management and employees, rather than the see-sawing power relationships which have so often been a characteristic of British industrial relations in the past.

Conclusion and the Need for Research

The principles behind achieving competitiveness are straightforward, but easily neglected. Whether at a macro-economic level or at a company level, people may not naturally want to face up to the difficult trade-offs involved, and it is the role of leadership (at both levels) to ensure a sense of longer-term direction.

Since the elements affecting competitiveness are multidimensional overall performance depends on the system as a whole. Economic choices which might enhance competitiveness will be wasted, if company strategies are woolly or lacking in commitment; but the benefit from more-effective company strategies will equally be wasted if, in the face of such increasingly intense international competition, the country makes inappropriate economic choices. Similarly within companies, it is easy for the various functional aspects to become out of balance.

The balance of importance between financial, marketing, operational and people considerations depends on a company's particular context and circumstances; but it is crucial to achieve a decisive overall strategy that provides a coherent 'match' between such internal policies and the continuously changing external business environment (Drucker, 1968; Ansoff, 1968; Argenti, 1980; Johnson and Scholes, 1984). Any failure to do so (looking at the business as a whole) is likely to lead ultimately to a process of continuous competitive retreat and decline, even though the position may sometimes appear to be well under control from a merely short-term point of view. Should an unduly financially orientated turnaround strategy, for example, merely sidestep critical though intractable production issues, retrenchment and rationalisation will only restore financial control at the expense of further competitive retreat in the market place: if real underlying problems are left unresolved, companies must eventually find themselves once again at the mercy of relentlessly increasing competition. Successful executives are those who, whilst remaining sensitive to the broader strategic issues discussed in the last section, also retain an entrepreneurial sense of long-term direction, based upon intuition, judgement and an intimate knowledge of the detailed workings of their own businesses, and where necessary they are prepared to override short-term financial considerations (Donaldson and Lorsch, 1984); whatever the risk, the alternative is the certainty of competitive decline. But particularly in the face of international competition, economic choices may also have a considerable effect on competitiveness, calling for an equal degree of leadership at a national level.

To appreciate the significance of such issues in practice requires a substantial research programme designed to examine the UK competitive position 'at the front lines', and the research approach adopted is described in the next section.

The Research Programme

Conceptual Approach and the Reason for Single Industry Focus

Research from particular disciplines, such as marketing (e.g. Doyle, Saunders and Wong, 1985), has contributed to an understanding of the problem of UK competitiveness. Many such studies are characterised by rigorous methodologies. Hypotheses, being well grounded in an established subject literature, can be carefully formulated and tested along fairly scientific lines and in a manner giving confidence as to the general applicability of research findings.

Yet depending on the nature of the research question addressed, even researchers pursuing a broadly single disciplinary approach frequently find it necessary to make use of more in-depth, research methods, centred on single cases. Those concerned for example with the organizational and decision making processes through which strategic change actually comes about, argue that to pursue such issues at the more general level would be sterile and inappropriate; the type of hypotheses that could be thereby pre-formulated and tested on a statistically representative basis would necessarily side step important aspects of the real picture, so as to render the research trite and superficial (Johnson, 1987; Pettigrew, 1985; Mintzberg, 1979; Scott, 1966).

Such researchers also argue that the choice of an in-depth case-centred approach need not preclude findings of wider relevance, provided such research is well constructed. This argument is supported by Yin's (1984) systematic treatment of the use of case studies as a research methodology. Yin evidences many examples of case studies which have advanced understanding not merely in an exploratory sense, but also in terms of providing rich descriptions of phenomenon, as with Whyte's (1943) 'Street Corner Society', rich explanations, as with Allinson's (1971) 'Essence of Decision Making : The Cuban Missile Crisis', and even in respect to the development of theory of more general applicability, as with Jacobs' (1961) 'The Death and Life of Great American Cities'. No-one would deny that such classic studies are statistically unrepresentative, nor would they deny the need for further testing; but neither should anyone deny their wider relevance.

Appropriate research methods depend on the question addressed. Some of the principles affecting competitiveness already discussed, particularly in the area of economics, are amenable to research approaches at the more aggregate level, to pre-formulated hypotheses tested in a manner representative of the wider economy.

Whilst the case of vehicle components has not (it should therefore be emphasised) been selected so as to be representative of the wider economy, it has nevertheless been chosen so as to increase the likelihood that the ideas and techniques developed will prove of more general relevance and applicability, in the context of the broader problem of Britain's competitiveness. I have deliberately avoided researching yet another unduly narrow industry sector, lest parochial substantive matters completely cloud out issues of more general interest.

The vehicle components industry is extremely complex and it mirrors a wide range of business characteristics within the economy: low but also high technology; small and large companies; product sectors which by their nature are likely to be more or less exposed to direct international competition; sectors where the pattern of competition is likely to be more or less concentrated; and so on - the 'industry's' diversity is almost unrivalled.

Furthermore its size and economic impact are both considerable. The techniques developed in this study would be equally applicable to the relatively small number of economic sectors, of comparable size, complexity and international exposure, which collectively dominate Britain's competitive performance. Thus the prospects of extending this research approach to cover the economy more comprehensively in the future would appear promising.

The choice of a single industry also involves an important issue of principle. Many suggested prescriptions for competitive success are based on research into companies, which neither share the semblance of a common business environment nor compete with each other, either directly or even indirectly (e.g. Peters and Waterman, 1984). Others do draw on examples involving real and direct competition, but establishing patterns of competitive success can be highly demanding. The empirical basis of examples presented is often extremely sketchy; not everyone would completely agree with the three page analysis of Caterpillar's competitive position vis-a-vis Komatsu, presented in Hout, Porter and Rudden (1982) in support of their ideas of how to play the 'global competitive game', in the light of subsequent events. The vehicle components industry on the other hand offers the opportunity to examine a rich variety of competitive strategies pursued by companies sharing a reasonably common business environment. By also focusing particularly on a few product sectors and employing field research, this study aims to examine much more closely the inter-reaction of real competitors, in Britain and also in key rival countries given the importance of the international dimension.

The final reason for choosing to focus on vehicle components is, that having worked for GKN (one of Britain's and indeed Europe's largest vehicle component manufacturers) for several years previous to commencing this research study more formally in 1980, my access to this industry has been fairly unique. The degree of subsequent access achieved nationally and internationally makes this study one of the few major empirically based studies of competition. Therefore I take Mintzberg's view (Mintzberg, 1979, p.vi) that my primary obligation as a researcher is to pursue to the limit a theoretical understanding of this particular context to which I have had access.

Having chosen to study the case of a single industry, I have found it necessary to pursue a 'grounded approach' (of the type suggested in Glaser and Strauss, 1967, p.277), guided by substantive issues as well as by more general theory. As they have argued, the criterion of methodological rigour then depends more heavily 'on the detailed elements in the actual strategies used for collecting, coding, analysing and presenting data' (Glaser and Strauss, 1967, p.224). Broadly my approach in researching such a complex industry has been 'embedded' (as discussed in Yin, 1984, p.45) in the sense of using field research centred on a few products to gain depth, complemented by different and more appropriate research techniques (using secondary data) in examining the industry as a whole. The more detailed elements in my research strategy are discussed in the next section.

The More Detailed Research Strategy

The competitive situation facing UK automotive

component manufacturers can only be understood in the context of the business environment to which they are exposed. I therefore analysed developments in the upstream vehicle assembly industry by reviewing academic and trade literature and other published sources such as official statistics. In addition I approached a number of vehicle companies (one in the UK, one in Germany, and five in Japan) to examine more closely issues of concern to the component sector.

Because of the scale and complexity of the UK automotive component industry, I chose a small number of product sectors for close examination. This raises more practical problems than taking a purely company based approach because companies such as GKN are engaged in a number of product activities. However, to address the issue of competitiveness it was essential to focus on situations in which manufacturers were directly competing against each other, so that 'winners' and 'losers' in the competitive game could really be distinguished. Also apart from the question of what one UK component manufacturer needs to do to outperform another, an important issue addressed by this study is what can be done to improve their collective performance. Comparisons with international competitors are more illuminating between manufacturers of the same products, actually in direct competition with each other.

Choice of Product Sectors

Product characteristics likely to affect the pattern of competition were derived partly from the academic literature and partly from an overview of the automotive components industry. Literature on business competition suggested different patterns of competition might be expected in cases of high versus low technology, of new versus mature products, of monopolistic versus fragmented industries. The impact of international competition might also be expected to depend on product related characteristics such as opportunities provided by technology or scale economies, or logistical considerations. An overview of the industry suggested an important distinction between original equipment and aftermarkets and also (Redden, 1975) indicated that a substantial proportion of automotive component manufacturers supplied only about 30% of their components to the automotive market.

The small number of product sectors examined in detail clearly could not be representative in any statistical sense but, as shown in Table 2.1, they were chosen to cover many of the range of characteristics expected to affect the pattern of competition.

Table 2.1: Characteristics of automotive product sectors chosen for close examination

Characteristics	Ball and roller bearings	Forgings	Electronic instrumentation	Exhaust systems	Spark plugs	Brake linings
Automotive dependance	only 30%	quite high	very high	very high	very high	very high
Expected radius of competition	very high	fairly low	medium	very low	very high	fairly high
Main market	original equipment	original equipment	aftermarket	aftermarket	aftermarket	aftermarket
Pattern of competition	oligopolistic	fragmented	fairly monopolistic but new entrants	oligopolistic OE but AM more fragmented	fairly monopolistic	fairly oligopolistic
Technology	medium	fairly low	high	low	medium	medium
Importance of scale economies	quite high	fairly low	high	low	quite high	quite high

Examination of Product Sectors

Individual product sectors chosen were first reviewed through desk research, market research and trade association reports where available, press and trade journal articles, official reports (e.g. the Monopolies Commission, the EEC and NEDO) and official statistics (e.g. Census of Production and trade statistics). Manufacturers were identified through national and international trade directories. Their annual reports were analysed and additional desk research was undertaken in the case of key manufacturers. The main perspective was on the period from the early 1970s, when UK vehicle production was at its peak, but some further historical context was built up where possible. Where, as in automotive bearings and automotive forgings, the automotive industry represented one of a number of markets, additional research was carried out into the component sector more generally.

I then carried out interviews with selected UK and overseas automotive component manufacturers, between 1981 and the first half of 1983. The purpose was to get an overall picture of the pattern of competition. Where only a small number of key UK competitors were involved, as in automotive ball and roller bearings, the aim was to visit as many as would allow access. Where large numbers were involved, as in automotive forgings, all major companies were approached, together with a selection of smaller companies covering the range of sizes. Overseas manufacturers approached included major competitors identified together with a wider selection drawn from international trade directories.

Because of the possible commercial sensitivity of competitive issues, companies were first approached at Chief Executive level and offered a veto, if necessary, prior to publication on any sensitive material contributed in the course of visits or interviews.

A structured interview approach was used. Companies varied considerably in their situations and issues discussed were rarely amenable to simple answers. A flexible approach was employed, using many 'open' questions in order to allow companies to focus on what they saw as their key competitive problems.

The pattern of these interviews varied, but generally included some discussion with either the Chief Executive or some senior company representative. I was then directed to appropriate company personnel to pursue questions on specific topic areas, typically executives involved in planning, marketing, product development and production. In most cases I was able to tour the factory to gain a fuller appreciation of technical and manufacturing developments. Where access was particularly good, repeat visits were carried out to add further depth to discussions.

To gain further understanding of the competitive situation facing UK component manufacturers, overseas manufacturers were also visited in Germany, Japan and the USA. Germany is the most significant competitor in terms of direct trade in automotive components. Indirect competition (via vehicle manufacturers) is also important. Since components represent some 70% of the manufacturing costs of Japanese cars, the competitive impact of their component industry on UK component manufacturers has (to date) been more indirect than direct. Similarly, US component manufacturers were visited because of the competitive significance of the US automotive industry.

Overseas interviews were carried out to complement the analysis of competitive situations affecting UK component manufacturers. In addition emphasis was placed on four main comparative themes:

a) comparison of productivity levels;

b) comparison of manufacturing developments underlying differences in production performance levels;

c) comparison of senior executives, production management and engineers, in terms of education, training and previous experience;

d) comparison of approaches to longer term planning and strategy formulation at senior executive level.

Despite the potential problem of confidentiality, access to companies was generally good as is shown in Table 2.2.

The automotive ball and roller bearings sector was given particular emphasis. Since product characteristics were conducive to international trade and competition, competitive developments in that sector were felt likely to indicate future developments in less internationally developed sectors. Access was achieved to all seven automotive ball and roller bearings manufacturers in the UK and to most of the major overseas manufacturers.

With over one hundred forging manufacturers in the UK alone it was impractical to visit all manufacturers. Three of the four largest companies were visited, including GKN Forgings which accounts for over 60% of UK automotive forgings production. A further cross-section of manufacturers was also visited to reflect the situation across the size range down to much smaller companies.

Both of the two independent UK automotive instrumentation companies were visited. They have since combined their operations.

Table 2.2: Number of companies accessed

	UK	Germany	Japan	USA
Automotive ball and roller bearings	7	2	3	2
Automotive forgings	11	1	3	1
Automotive instrumentation	2	-	2	-
Automotive exhaust systems	8	-	1	1
Automotive spark plugs	1	-	1	1
Automotive brake linings	1	2	2	-
Other automotive components	-	2	1	-
Vehicle customers	1	1	5	-

In the automotive exhaust system sector, which is fairly fragmented, the largest UK manufacturer and six others (across the size range) were visited.

Briefer studies were also carried out in two other sectors. The largest independent manufacturers of automotive spark plugs were visited in the UK, the USA and Japan. In brake linings, access was only achieved in the case of one out of the three major UK manufacturers but useful comparisons were drawn from visits to manufacturers in Germany and Japan. A small number of overseas visits was made to manufacturers of other automotive components, principally axles, brake assemblies, and wheels.

Interviews were also carried out with representatives from trade associations, consulting companies, specialist research centres and relevant government departments, and with academic researchers, both in the UK and overseas.

Checking for Generality

Initial research overviewing the automotive components industry was later extended in order to check whether research themes emerging from the product sectors examined applied more generally. Some themes, such as the strategic importance of developments taking place in the area of production, are inherently difficult to check at an aggregated level. It was however possible to review other relatively well-documented automotive product sectors, such as engines and tyres, making extensive and fairly comprehensive use of secondary data sources such as market research reports and journal articles. The *Financial Times*, which proved particularly valuable, has been scanned systematically and continuously since beginning this research in 1980, yielding well over a thousand articles. I also made use of a small number of visits to miscellaneous automotive component companies.

The pattern of company performances across the industry more generally was analysed by aggregating performance figures published by Inter Company Comparisons: for strategic assessment, data is needed over a reasonable time period and I was able to use continuous data over 9 years for 66 companies and over 14 years for 24 companies.

For all products for which data was available, Census of Production data over many years was analysed in conjunction with trade figures, so as to complete market analysis as far as possible. This data enabled me to examine the industry's collective international performance.

Finally, another theme emerging from the study was the importance to this industry's competitive situation of UK economic choices more generally (particularly in respect to pressure on real wage levels). To examine this issue I again made use of aggregated data.

The final and most up-to-date source of research data has been provided by the House of Commons, Trade and

Industry Committee (1987) enquiry into the UK Motor Components Industry between 1986 and 1987. In 1987 senior executives from 13 major UK vehicle component manufacturers, and from 8 vehicle assemblers, were called in as witnesses in this enquiry, as were other major bodies concerned with the industry including for example the Department of Trade and Industry, trade union officials, SMMT and BAPPC. In November 1986 officials representing the Committee also visited and interviewed continental European customers, including Volvo, Saab/Scania, Opel, Daimler Benz, Porsche, PSA and Renault, and their report (Houses of Commons, Trade and Industry Committee, 1987, appendix 1) contains an up-to-date, international perspective.

3
The Vehicle Industry

This chapter reviews upstream developments in the vehicle industry, which affect the competitive situation of UK component suppliers.

Since OE components represent about 55% of most European vehicle assemblers' costs (Central Policy Review Staff, 1975, p.75), the competitive fortunes of UK assemblers and their suppliers are in fact highly interdependent. The competitiveness of the component industry is critically dependent on the strength of its home market base. Likewise any erosion in the competitive position of UK vehicle assemblers is likely to reflect at least in part weaknesses within the supplier sector, which if not resolved must threaten any recovery.

Historical Perspective

At the turn of the century Europe was still pre-eminent. In 1906 France and Germany accounted for 58% of worldwide vehicle production (Altshuler, Anderson, Jones, Roos and Womack, 1984, p.14). Its position also being strong, Britain strongly advocated free trade and maintained no tariffs on auto imports until World War I.

An almost revolutionary change then took place in the pattern of competition, transferring the competitive lead to US manufacturers. Ford's Model T marked radical changes both in production methods (with the introduction of continuous assembly) and also in the approach to management and organisation. Between 1910 and 1921

Ford fully exploited experience benefits associated with volume, by modernising plants, vertically integrating to reduce purchasing costs, eliminating model changes and by increasing the division of labour. Costs were cut by three quarters as US market share increased from 10 to 55% (Abernathy and Wayne, 1974). This more 'scientific' approach to management, based on the division of manufacturing skills and routinisation of complex tasks, was further developed during the early 1920s by Alfred Sloan at General Motors. The US competitive lead, encouraged by a substantial home market, continued until almost 1955. The development of competition over this period was dominated by adjustments taking place in other countries as they sought to deal with this competitive gap. American domination in car production over this period is shown in Table 3.1 which summarises the main trends over this period.

Table 3.1: Car production 1929-1955 (thou' units)

Year	1929	1938	1950	1955
World	5,355	3,074	8,168	11,015
N. America	4,791	2,143	6,950	8,295
W. Europe	554	879	1,110	2,486
Japan	-	-	2	20
UK	-	341	523	898
N. America/world %	89	70	85	75
W. Europe/world %	10	29	14	23
UK/W. Europe %		39	47	36

Source: SMMT Yearbooks

The US also led in commercial vehicles, but the UK position here was stronger. In 1955 the US produced 1,250,000 commercial vehicles compared to 340,000 in the UK and only 49,000 in Japan.

Faced with so large a competitive gap all major European countries and also Japan responded with high tariffs and other protective measures. Even Britain sustained a

33.3% tariff (originally introduced as a wartime measure in World War I) up until 1960. In addition, it introduced a horsepower tax disadvantageous to the US and steep tariffs were extended to tyres and other components.

Both Ford and General Motors responded by establishing manufacturing operations in Britain and Germany between 1925 and 1934; but stronger protectionism in Japan went further and prevented such moves. The US presence in Europe spurred efforts to bridge the gap with world 'best practice', both as regards new technology and new managerial approaches. US multinationals were also an important influence in the supplier sector, for example Champion (spark plugs), Timken (tapered roller bearings), Borg Warner (gearboxes), and Cummins (engines).

Since the introduction of Ford's Model T volume has been an important factor shaping competition. Specialist manufacturers of highly differentiated products (e.g. Morgan, Lotus and, on a larger scale, Mercedes) have been less affected than 'volume producers' who represent the bulk of the market. However, even volume producers have always had to balance the pursuit of scale economies associated with volume against the need to preserve flexibility, both in terms of marketing and manufacturing policies. In 1927 the insensitivity of Ford's extreme volume orientated approach to a changed pattern of market demand led to a one year close-down as the company was finally forced into retooling for a completely new model, and a total reversal in the market share position against General Motors (Abernathy and Wayne, 1974).

Nevertheless, rationalisation and concentration have generally been driven by the search for scale economies, even sometimes at the expense of flexibility. OECD (1983, p.11) points out that the number of US automakers fell from 80 in 1920 to 30 in 1930 and about 9 in 1950 (today the top 3 produce 95% of US cars), and they argue that a similar process of concentration has taken place in Europe and Japan.

Heterogeneous markets within Europe appear to have frustrated the achievement of scale economies comparable to the USA, despite progress in other respects. The competitive gap just before World War II was still evident: even Ford's modern facility at Dagenham had higher delivery costs in Europe than vehicles brought in from Detroit despite shipping rates and higher US wages (Altshuler, Anderson, Jones, Roos and Womack, 1984, p.18).

However, by 1955 the European vehicle industry had virtually recovered from the effects of war. During the next 15 years its share of world output rose substantially whilst the American position waned, as shown in Table 3.2.

Table 3.2: Car production 1955-1970 (thou' units)

Year	1955	1960	1965	1970
World	11,015	12,985	19,281	22,755
N. America	8,295	7,001	10,016	7,491
W. Europe	2,486	5,120	7,519	10,379
Japan	20	165	696	3,179
UK	898	1,353	1,722	1,641
N. America/world %	75	54	52	33
W. Europe/world %	23	39	39	46
Japan/world %	0.2	1	4	14
UK/W. Europe %	36	26	23	16

Source: SMMT Yearbooks

Europe's fast-growing markets were still protected by high external tariffs until about 1960. Even then manufacturers in America took little interest in European markets, which were distinctive in terms of consumer tastes (particularly in respect to size) and still relatively heterogeneous.

Intra-European trade grew rapidly, encouraged by falling internal tariff barriers. This enabled manufacturers to sell their more specialised products in all the markets of Europe in sufficient quantities to realise reasonably good production economies. As its volume situation improved, the European industry also gained in competitive strength because of its flexibility. Manufacturers, still more numerous than in America, competed vigorously in the face of a wide range of design requirements. Though partially offsetting improvements in terms of volume, this generated equally wide ranging and often highly innovative technical solutions, such as front wheel drive. Following the General Agreement on Tariffs and Trade (GATT), technological innovativeness and overall flexibility helped European manufacturers both in defending their own fast growing markets, and also in counter-attacking particular segments of US competitors' own markets. Later, in the wake of the oil crisis, flexibility (as well as a focus on smaller vehicles) was to prove even more important.

Britain, partly because of its isolated position in Europe and partly through problems of its own making, did not fully participate in the resurgence of European competitiveness. Its share of Western European vehicle output fell steadily from 36% in 1955 to 16% in 1970, as was shown in Table 3.2.

The Rise of Japan

Though the competitive gap against the US had been bridged, Europe's resurgence was more due to its ability to defend its own fast growing markets, than to any competitive supremacy capable of dominating rivals elsewhere. Yet Japan's almost exponential rise in vehicle output, already evident in Table 3.2, reflected a transformation in the competitive situation as significant as that instigated by US manufacturers earlier in the century (Altshuler, Anderson, Jones, Roos and Womack, 1984).

As Shimokawa (1982b, p.274) argues, 'both macro and micro factors have increased international competitiveness in the Japanese auto industry'. Without commitment at government level to the protection and development of this industry, Japanese manufacturers could never have survived Western competition at any time up until the late 1950s. They were behind on technology and beset with industrial relations problems affecting both quality and efficiency. The government fostered the industry's development through assistance on licencing overseas know-how and through the provision of scarce financial resources (McArdle and Jones, 1984, pp.47-48). Their system of industrial and conglomerate groups, in turn supported by the banking system, also helped directly. The Ministry for International Trade and Industry (MITI) attempted, at an early stage, to rationalise vehicle assemblers by reducing their numbers and also to encourage the development of an independent supplier sector. Both attempts were aimed at benefits from volume more comparable to those of Western competitors; but both failed. The main contribution made by Japan's unique industrial system was that it actually succeeded in fostering virile domestic competition, whilst at the same time providing a system of close collaborative relationships between businesses, and particularly assemblers and suppliers (Shimokawa, 1982b). Japanese economic choices, such as their high savings ratio, allowing low interest rates and low (certainly until recently) exchange rates have also produced a conducive climate for business growth.

At the micro level, following the break-up of the intense Nissan strike in 1955, the Japanese modelled a unique labour relations approach, aimed at gaining much greater participation and flexibility on the shop floor. Lifetime employment and unique payment schemes played an important role. More fundamentally, however, they turned upside down conventional organisational approaches based on the division of labour and scientific management. The number of layers of management were drastically reduced (just as Nissan has been doing more recently in the USA, *Financial Times* 17 February, 1985, p.8) and a new approach was developed with attention focused onto shopfloor work groups.

In this context it was possible to adopt a new manufacturing philosophy, though progress was slow and incremental, taking effect over a matter of 20 years. The approach was characterised by a commitment to securing long term benefits of organisational learning even at the expense of short term problems. Concepts such as 'total quality' and just-in-time systems of stockless production (linking in suppliers also) turned established US manufacturing ideas upside down.

Not only do the Japanese lead best practice in respect to specific issues such as quality, but their whole approach to management in reversing several previously accepted managerial assumptions would seem to represent a step forward in managerial best practice. Indeed Japan's competitive lead today is the result of a transformation as revolutionary as the one which gave the USA its original domination over the industry:

> ... this new system utilises several key concepts that turn old ideas about production organisation upside down. The notion that quality costs more has been reversed. Defect prevention turns out to cost less. Similarly the traditional assumption that large inventory buffers are needed for high process yield has been turned around. High yield, defined as a large number of good parts per unit of operating time, seems most likely to be obtained with very low buffers. Yet another notion that has been reversed is that output can be increased and information about factory conditions can be obtained only through an independent system of supervision and information reporting. Instead of sending manufacturing orders from the top down and bringing information from the bottom up, the Japanese producers have learned that moving knowledge, skills and decision making down the system into the hands of the primary work force makes the old supervision and information-gathering systems redundant. Between the assemblers and suppliers the Japanese have also pioneered new techniques. The old ideas that financial integration, top-down decision making with tight control of product information, multiple sourcing, and geographic dispersion are the keys to production efficiency have given way to operational coordination combined with financial disaggregation, increased single sourcing, and geographic concentration.
> (Altshuler, Anderson, Jones, Roos and Womack, 1984, pp.146-147)

Despite high volumes on some models, Japanese competitive strength has generally relied less on a crude volume approach and more on subtler issues such as the flexibility yielded by their alternative approach. The Japanese vehicle industry resisted concentration, which might have improved volumes, and also world car approaches.

The system has yielded levels of quality, productivity, efficiency and flexibility (both in terms of varying orders and in terms of the ability to handle an increasing variety of new products) as yet unmatched elsewhere. By the early 1980s the Japanese cost advantage over US manufacturers in small cars was estimated at $1,500 (at 215 yen/$; Altshuler, Anderson, Jones, Roos and Womack, 1984).

As international trade barriers fell the impact was felt initially in particular market segments, but became more significant after the oil crisis and as successive generations of products have gradually been introduced. Table 3.3 shows the division of world auto production in more recent years and the likely future situation.

Table 3.3: Car production 1970-1992 (thou' units)

Year	1970	1978	1986	1992*
World	22,755	31,226	32,484	35,096
N. America	7,491	10,315	8,890	7,579
W. Europe	10,379	11,321	11,805	12,493
Japan	3,179	5,748	7,810	7,816
UK	1,641	1,223	1,019	1,396
N. America/world %	33	33	27	22
W. Europe/world %	46	36	36	36
Japan/world %	14	18	24	22
UK/W. Europe %	16	9	9	11

* Forecast for 1992 from DRI Europe's World Automotive Forecast Report November 1987. Other data SMMT.

Japan's share of world production, which in 1960 had been just over 1%, actually caught up with North America in 1982. Subsequently the position has been slightly obscured by trade restrictions and by Japanese companies switching to overseas production. Direct Japanese imports into the important US market only rose from 1.6m to 2m during the eight years to 1987, and are expected to stabilise. Nevertheless the Japanese share of this market rose from 15% in 1979 to over 20% in the first half of 1987 and was still rising in spite of the dramatic rise in the yen-dollar exchange rate. DRI also argue (*Financial Times*, 27 April 1987) that by 1990 their share could rise to 37%, even holding export shipments to 2.3m, through building 1.3m in the USA and by further supplying 0.3m cheap cars from other East Asian countries. South Korean production, which is mainly for export, poses a threat in its own right: this increased from only 57,000 in 1980 to 457,000 in 1986 and is forecast by DRI to reach 1.36m in 1992 (catching up with Britain).

In spite of GATT and free trade rhetoric European governments responded, just as they had had to when faced with the earlier rise in US competitiveness, with measures aimed at some degree of protection. This has helped to stabilise the European position. Restrictions have so far held the Japanese share of the European market to about 11%, whereas General Motor's Chairman, Roger Smith, has estimated that unfettered this share could rise as high as 30% (*Financial Times*, 16 March 1988). Japan's bilateral accords with France and Italy currently restrict its market share to 2.9% and 2,500 cars respectively, but in freer markets such as Ireland its share in 1986 rose to 43% (*Financial Times*, 30 April 1987). In the first two months of 1987, Japanese car shipments to the EEC rose 34% in spite of a steep rise in the yen.

History suggests that although protection can play an important role for a time, it can only stave off an inevitable process of adjustment. Disparities in the situations of individual member countries have made it difficult for the EEC to achieve any coherent overall political response. There is also some recognition, shared by the US government which in 1985 abandoned the 'voluntary restraint agreement', that the scope for such measures is ultimately limited though attitudes on both sides of the Atlantic are undoubtedly hardening.

European manufacturers cannot escape Japanese competition either in the US market, or in other markets.

Since the early 1970s European car exports have fallen from 3m to 1.3m units in 1984. In the same year, Ford claimed Japanese manufacturers alone eliminated 1.6m European exports as well as taking 1m car sales in the European home market (*Financial Times*, 16 Oct. 1984, p.I). This exacerbated European overcapacity, estimated at 2.3m units or nearly 20% (*Financial Times*, 16 Oct. 1984, p.IV), and led to vicious price competition. Better market conditions have slightly alleviated the situation more recently, with European production expected to be about 12.2m in 1987. However, DRI predict this figure will fall by some 0.3m by 1989. Equivalent to the annual output of a medium-sized car plant, this would again prompt anxieties about excess capacity.

Many progressive European manufacturers (e.g. Ford Europe) are pursuing competitive standards set by Japan and finding the lessons applicable to their own European situation. Thus any European country or company which does not rapidly close the competitive gap with Japan faces inescapable competition from other European competitors who are doing so, as well as increasing Japanese competition based within Europe itself (probably from Toyota and Mazda in the near future as well as Nissan and Honda). As shown in Table 3.3 the UK vehicle industry's share of West European production fell back to just under 9% in 1986. Although the overall position will be boosted by rising production from Japanese and other multinationals, the situation of the UK owned industry (notably Rover) would seem particularly precarious.

Internationalisation of Competition

Most commentators would acknowledge the pressing need for vehicle assemblers (and indeed their suppliers) to bridge the competitive gap with Japan; but whether or not these new developments will lead to further concentration in the world vehicle industry is more contentious. Following the first impact of Japanese competition, many felt the answer to be yes. Moves to smaller, more fuel-efficient vehicles seemed to be bringing world markets closer together. General Motors (GM) and Ford responded by attempting to exploit benefits associated with internationalisation and volume by developing 'world cars' such as GM's 'J' car and Ford's Escort. In addition major international link-ups such as between GM and Toyota seemed to confirm 'world car scenarios' of increasing internationalisation and rationalisation. Japanese competition was seen as merely catalytic to this process.

Given the weak position of British manufacturers such as Rover, the issue of any further concentration of the world industry is as critical as it is contentious. This section therefore attempts to provide a balanced appraisal of this issue before assessing the future of the British industry.

The picture of increasing concentration of the world car industry appeared evident in OECD findings (1983) discussed earlier in this chapter. The need for volume, not only in pursuit of crude production economies but also to fund new model programmes and other investment demands such as distribution networks, overseas plants, promotional activities and more generally in keeping up with technology, has always been an underlying issue. OECD (1983) see the process of concentration continuing on an worldwide basis, with internationalisation being further propelled by three other factors: the development of the EEC, the impact of Japanese exports, and the advantageous cost position of many newly developed countries. In fact Marfels' (1983) more recent empirical evidence indicates no increased concentration within Europe between 1970 and 1979, but suggests that the industry did anticipate that increased US and Japanese competition would result in further concentration and rationalisation in the 1980s.

MIT's team, however, point to a radically different scenario in the wake of the transformation they see as having taken place in the pattern of competition (Altshuler, Anderson, Jones, Roos and Womack, 1984). Improved methods developed by the Japanese now place a premium on flexibility; crude volume orientation may be dangerous, as it proved to be for Ford in 1927.

Europe, the largest market, still displays distinctive preferences and different patterns of segmentation. French customers still prefer their own distinctive styling, and Italians prefer smaller cars suited to their narrow streets, whilst the German market tends to polarise between good quality, fairly practical cars (e.g. the VW Polo) and more expensive, luxury, high-performance cars (e.g. BMW and Mercedes). National companies still orientate their models primarily to their national markets.

Market segmentation has become even more complex, with differentiation not merely on the basis of size but also along entirely independent dimensions of luxury, utility, economy and performance. 'Down-sizing' has compressed model ranges, but intensified competition has led to an increased variety of product offerings, as even volume manufacturers such as VW/Audi, Renault, Fiat and Peugeot have placed greater emphasis on product differentiation. Also ARMC (*Financial Times*, 2 August 1985) have suggested that a large proportion of any increased European market demand is going to specialist producers such as Mercedes, BMW, Volvo and Saab rather than to volume producers. Specialist segments have also become more profitable.

These developments have been supported by much more flexible systems of vehicle manufacture; Bessant, Jones, Lamming and Pollard (1984) argue, for example, that new tooling systems and manufacturing methods (along lines pioneered in Japan) have enabled BL (now renamed as Rover) to reduce the critical level for scale economies.

There has been an explosion of technological innovations:

- electronic developments aimed at fuel economy (engine/drive train management systems), safety (anti-skid systems) and product differentiation and convenience (instrumentation)
- use of new materials aimed at weight reduction (plastics) or safety (windscreen materials)
- new concepts in vehicle design

Patenting activity has increased sharply in Japan, the USA and Germany, though Britain appears to lag behind (Jones, 1983a, p.227; Patel and Pavitt, 1987).

The conflicting demands of volume and flexibility have been partly reconciled by an emerging pattern of both competition and cooperation between vehicle assemblers and also component manufacturers, analogous to the pattern of competition which has for many years existed in Japan. Extensive joint ventures, such as between BL and Honda, are already widespread (e.g. joint engine development by Renault, Peugeot and Volvo) and seem likely to increase. The same pressure is forcing much closer cooperation between assemblers and their suppliers (e.g. BL and Perkins on diesel engine development for the Rover V6) and also between component manufacturers themselves.

Ultimately the priority is for other manufacturers to catch up with best practice, now established by Japan rather as in the past the USA. Yet political intervention may still play some part in any adjustment process, just as historically all countries in both Europe and Japan took measures to protect their home industries when faced with such radical improvements by the US industry.

These factors modify any scenario of increasing concentration (even among volume producers). Altshuler, Anderson, Jones, Roos and Womack (1984, p.183) argue that this and the likelihood of, if necessary, protective intervention mean 'there are likely to be about as many automakers 20 years from now as today'. On this basis prospects for medium volume producers such as Rover are much brighter. Similar thinking led Bessant, Jones, Lamming and Pollard (1984, p.23) to expect Rover's output to increase from 360,000 vehicles in 1982 to 575,000 in 1986.

MIT seem to have been correct in debunking more extreme world car scenarios. The Japanese competitive advantage does appear to be based more on flexibility than on volume, as Bhaskar (1984) would also seem to argue. GM and Ford do seem to have misjudged the market in introducing their world cars. For example, the US market moved sharply away from European-type small cars just as the Escort/Lynx and ideas of rationalising parts between Europe and America did not work out in practice. Bannock (1983, p38) pointed out that 95% of components for the US version were sourced locally. A *Financial Times* survey (11 Sept. 1985, p.X) summarised the situation: 'The first world cars appeared as recently as 1980 but already the concept seems to be as old-fashioned and outdated as a model T Ford'.

Yet whilst they are correct in pointing out the dangers of simplistic scenarios and of crude volume-orientated strategies, I believe they may have understated the significance of volume in a broader sense. Bessant, Jones, Lamming and Pollard's (1984) conclusions about the prospects for medium-sized volume car producers have in fact proved substantially over-optimistic. Despite market recovery, Austin Rover's growth in output between 1982 and 1986 was actually 12% rather than their anticipated figure of 60%.

Knibb(1982) and Marfels(1983) foresee further concentration in the world industry. Bhaskar likewise argues that overcapacity by 1990, together with investments demanded by the accelerated pace of technical innovation and the need for new plants and models, will force further rationalisation (*Financial Times*, 11 September 1985, p.11). Japanese rivals have invested heavily in product improvements such as style, comfort and handling, cost and maintenance, and in quality and reliability where they are increasing their lead (Bhaskar, 1984, pp.12,301-303). US rivals have followed suit placing further pressure on European manufacturers to keep up with new model programmes despite their weak financial positions: 'The average expected product sales life in Europe is still currently 8 years, when Japanese competitors are moving towards 4 years (as for instance Mazda with the 323). G.M.'s replacement of the Kadett after just 5 years has set a new standard in Europe.' (DRI Europe, 1985). European manufacturers are also finding it a struggle to keep up with the level of overseas investments now necessary, particularly if they are to keep up with the Japanese. Gooding (*Financial Times*, 3 May 1985, p.13) suggests that the only car assemblers with credible multinational operations in the 1990s will be VW in Europe, GM and Ford in the USA, and Nissan, Toyota, Mitsubishi and Honda in Japan. VW's Chairman Carl Hahn also warns that even the emergence of further collaborative arrangements between assemblers (and their component suppliers) will not stave off such pressures (*Financial Times*, 3 May 1985, p.13).

DRI Europe (1985, p.17) specifically refute another

plank in MIT's argument, that FMS production methods will enable medium-sized volume producers, such as Rover, to obtain production economies with plant output as low as 240,000 cars p.a. and conclude that 'major changes in the relative share of each volume manufacture are liable to take place':

> The leap between current practice and this Utopic future (heralded for instance in the MIT study) and where sixteen passenger car manufacturers could theoretically all operate at competitive production levels by utilising the latest manufacturing technology is a very long one and probably beyond the ability of many participants to fund.

Rover has achieved some real progress towards flexibility, for example in cutting its 'concept to production' time down from 5 to 3.5 years. Yet as Williams, Williams and Haslam (1987) argue, much of their investment has also gone into less flexibility assembly methods and capital productivity has proved far less impressive than highly publicised achievements in respect to labour productivity.

Thus, whilst crude volume orientated strategies such as 'world car' developments may well be as dangerous as MIT indicate, the scenario of further concentration in the world industry cannot be entirely dismissed. Buoyant market conditions in the last few years may have even encouraged some proliferation (Scott, Ward and Way, 1988), but European manufacturers are likely to enter the next downturn without the benefits of the financial reserves built up by other groups according to Roger Vincent, Bankers Trust Managing Director (*Financial Times*, 11 September 1987). This will increase the pressure for rationalisation. European harmonisation is also likely 'to have a negative effect on weaker manufacturers, and in extreme cases might force manufacturers out of business' (Motor Industry Research Unit, 1988). On any such scenario the prospects for UK vehicle assemblers such as Rover (and for their suppliers) must appear vulnerable, once the immediate upturn is over.

The UK Position

Despite Japan's rise, W. Europe has broadly held its own. Its share of world car production, having perhaps peaked in 1970, was in 1973 39%, the same level achieved throughout the 1960s. By 1978, this had slipped slightly in the face of Japanese competition to 36%, but since then (as shown in Table 3.3) it has remained at the same level and is not expected to change in the next few years.

Britain's problem is that it has not been able to keep up with the rest of Europe. In 1955, its share of W. European production was 36% only slightly below its position before the War. This fell steadily to 16% in 1970 and 11% in 1978.

Central Policy Review Staff (1975) incisively summarised many key competitive issues then facing UK vehicle manufacturers: poor distribution networks, inadequate products on offer, poor quality, late delivery, lack of capital investment, poor industrial relations and excessive manufacturing costs reflecting poor productivity. It was also clear that the industry had been seriously damaged by an unfavourable political and economic climate, due to stop-go policies, sharply varying taxation and hire purchase arrangements, and regional policies (Dunnett, 1980).

Though effectively nationalised as British Leyland in 1975, the problems of the UK-owned sector of the industry, were not resolved by the Ryder Plan's combination of government funds and a softly-softly managerial approach, which merely led to a further profits crisis (Williams, Williams and Haslam, 1987). The combination, however, of government funds and a much more determined managerial approach under Michael Edwardes's leadership showed greater promise, though the financial position was again damaged by Britain's exceptional economic climate. Apart from there being room for further improvement on quality, Bhaskar (1984) indicated substantial progress on many of the other problems identified by the Central Policy Review Staff report.

Bhaskar (1984, p.295) nevertheless showed, that in the years immediately following 1979, there was still a major problem of manufacturing costs because of the country's economic choices: 'Since 1978, monetarism and North Sea

Oil have contrived to introduce a new element which completely swamped the competitiveness of the motor industry'. Real exchange rate movements were reflected in much higher UK vehicle cost levels and prices (see for example Ashworth, Kay and Sharpe, 1982). In spite of improved market conditions Bhaskar warned that, with the Japanese threat, there was little room for complacency either by management or by government.

By 1982, Britain's share of European car production had slipped back to 9% and this was indeed partly due to the deterioration in Britain's general cost position as a result of exchange rate movements. The increased proportion of 'tied imports' shown in Table 3.4 demonstrates that even multinational companies such as Ford and General Motors were finding Britain uncompetitive as a manufacturing location at this time.

Table 3.4: UK market shares (%)

Year	1973	1978	1982	1986
UK made				
Austin Rover	31.9	23.5	17.2	15.6
Ford (UK)	22.6	16.1	15.7	17.6
GM & Talbot (UK)	18.7	12.0	8.6	10.1
Imports:				
Ford	–	8.6	14.8	9.8
GM & Talbot	0.3	4.4	7.9	9.6
Other European	20.9	24.5	24.2	26.1
Japanese	5.6	10.9	11.6	11.2
UK made	73.2	51.6	41.5	43.3
Captive imports	0.3	13.0	22.7	19.4
Other imports	26.5	35.4	35.8	37.3

Source: Bessant, Jones, Lamming and Pollard (1984, p11) and SMMT

Subsequently the exchange rate improved, particularly in 1986 when the pound fell 25% against the West

German D-mark. Captive imports have continued to decline as Ford and General Motors both substantially increased UK content, and such moves by multinationals explain why UK car production is expected to rise from 1.0m in 1986 to 1.4m by 1992 as indicated in Table 3.3. Such an outlook could prove vulnerable however. In the first half of 1987 the market share of UK made cars advanced to 50%, but already in the first half of 1988 a combination of strikes and a less competitive exchange rate has reduced this share to 45% (*Financial Times*, 7 July 1988, p.8).

For suppliers a critical problem has been the continuing decline of Rover, particularly in view of its unique near 100% UK component content. Between 1973 and 1982 its market share fell from 32% to 15.6% in 1986. This may have been a bad year, but although it has finally broken back into profits, market share again fell in the first half of 1988 to 15.1%. DRI forecast an increase in Rover's output from 0.40m cars in 1986 to 0.50m in 1992, with half the increase coming from Honda, though this would imply a further fall in UK market share to 13.2%. Despite the fact that modern technology is estimated by some to have reduced optimal plant size to about 0.4m cars a year (Rhys, 1984), and despite collaborative agreements, Rover does as the last section concluded still face a problem of volume. Japanese market share has only been held at 11% as a result of a strict SMMT/JAMA agreement on imports, but this will rise as UK-based production builds up. Rover's progress in the market place is becoming stymied by competition from GM and Ford, which can only further intensify. At the same time imports from other companies are still edging up and Rover's funding position looks very weak at a time when further investments will have to be made in new model programmes. Given an effective subsidy, the group as a whole may offer adequate attraction to British Aerospace; but ultimately the car side will have to stand on its own feet, and this consolidation does not appear to offer synergies that might enable Rover to address its underlying competitive difficulties any more effectively. Indeed corporate plans released to the European commission now indicate Rover's decision to switch from being a volume car producer to a smaller specialist producer, and plans to reduce capacity by over 30% which will affect both assembly and in-house component production (*Financial Times*, 15 July 1988, p.6). Even allowing for the revelation, that year's capacity utilisation was under 60%, future prospects from the viewpoints of suppliers must now look distinctly gloomier.

Thus although some progress has undoubtedly been made in absolute terms, the British-owned car assembly industry is still losing ground in international terms, and the overall outlook is considerably more vulnerable than projected UK production levels might at first sight suggest.

The Relationship between Vehicle Production and Component Markets

The impact of such developments in the upstream vehicle assembly industry upon UK suppliers depends on the relationship between the two sectors, and in particular upon assemblers' sourcing policies and domestic content levels.

Despite the fact that components represent some 55% of vehicle costs, the relationship between assemblers and suppliers was traditionally regarded as 'arms length'. Traditionally UK suppliers perceived their relative independence, as compared with continental rivals, to be a positive advantage. A greater degree of out sourcing by UK car assemblers, and also by related upstream industries such as engines, trucks and tractors which were still relatively large, meant that the UK vehicle components market (here broadly defined) in 1981 was larger than suggested by vehicle production levels, as shown in Table 3.5 (source: Knibb, 1982).

Relative independence was also expected to help UK suppliers to gain from the fact that international trade in parts has increased more rapidly than vehicle production. Between 1974 and 1979 original parts imports rose 270% in Germany, 100% in France and 60% in the UK, compared with vehicle volumes up by 37%, 18% and -26% respectively (Knibb, 1982). Trade is expected to increase further as is shown in Table 3.6.

Table 3.5: Sizes of main European markets for original equipment vehicle parts in 1981

Country	Value £bn	European share %
Germany	6.3	33
France	3.6	19
UK	3.1	16
Spain	2.1	11
Italy	1.9	10
Rest of Europe	2.1	11
Total	19.1	100

Table 3.6: Trade trends in European component markets

Year	1981	1990 (forecast)
European market, 1981 £bn	19.1	22.0
Non-European trade %	1	2
Inter-European trade %	9	23
Domestic %	90	75

Source: Knibb (1982)

Of the projected market increase between 1981 and 1990 only £1.7bn is expected to derive from rising vehicle production and £1.2bn is expected to come from greater outsourcing by vehicle manufacturers (Knibb, 1982). Accelerated technical change and a poor funding position were also considered likely to increase European assemblers' reliance upon suppliers.

Yet both assemblers and suppliers were cushioned from international competition by UK tariffs up to 1960. Suppliers were also cushioned by established and sometimes monopolistic customer relationships. As a result both sectors tended to be complacent about their effect on the other's competitiveness, which may have been damaging to both. The MIT report already discussed stresses the close interdependence which has played such an important part in the competitiveness of both Japanese assembler and supplier sectors. On balance only a very few UK suppliers may be strong enough to gain on balance from pursuing a more independent stance; most might perhaps be better advised to concentrate on developing closer relationships with UK-based car assemblers. For their part, the need to foster an internationally competitive domestic supplier industry has also been a central consideration in the changes which have taken place in car assemblers' sourcing policies over recent years.

Sourcing Policies

In the past assemblers' sourcing policies were relatively stable and UK suppliers may have felt able to take their home market to some extent for granted. In the early 1970s faced with international competition, UK assemblers turned increasingly to dual- and multi- sourcing, partly initially to improve security of supply on key components, but increasingly to secure a more internationally competitive service and in particular to reduce costs. Alterations in sourcing policies have been the practical way in which assemblers have passed onto UK suppliers the need to become more internationally competitive.

As multi-sourcing was extended later in the 1970s this increased negotiating power, and so reduced costs in the short term, but at the expense of weakening the supplier network. Suppliers were hit by falling production volumes, with the remaining business increasingly split up (further offsetting scale economies) leading to more rivalry among suppliers. After 1979 worldwide recession in the motor industry and growing overcapacity stepped up international competition just as the cost position of UK assemblers and suppliers was severely eroded by a soaring exchange rate. This led to further more radical changes in sourcing policies and also involved substantial overseas procurement.

Both BL and Ford conducted detailed international surveys comparing component costs. BL's Chief Executive, Ray Horrocks (CBI/SMMT conference, London, 16 May 1983), described how they had 'found that, virtually across the board of electrical, mechanical, trim and body components, Japanese produced parts were between ten and thirty five per cent cheaper than the cost of their European equivalents ... Indeed if sheer commercial logic was to be the sole criterion then a large proportion of our components business would have left the UK at the time'. Ford's Chief Executive, Sam Toy also pointed to the fact that UK suppliers were responding inadequately to international standards of competitiveness in three key respects: consistent quality, delivery and price. He acknowledged there had been 'some drop in our level of UK sourcing' and stated that:

> Because we are making our vehicles to European quality standards not British ones; we have to survive out there ourselves - and there has been some improvement but there are still too many British suppliers who cannot give us competitive standards of quality. And even when they do they often can't deliver the quantities we need when we need them.

Vehicle companies were prepared for drastic action to ameliorate the competitive gap which had emerged on components after 1979. Jones (1985b, p.9) summarises the impact on component markets:

> The volume of UK components supplied to UK car assemblers in 1984 was as a result only 33 per cent of the 1972 level. Between 1972 and 1979 the collapse of the component market was almost entirely due to the fall in the numbers of cars produced in the UK. However, since then imported components accounted for half the drop in the component market. There is little doubt that the UK components industry suffered the biggest collapse of any car producing nation in the world.

Much of this was due to multinational vehicle assemblers, Rover's volume adjustments having been more conservative. Although international procurement became critically important, the actual volume of business involved was no more than 10 to 15% in 1983 (Bessant, Jones, Lamming and Pollard, 1984 p.26). Yet changes in market volume are only one way in which suppliers have been affected. More significantly, in the context of overcapacity in the component sector, Rover's move back to single sourcing, its threat and occasionally use of overseas sources enabled its purchasing department to completely reverse the bargaining positions of the two sectors: 'most components have been subject to a four year price freeze and some are even cheaper now than their 1979 prices' (Bessant, Jones, Lamming and Pollard, 1983, p.61). The UK general wholesale price index rose just over 46% over this period. Whereas UK component companies averaged about 18% return on capital employed during the 1970s (see page 186) over twice that for UK assemblers, for the first time ever they actually averaged losses just as BL's financial performance was beginning to improve.

BL has recognised that such policies weakened the technological capability of its supplier base and led to a deterioration in supplier relations at precisely the moment when it needed greater supplier collaboration and technological support. Yet comparing overseas component prices, Rover estimated that in the four year period after 1979, it effectively subsidised UK suppliers by about £30m p.a. even after its drastic cost reduction programmes, giving it little room for manoeuver (Bessant, Jones, Lamming and Pollard, 1984, p.62). Since then, like other assemblers, it has been attempting to move towards a closer more collaborative relationship with suppliers.

More recently the international competitiveness of UK suppliers has improved, though thanks in large part to somewhat fragile exchange rate movements. Both Rover and Ford are entering into longer-term agreements, though with a smaller number of suppliers. They are demanding high standards of supplier service and involvement, through from quality assurance, technological support, the taking of responsibility for a much more flexible service (inventory costs being made a supplier responsibility) and a greater degree of local manufacturing support. But in return the relationship is gradually becoming more two-way, with assemblers offering longer-term assurances and being much more prepared to offer suppliers more detailed information and greater involvement in regard to their own plans. Outsourcing is expected to increase (Sleigh, 1988), particularly perhaps at Rover. GM is the most vertically integrated assembler, building up to 70% of its cars from internally sourced components, compared with about 50% for Ford and even less in the case of Chrysler and the Japanese (*Financial Times*, 14 June 1988); however only about 2% of GM's supply is likely to be affected in this way. Some suppliers are already exploiting the trend towards 'black box' engineering, whilst others are seizing the opportunity to offer a more overall 'systems engineering' support service. Gains from collaboration (e.g. on cost reduction) are now being split more equally between the two sides.

Such a relationship has been crucial in Japan to developments which have led to an extremely competitive vehicle industry, such as complete just-in-time systems of manufacture, operating through from assemblers, to suppliers, and to suppliers' suppliers. For UK component manufacturers a closer relationship has become particularly vital. On the one hand multinational assemblers are increasing their grip on the home market, whilst at the same time affording improved access to overseas operations; on the other hand, there is still little sign of other continental component markets (let alone Japan!) opening up anything like as quickly as the UK.

Domestic Content

Taking a number of common models UK content of British cars in 1987 averaged 90% for Rover, 80% for Ford, 62% for GM's Vauxhall, 58% for Peugeot and was 45% for the Nissan Bluebird (analysis of Rhys' figures in *Financial Times*, 14 May 1987 p.8, based on ex-factory prices). Rover expected to maintain its high level of content, whilst that of a number of these GM and Peugeot models was expected to increase by around 5% by 1989. Nissan's content was expected to rise to 54% in 1988 and around 70% by 1991. UK-based multinationals also use British components on overseas-made cars but here UK content is generally below 5%.

The reason UK suppliers cannot take their future market prospects for granted is that as discussed in the last section most of the increase in UK car production over the next few years is expected to come from the multinationals, whose content levels are relatively lower. Rhys argues that UK suppliers only really benefit when content levels reach about 80%. 'Only then will sophisticated, high technology, high value-added items related to power train (engines, gearboxes, etc.) and suspension be bought'. The effect of lower levels he stresses would be disproportionate: a 60% ex-works content can result in only about 20% of components and materials being sourced locally. In addition overseas multinational assemblers are bringing overseas suppliers in their wake. Some 20 French, German and Japanese component companies are actively seeking locations for plants in the UK currently (Sleigh, 1988). UK supplier prospects are thus more than ever contingent upon their ability to offer a fully internationally competitive service.

Structural Influences

The process of internationalisation, which has been a feature of upstream developments, is today mirrored by a similar phenomenon in the downstream components industry - a phenomenon given greater impetus by multinational assemblers' decisions radically to reduce supplier numbers worldwide. Relatively isolated even as late as the 1960s, UK suppliers today face gruelling quality and efficiency audits, designed to weed out all but the most internationally competitive whether they are supplying multinationals or even nationally owned customers such as Rover. Even the Japanese now look set to internationalise their supplier base, and such moves will also accelerate the threat of low cost Asian competition, particularly from Korea.

Suppliers who wish to remain in the business cannot afford to escape the opportunities which are emerging, but nor can they escape the increasing level of demands thereby placed on their resources. Given that most UK suppliers seem insufficiently invested to meet such demands, Sleigh (1988) therefore sees further structural change, leading to greater concentration and favouring larger companies. Size again is suggested as a critical issue. Only 60 suppliers in the UK are regarded as 'viable', in terms of having automotive sales of at least £10 million p.a, the same number as seven years ago; but the number British owned has fallen from 68% to just over 50% as overseas multinationals have increased their grip. Only five British suppliers (Lucas, GKN, T&N, Pilkington and BBA) are seen as potentially genuinely global players; although other niches exist Sleigh argues that, with only 32 companies accounting for 93.3% of these 60 companies' automotive turnover, the stage is set for further concentration with larger companies expected to win out.

Such arguments pose important strategic questions for those concerned about the competitiveness of the UK industry, but they have to be answered carefully. Patterns of emerging competition can often prove more complex in practice, with the result that crude volume orientation can often prove a mistake (as we have seen happen in the upstream assembler industry). The characteristics of particular vehicle components also vary enormously, in respect to scale economies and their exposure to international trade. What is needed is a careful analysis, taking into account such factors, firstly into the real causes behind competitive decline in the past (was the problem really merely one of scale?) which will be comprehensively examined in Chapter 4. In this light, we can then proceed to a briefer analysis of recent developments in the vehicle component industry, which will be covered in Chapter 5. Finally in Chapters 6 and 7, we will return to the broader issue of British competitiveness.

4
The Vehicle Components Industry: Roots of Decline

4.1 The Position in Selected Product Sectors

This chapter presents the results of a detailed study of the UK automotive components industry's competition position carried out between 1980 and 1984, a period characterised by severe performance problems. The focus is on gaining an understanding of the competitive problems at that time and of what needed to be done. The first section is based on indepth case studies of four product areas; the second deals with the situation overall. Chapter 5 will deal with the most recent position and address the question of the extent to which the necessary steps have been taken, but it is hoped that this chapter is not just a dry ex-post analysis relying on the benefit of hindsight. It is based on international comparisons at the time (supported by a more historical analysis of events), with conclusions being forward looking. It is therefore written in the present tense and the reader will be able to judge for himself whether or not the results of the analysis are borne out by subsequent developments.

4.1.1 Automotive Ball and Roller Bearings

The UK Market for Bearings

To understand the situation in automotive bearings it is first useful to examine the UK market for all types of bearings. This is analysed in Table 4.1

Table 4.1: UK ball and roller bearings market by value (£m)

	1970	1974	1978	1980	1982	1983
Sales by UK mfr's	315	280	243	239	161	142
Less exports	82	98	104	113	92	83
Plus imports	68	151	149	132	118	116
= Home market	302	333	288	258	187	175
Import share %	23	45	52	51	63	66
Japan's share %			3.2	6.6	6.4	7.1
Exports/sales %	26	35	43	47	57	58
BoT/home market %	+4.5	-16	-7	-14	-19	

All figures have been adjusted to 1980 prices. Import figures have been increased consistently by 35% in line with the trade association correction to raise import prices to market prices.

Source: Business Monitor

Allowing for inflation, the home market by 1983 had fallen to 58% of its level in 1970. Gradual market decline up to 1980 is understandable given UK vehicle production levels for example nearly halved between 1973 and 1980; but such steep decline after 1980, when UK vehicle production in fact remained stable, would seem to reflect more fundamental problems in the UK, and not merely recession either.

The market comprises direct automotive sales (28%), mechanical engineering (25%), agricultural machinery (8%), aero (6%), other transport industries (5%), and electrical appliances (5%). The remaining 23% is directed through distributors. Of this about 2% is for the automotive aftermarket, so that bearing manufacturers depend on the automotive market for only about 30% of their sales. Potentially, bearing manufacturers might have been expected to have had more scope than other component manufacturers for offsetting automotive decline by increasing other activities. In fact, the market split is considered to have remained fairly stable. The market base has therefore been eroded by comprehensive decline among UK customer industries, allowing little scope in this direction.

The impact of direct international competition has increased substantially. Import penetration increased from 23% in 1970 to 66% in 1983. Although UK manufacturers' export ratio increased from 26% to 58%, export volume actually remained flat.

Thus business competition in this sector is now much more international. Market performance has been damaged both by direct international competition, this being reflected in the declining position on international trade, and indirectly, due to comprehensive decline among UK customer industries, themselves also highly exposed.

The Direction of Trade and Competition

Table 4.2 analyses the source of imports and the destination of exports.

Table 4.2: Source of UK imports and destination of UK exports

	% of UK imports		% of UK exports	
	1970	1980	1970	1980
EEC	33	55	22	45
USA	33	16	10	8.5
Japan	11	14	-	-
Germany	26	30	5	14
France	3	10	6	12
Italy	3	11	5	11
Sweden	10	6	3	5

Source: Customs and Excise

US trade has reduced in significance, whilst Japanese competition has become more important. The major focus of both trade and competition is now Europe.

Competing Companies and Market Performance

Table 4.3: Sales performances of companies and of UK subsidiaries

Company and base	Units	Sales 1970	Sales 1980	Sales 1983	Growth 1970-80 %pa	Growth 1980-83 %pa	Sales 1983 £m
SKF (Sweden)	kr/m	4,758	12,512	16,191	0.1	(0.02)	1,390
Timken (USA)	$m	365 (1972)	966	na	2.68	na	560 (1981)
FAG (Germany)	DMm	1,680	1,950	1,710	(3.03)	(7.44)	430
NSK (Japan)	y'000	52.27	167.7	185.6	6.92	2.87	550
Koyo (Japan)	y'000	51.9	110	126.7	1.18	4.34	375
Federal Mogul (USA)	$m	251.1					
Torrington (USA)	$m	n/a					
Nachi-Fujikoshi (Japan)	y'000	48.3	91.15	91.48	0.98	(0.05)	270
NTN	y'000	45.3	149.1	184.9	7.36	7.23	550
INA (Germany)	DMm	n/a					
N Thomson (Japan)	y'000		12.2				
SNR (France)	FFm	n/a					
RHP (UK)	£m	40.1	120	102.4	(1.91)	(10.85)	102
SKF UK	£m	22.19	71.78	66.37	(1.25)	(8.97)	66
Torrington UK	£m	6.608	24.1	25.85 (1982)	(0.13)	(0.53)	26
INA UK	£m	4.279 (1971)	11.6	17.22	(2.01)	5.78	17
NSK UK	£m		6.88 (1979)				
Timken UK	£m	n/a					

Source: company accounts

*Note: growth rates calculated after adjusting for inflation

of domestic currency by means of wholesale price indices. 1983 exchange conversions based on sterling at: $1.4514, 337.0 yen, FF12.1147, 2408.6 lira, DM3.9536, 11.6125 Swedish kronor.

In 1969 the three remaining major UK-owned bearing companies merged, with assistance from the Industrial Reorganisation Corporation, to form RHP. Other UK manufacturers of automotive bearings are subsidiaries of overseas companies.

Table 4.3 gives performance details for the most important world competitors in this sector. Some details for UK subsidiaries are also included to give a better appreciation of the UK situation. These should be treated cautiously as their results reflect parent company marketing operations in addition to UK manufacturing.

Poor UK sales performances (with the exception of INA recently) reflect the poor domestic market situation already discussed. Although RHP is the UK market leader, it is considerably smaller than the parent companies of key competitors taking an international perspective. Most are supported with UK and other overseas manufacturing operations: SKF, Timken, Torrington, INA and NSK.

As the radius of competition has become more international RHP, which lacks an overseas manufacturing capacity, has found its competitive position against world competitors increasingly vulnerable. Between 1970 and 1980 total sales volume fell back relative to other competitors, and also in absolute terms, at about 2% per annum. Between 1980 and 1983, as competitive conditions intensified it fell back even more sharply: total sales volume declining at about 11% p.a., despite non-bearing activities increasing to 27% of sales.

Competitor positions in the UK and other major European bearing markets are shown in Table 4.4, and show the strength and international integration of RHP's main competitors. Furthermore, as will be explained later, most have achieved defensible positions, coherent in international terms. Some indication is given in Table 4.5.

Table 4.4: European markets: positions and percentage shares

UK		Germany		France		Italy		Spain
RHP*	22	FAG*	~35	SNR*		SKF*	70	SKF
SKF*	18	SKF*	~35	SKF*	~33	FAG	15	FAG
Timken*	14	INA*		INA*				
Japan*	8	Japan*		Timken*				
FAG	5	Timken		SNCF*				
Fafnir	4	SNR		Japan*				
INA*	4	RHP	<1	Nadella*				
Others	25							
(Others are principally Torrington* SNR and then a host of specialist mfrs)		In 1968 FAG and SKF held about 40% each but have lost share to INA and Japan.						
Automotive only:								
RHP	~25	Vehicle customers more 'open' but competition among mfrs duopolistic		SNR owned by Renault and close links with Peugeot		SKF's plant closely linked with Fiat		SKF has strong position with SEAT (Fiat link) and GM
SKF	~20							
Timken	~16							
Torrington								
INA Japan	~2							
RHP link with BL fairly strong								

* denotes market support through manufacturing operations

Such coherence, in international terms, is less evident in the case of FAG, SNR, Nadella and RHP and this tends to be reflected in poorer long-term performance. Their competitive positions were undoubtedly stronger and more coherent whilst competition was largely fought on a country by country basis. France's Nadella, in needle bearings, is too weak to survive competition from INA and Torrington and at some stage may well be taken over. FAG is still extremely powerful because of its strong German home market base and because of its highly successful exporting performance.

France's SNR, whilst weaker, is nevertheless supported by its closely tied relationships with French vehicle manufacturers. RHP has a fairly close relationship with BL, but given a small and declining home market its position in international terms has been weak.

Key Issues

Changing pattern of competition generally

In the late 1950s and early 1960s (prior to Britain's entry into the EEC) British bearing manufacturers remained fairly isolated from European or Japanese competition. Imports were mainly limited to specialist bearing types, mainly from the USA through Timken (tapered roller bearings) and Torrington and some from SKF in Europe. Most of these companies' sales, though, were based on production from their UK factories and competition was on a national basis. Exports to soft Commonwealth markets more than covered any net imports from these companies, and the international competitive position of the sector was strong.

Yet an undercurrent of change was taking place in the pattern of competition. Exports to Commonwealth markets were declining; but in Europe, now their main destination, Britain faced powerful competitors. At the same time the first tremors of Japanese competition signalled a step change in the intensity of competition among the major world bearing companies. This in turn was to lead to international rationalisation in the industry.

The key development involved was a change in manufacturing processes. The Japanese mounted their attack on the European market on a few popular size ranges of radial ball bearings, the main application being electric motors. Given long production runs they moved from batch production, which made use of fairly basic flexible equipment, to a flow line operation employing dedicated equipment. Although raising investment requirements this resulted in a step change in the productivity both of labour and working capital. Gearing up manufacturing operations accordingly the Japanese aggressively pushed down costs as cumulative production volume rose, in the manner of the 'experience curve'. (Boston Consulting Group, 1975, estimate the gradient for Japanese radial ball bearings at 73%). Japanese manufacturers were assisted by a fast-growing home market, which if not as large as Europe was substantially more homogeneous. Moreover the structure of their industry was less fragmented: in 1977 for example four companies accounted for 90% of total sales and 95% of exports.

The initial British reaction was one of almost amused complacency as the Japanese struggled unsuccessfully to come up to European quality standards. What then surprised many was the degree of commitment with which the Japanese pursued their strategic thrust. To achieve the required quality they broke industry quality/cost trade-off norms, accepting a substantial (in the short-term) cost penalty by using extensively expensive operations such as honing. Having finally met quality standards and established a foothold in the market they were gradually able to exploit experience effects to improve cost levels and quality levels still further.

As the Japanese competitive position gradually strengthened British manufacturers, slow to respond, were cushioned for a time by lower capital charges resulting from depreciated equipment. One Japanese executive who had visited British plants recalled how he had envied such low capital costs at the time, though not with the benefit of hindsight.

The effect on sales volume was fairly small, particularly in the automotive market, starter motor / alternator bearings being a fairly minor market segment. Financially, however, such long order runs represented 'cream' business and multinationals such as SKF were quick to respond with their own manufacturing changes. Manufacturers finding profit margins under greater pressure recognised that similar productivity and cost improvements could be made in other market segments. The name of the game, at least for the more powerful competitors, seemed to be 'volume', the means being to standardise onto fewer product ranges. This became a crucial factor driving rationalisation within Europe.

Table 4.5: Strategies of major international competitors

SKF	TIMKEN	NSK	TORRINGTON	INA	FAFNIR
World market leader	US market leader	Japan market leader	US leader in needle bearings	European leader in needle bearings	World leader in aero market
Full range except tapered roller bearings	Tapered roller bearings only and world leader in this segment	Full range except tapered roller bearings, but European strategy focused on metric ball bearings, volume ranges such as electrical applications	Focused on particular applications	Similar applications approach to Torrington	Strength in pulley block bearings
Integrated manufacturing facilities in all major European markets	Major base is USA, but operations supported by plants in UK and France	European position supported by modern UK plant dedicated to volume metric	Strength in applications engineering and customer support on more marginal business	Supported with manufacturing operations throughout Europe and rest of world	
Manufacturing support in USA and in some other parts of world			European position in this niche 2nd to INA but supported with manufacturing facilities in UK and Germany	US position in this niche 2nd to Torrington but supported by manufacturing operations	
Metric bias	Imperial bias	Metric	Imperial bias	Metric bias	Imperial bias
Diversified (28%) into related steel activities	Diversified (32%) into related steel activities	Diversified (31%)			

One by one the multinationals reorganised their manufacturing operations in the face of international competition intensifying as companies scrambled for volume order business. No longer content to compete on a country by country basis, SKF between about 1968 and

1975 radically integrated manufacturing operations within Europe to obtain the maximum benefits of volume. Their new 'global forecasting supply system' (GFSS) put planning and scheduling on a European basis. Timken reorganised its British and French plants, hitherto fairly autonomous, into Timken Europe and a new chief executive was appointed with a brief to 'bring down the walls in Europe'.

INA and Torrington, though powerfully supported by overseas manufacturing operations, responded more cautiously. Both stressed applications engineering and the provision of a more flexible customer service. They have therefore been wary of becoming too orientated towards volume order runs, and have so avoided head-on collision with SKF for example except in their more specialist applications. Nevertheless by the end of 1982 Torrington USA had finalised its plans to coordinate international operations much more closely, mirroring many of the manufacturing changes at SKF (e.g. commonality of tooling). INA has also become more integrated internationally.

Thus as the radius of competition became more international in volume segments, companies have generally had to adjust their strategies. The choice has been to orientate operations more internationally, reorganising where necessary to secure maximum volume benefits, or to develop roles still coherent internationally but avoiding head on competition with powerful international competitors.

Response to automotive developments

Ford and GM have moved to centralised purchasing within Europe and multinational bearing companies such as SKF and INA have adapted their operations to provide better support internationally. This has meant ensuring commonality of design and quality standards so that no matter where Ford is assembling or where SKF is manufacturing, bearings will fit and function properly: a left hand bearing made in one country may also have to match a right hand bearing made in another. Commonality is particularly important in the context of an increasing number of international joint ventures among customers, for example gearboxes which incorporate bearings.

An effect has been to raise minimum acceptable quality standards in all manufacturing countries to common norms, these being above those acceptable in Britain in the past.

SKF now sets price levels against local market conditions (UK price levels were about 12% higher than elsewhere in Europe in 1981 due to exchange rate movements). In the short-term this involves riding cost variations between different countries and affords some cushioning to countries such as the UK which have allowed relative cost levels to rise. Having rationalised manufacturing operations internationally, they want to minimise disruption. However, in decisions with longer-term implications such as major investments or closures, they are now much more sensitive to the issue of cost competitiveness (as indeed are all their customers). SKF has reorganised formally to mirror increasing integration in the world vehicle industries, and sees further changes in the future.

Vehicle customers are requiring increased technical support and this has been reflected in component company strategies. Timken has stepped up R & D considerably. SKF's move, up-value-added, into integrated wheel hub bearings represented an investment of about $25m, a step change well beyond levels affordable by Britain's RHP and recoverable only in the context of a more international market. Similarly, INA is placing still greater emphasis on applications engineering such as its successful clutch release bearing, an innovation saving Ford substantial warranty costs.

The bargaining position of vehicle customers has increased, forcing these suppliers to reduce margins in real terms, whilst reflecting customers' needs much more closely. For example the cost of stock holding, as a buffer against varying vehicle production levels, has been passed back to suppliers. Given fewer major vehicle purchasing departments, and their wish to deal with a smaller number of suppliers, there is pressure to squeeze out marginal international competitors. In such a capital intensive industry this competitive pressure is of course increased by overcapacity. Intensified competition has raised the cost of complacency: for manufacturers not responding adequately to new developments now face not merely suboptimal profit levels, but the threat of closures and asset write-offs.

Thus customer demands have forced a more international pattern of direct competition, both because in many cases they required international support from component manufacturers, and because they were increasingly able to insist on international standards of service and performance.

Productivity

Some indication on productivity is given in Table 4.6. This suggests that RHP's productivity growth has been reasonable compared with other major companies. This is partly because RHP has diversified into higher value-added electronic activities. However, its productivity level of about £16,000 sales/employee still appears well below that of other competitors in other countries.

Productivity performance appears better for UK subsidiaries of overseas companies, but an increasing proportion of their UK sales is made up of products manufactured overseas.

The operations of multinational companies in different countries provide better evidence on this issue. Two plants, one in Britain and one in Germany, belonging to one company, were engaged as 'dual sources' on the same automotive bearing product. Design, quality specifications and production runs were identical. I visited both plants to investigate productivity levels. An executive with experience of working in both plants stated that manning levels in the German plant were approximately 40% lower than in the British one. One factor was that German unions were more flexible, reflecting a much healthier industrial relations climate. A second factor was that responsibility for a wider range of production tasks was vested in the production operators themselves, and they were more actively willing and more appropriately trained for this responsibility (e.g. German operators involved were dual skilled).

I visited both British and German plants belonging to a second company and found executives held similar views on the scale of productivity differentials and also on the causes. German executives in both companies were critical of complacency by UK production management. This was felt to reflect inadequate pay levels, and inadequate board level attention to the production function.

Table 4.6: Company productivity performances

Company	Employees			Productivity growth			Sales/
	1970*	1980*	1983	70-80 %p.a.	80-83 %p.a.*	70-83 %p.a.	employee 1983/£*
SKF	67,375	56,501	45,683	2.04	5.33	3.05	30,400
Timken	22,433	22,874		3.04			29,100
NSK		7,006	7,363		1.11		74,800
Koyo		5,487	5,510		4.19		68,200
Nachi-Fujikoshi		5,000	5,032		(0.71)		53,900
NTN		3,981	5,949		(15.56)		
RHP	14,830	9,647	6,267	2.44	1.28	2.25	16,300
SKF UK	5,486	2,532	1,524	8.96	7.15	10.00	43,500
Torrington UK	1,560	1,607	1,217	(0.42)	5.99	1.00	21,200
INA UK	358	377	237	1.28	28.89	8.51	72,700
NSK UK			153				59,000
Timken UK		4,000					

Notes: Productivity growth rates calculated after allowing for inflation of domestic currency by means of wholesale price indices.

Figures not available for: FAG, Federal Mogul, Torrington, INA, N Thomson, SNR

* Exceptions to dates given:

1970 employees - figures for Timken and INA UK are 1972
1980 employees - figures for Koyo and NTN are 1981
1980-83 productivity growth - NTN is 1981-83 growth
Sales/Employee 1983 - Timken is 1980, NSK UK is 1978

Source: company accounts

Both companies reflected criticisms, made by German and Japanese executives, of an exploitational style of management in Britain. They felt it was impossible to gain fuller and more active participation from production operators in an atmosphere in which productivity gains so frequently resulted in unemployment. Frequent recourse to unemployment was perhaps inevitable so long as British management were content to allow their competitive position to be eroded.

There was, however, evidence that multinational companies, faced with increasingly severe UK conditions, were moving sharply to deal with such productivity differences. Until 1979 UK relative wage rates were on a downward trend sufficient to cushion this problem. By 1981 a rise of almost 40% reduced the gap between UK rates and those of its overseas competitors. Multinationals generally, stung by the effect this had on financial performance, adopted a much stronger line insisting that UK manning levels come into line with levels in other European countries: an example being SKF UK's January 1982 ultimatum to its workforce that unless this happened the plant would close. Productivity differentials within multinational companies could now be expected to be significantly lower, at least for comparable situations.

One Japanese company visited did not feel its UK plant (though under Japanese management) was behind Japan on productivity. The situation was not altogether comparable. The UK plant was small, very modern, and established on long production runs, and productivity was to a substantial extent process determined. However, like the Germans they found UK operators individually competent and efficient. Using Japanese managers they seemed to have succeeded better at harnessing the loyalty, flexibility and active participation of their UK workforce as a whole.

Thus UK management has been complacent on the issue of productivity, especially until recently, so that as UK wage rates moved more closely into line with international rivals' in 1980, international competitiveness and profitability declined sharply. British managers need to achieve the more constructive partnership with employees fostered by their German and Japanese counterparts.

Other production issues

The issue of manning is important in itself, but it is also symptomatic of a wider malaise that has plagued UK manufacturing. Where there is not the will, either by management or by employee representatives, to insist on even sensible manning levels, there would seem to be little hope of matching concepts such as 'built-in quality' that characterise German and Japanese manufacturing operations.

Such approaches, which would also seem critical to success in this sector, demand not merely even passive acceptance of change, but positive and committed pursuit of change by large numbers of production personnel. Progress here is more demanding, often taking several years of sustained and patient effort. Two things seem important.

First, top management in the UK need to recognise that in the context of this particular industry they cannot afford to treat such progress in production areas as a merely operational matter, viewed in the perspective of fairly short-term operating budgets. For example, this sometimes involves intractable industrial problems. From an operating perspective, resolving these may be unattractive because of obvious risks, but establishing more healthy 'precedents' may be vital to further progress and therefore ultimately to competitive survival. Where necessary resolution of any such problems must be viewed as a strategic, longer-term objective.

Second, and perhaps paradoxically, they need to rely less on externally imposed managerial control systems (e.g. ex-post quality control checking systems) and to delegate more authority (and recognition) to production personnel. UK production management is poorly trained technically in comparison with Germany, and also in comparison with the USA on more general managerial issues; the main problem, however, is the poor level of morale in comparison with Germany and especially Japan (where training is not well developed). However, increased delegation of power and authority is unlikely to be effective unless there is first a better partnership between management and employee representatives; without this production managers are likely to be swamped by the task presented to them.

Methods of production seem likely to change in two directions. The first, only appropriate to extremely high volume order runs, is the introduction of a third virtually unmanned 'ghost shift', a development pioneered by German manufacturers. This technology though is appropriate to few automotive bearings. It is not appropriate to UK manufacturers, given their withdrawal from volume market segments, and given a weak technological and financial position.

The other more appropriate challenge is to secure similar benefits to those presently obtained only with the advantage of long order runs on much lower order runs. This is inherently difficult in bearings and represents both a technological and an organisational challenge: much progress can only be incremental and depends on wholehearted support by production personnel.

Although FMS technology might seem to benefit smaller producers particularly, the immediate outlook is that it is the larger companies who are best able to afford the investment that in this sector will probably be needed.

Changes in production technology appropriate to automotive bearings are likely to take place fairly slowly, but will probably encourage further international rationalisation.

Decline of Multinational Companies' Manufacturing Operations in the UK

SKF

The coherence of the parent company SKF's strategic position is readily comprehensible in an international perspective. As the world market leader, it offers the most comprehensive product range, is strongly supported internationally, and has integrated its operations to exploit benefits associated with volume. This has substantially cushioned its UK manufacturing operation against the decline in the UK market. In 1970, almost 90% of SKF (UK)'s bearing sales were UK sourced. By 1981, largely as a result of the 'Global Forecasting and Supply System' programme (completed earlier), the majority of UK sales were sourced from overseas; but, conversely, most UK production was destined for overseas, so that dependence on the UK market was reduced.

Along with most other companies, SKF has found the UK an increasingly unattractive base from which to source bearings. Table 4.7 shows company profit performances.

Table 4.7: Company profit performances (pre-tax)

Company	Av. Profit/sales		ROCE	
	1970-80	1980-83	1970-80	1980-83
	%	%	%	%
SKF	6.4	5.0	5.7	6.0
Timken	10.1		13.4	
FAG	2.2		3.2E	
NSK	5.0	4.1	5.8E	
Koyo	1.9	2.1		
Federal Mogul	9.2		13.2	
Torrington	n/a			
Nachi-Fujikoshi	2.3	3.1		
NTN	2.6	6.3		
INA	n/a			
N Thomson	3.9			
SNR	n/a			
RHP	5.1	3.5	8.2	5.1
SKF UK	1.0	(2.3)	(0.5)	(3.7)
Torrington UK	4.4	1.5	5.4E	1.6
INA UK	8.0	12.1	18.8	21.5E
NSK UK	(8.4E)		(18.9E)	
Timken UK	n/a			

Source: company accounts

SKF (UK) averaged pre-tax losses on capital employed of 0.5% between 1970 and 1980 and 3.7% between 1980 and 1983, during which periods the parent company averaged profits of about 6% ROCE. SKF (UK) remained profitable from 1970 to 1975 after which financial performance fell alarmingly: apart from a marginal profit in

1980, it declared pre-tax losses (even on a historical cost basis) in every year from 1976 to 1983! These results also incorporate marketing activities on behalf of the parent company which are said to be more profitable than manufacturing operations.

SKF (UK)'s sales do not reflect UK manufacturing output and changes in employment levels give a better indication of SKF's commitment to manufacture in the UK in comparison to other companies. One should strictly allow for any differential growth in UK productivity as compared with other SKF plants, but this effect is small in comparison to employment changes.

Employment in SKF (UK) has fallen from 5,500 in 1970 to 1,500 in 1983; by comparison, SKF's employment worldwide fell from 67,000 to 46,000 over the same period. Table 4.8 shows employment for bearings activities only over the last five years, and compares the UK with SKF's other European operations.

Table 4.8: Employment in SKF's European bearings plants

	1978	1983	Reduction
Germany	10,180	8,188	20%
Italy	7,563	6,100	19%
France	5,754	3,685	36%
UK	3,440	1,162	66%
Other European	5,288	4,332	18%
Total European	32,225	23,467	23%

Source: company accounts

UK employment in bearings alone has been reduced to one third of its level five years ago, a reduction unmatched in any other European country. The UK operation has now retrenched onto a single plant at Sundon, having closed a second plant in the same area and its Scottish plant at Irving.

SKF's threat in January 1982 to close this last remaining plant, the first such ultimatum in fourteen years, demonstrated even its precarious position.

A more recent changeover of the major UK production lines demonstrated how marginal the UK operation has become from the parent company's viewpoint: in the weeks involved manufacture was transferred to other European plants which absorbed the additional production without apparent problems.

SKF's automotive bearing manufacture, its major UK manufacturing activity a decade ago, has changed significantly: only a few automotive bearings are now manufactured in substantial volume. Significantly SKF's recent quotation for a volume order for BL Austin Rover was based on manufacture in Italy. The major factors keeping some manufacture in the UK are first that some local manufacturing capability is useful marketing support and, second, political particularly in view of employment implications.

Timken

Timken worldwide enjoy a unique niche, specialising in tapered roller bearings. They are the market leader in the US market and are supported by overseas manufacturing operations. The coherence of their position in international terms has been reflected in consistent success, in terms of market and financial performance, and on other indicators such as employment and productivity, as shown in Tables 4.3, 4.6 and 4.7. Its US base is reputed, however, to have been more profitable than Europe. In 1977 the company employed about 23,000 people in the USA, 4,000 in the UK at two plants, Duston and Northampton, and 1,300 in France. It also has other manufacturing operations outside Europe and the USA. The UK operation is helped by the strength of its parent company and also by its historical position as the main base for the parent company's attack on the European market.

However, Timken's parent company is perhaps even more sensitive than SKF to what it perceives as a decline in the UK's attractiveness as a manufacturing location. SKF has integrated international manufacturing operations so as to maximise the long-term benefits, associated with scale and experience effects, resulting from plant specialisation: so it is less inclined to move production between countries when the relative cost position changes. SKF's structure also provides some cushioning against the effect of exchange rate movements. Losses in one country are partially offset by gains in other countries. Also if sterling rises any losses on UK manufacturing operations tend to be offset by additional profits on UK marketing operations, since a high proportion of their sales are sourced overseas. Timken is less internationally integrated and they are therefore highly sensitive to the UK's relative cost position.

Timken specialise in tapered roller bearings (about 20% of the market) and their products are heavily automotive orientated. They point to a step change in the cost of keeping up with new technological and manufacturing developments in automotive bearings, and foresee an intensification of international competition as leading to a 'shake out' of less competitive operations.

For this reason Timken UK is particularly critical of UK economic choices that have rendered UK operations less internationally competitive. Their cost position has been influenced by real exchange rate movements (nominal rates adjusted for differential inflation rates). Thus in 1973 they wanted to source as many bearings as possible from the UK following the fall in sterling. By contrast at the real exchange rate prevailing in 1981, the CEO's review of his UK operation suggested that the UK simply did not constitute a competitive base from which to manufacture. He felt the country had effectively made the decision to trade North Sea Oil off against a substantial part of the industrial sector. Automotive bearings are especially vulnerable to such economic issues because they are price sensitive and transport costs, even as far as America, represent only about 5% of sales value.

Graphs showing trends in relative UK labour rates in manufacturing were shown in Figure 1.2 in Chapter 1 on page 10. They confirm that a substantial drop in UK competitiveness took place between 1979 and 1981, making a discontinuity with trends over the previous twenty years. Since then there has been some return to past trends in the UK's relative position against the USA and to a lesser extent against Japan. This should improve Timken UK's position as against US manufacturing operations. However, the UK cost position is still seriously out of line with European countries. Not only does this create an incentive to transfer production to France, but it continues to undermine Timken's position against its key overseas competitors who are European.

It was also a question of market attractiveness, but Timken UK's customers were also manufacturers highly dependent on their international cost position; the declining customer base reflected similar problems. Competitive decline in the UK was a collective phenomenon affecting manufacturing generally.

Timken see their own competitive position in automotive rolling bearings as stronger, due to parent company support, than any other UK manufacturer. Nevertheless they did not see UK manufacture of this product continuing on any substantial scale in the long-term, unless the business environment became radically more favourable.

Other multinational operations in the UK

A detailed analysis of other multinational companies' UK bearing manufacturing operations is given in Carr (1985) Appendix B.3. For reasons of brevity the fuller account will here be omitted, though Tables 4.6 and 4.7 have provided an indication of profit and productivity performances in comparison to key international competitors. The analysis, however, supports two clear conclusions from this section.

First, multinational companies have had to reorientate their international operations in order to face intensifying international competition. Second, operations marginally competitive internationally have suffered disproportionately. This has applied to virtually all UK subsidiaries, and partly reflects a UK business environment unfavourable to international competitiveness.

RHP's Overall Competitiveness

As the only British-owned manufacturer of automotive bearings and the UK market leader, RHP's competitive situation will now be examined in detail.

As international competition intensified during the 1960s, Britain's competitive position declined. Exports of bearings, over 75% greater than imports in 1963, were only 36% greater by 1969. In such circumstances the Government viewed with alarm a takeover bid by SKF (UK) for Ransome and Marles, the largest of three major national bearing companies, which would almost certainly have left Britain with no viable UK-owned companies in the industry.

The resultant strategy, supported by financial assistance from the Industrial Reorganisation Corporation, was a merger of the three remaining UK-owned companies to form RHP and this was followed by a programme of consolidation and rationalisation. Such a broad strategy was to some extent dictated by a situation in which the competitive position of the UK industry had been allowed to weaken seriously. It was predicated on the assumption that the key weakness was one of scale and over-fragmentation: consolidation rigorously pursued promised to alleviate this weakness, and provide a stronger base for exports.

British productivity was recognised to be weak and key manufacturing developments being pursued by other world companies offered the promise of radical improvements. The seductive simplicity of such broad strategic thinking has ultimately proved superficial and misleading. By effectively mimicking their strategies RHP has plunged into head-on competition with powerful world (not merely national) market leaders. This almost inevitably has contributed to deterioration in its competitive position in virtually all the major automotive bearing market segments, leading to a costly (in both financial and human terms) process of retrenchment.

A key target in this strategy was to achieve longer production runs. This was done successfully by standardising the product range: the number of product variants being reduced from about 15,000 to 5,000 within just a few years. Factories were accordingly reorganised, so that production lines could be developed focused onto particular bearing types so as to exploit the advantages of experience effects and longer production runs.

Bold export targets were set, as the company

optimistically planned to take advantage of Britain's entry into the EEC and a more international pattern of business.

RHP's subsequent performance is analysed in Table 4.9.

Table 4.9: RHP's performance 1970-84

Year to 30 Sept	Sales £m'80	Profit £m'80	Margin	ROCE	Sales/ employee £'80	Exports £m'80	Non-bearing activities % / sales
1970	148	7.0	4.7	3.1	10,000	24.7	-
1971	150	8.5	5.7	4.7	10,800	32.0	-
1972	135	3.5	2.6	2.6	10,900	24.3	-
1973	141	2.4	1.7	2.3	12,700	26.6	-
1974	126	6.8	5.4	4.6	11,800	29.1	-
1975	125	11.5	9.2	8.4	11,900	24.9	4
1976	132	8.6	6.5	5.9	12,500	23.8	12
1977	119	7.2	6.0	4.8	11,300	23.8	14
1978	114	4.9	4.3	3.2	11,600	24.2	14
1979	114	6.1	5.4	6.3	11,700	28.4	18
1980	120	11.0	9.2	17.5	12,400	31.1	21
1981	105	0.7	0.6	1.2	12,300	25.2	24
1982	91	3.3	3.6	6.5	12,900	20.1	27
1983	81	0.5	0.7	1.1	12,900	17.6	29
1984	79	4.6	5.9	9.8	13,800	18.6	27

Source: company accounts

Allowing for initial disruption, results in the first few years looked promising. Under favourable market conditions sales volume fell only slightly as product lines were rationalised, and by 1973 productivity had been pushed up about 27% above 1970 levels. ROCE recovered, after being depressed in 1972 and 1973, peaking at just over 8% in 1975.

By 1974 a fundamental weakness in this volume-orientated strategy was becoming evident. The benefits associated with volume seem greater in this sector than for many other components. Had competition remained predominantly UK, this strategy would probably have continued to serve RHP (as the UK market leader) extremely well. Yet in the volume market segments particularly, RHP faced increasing competition from more powerful international competitors, better supported internationally to pursue precisely the same benefits associated with volume. The prospect of cost reduction had seduced RHP into head-on confrontation with international competitors that it was unlikely to be able to match.

RHP's competitive problem was by 1974 already apparent in popular metric segments of the market, where production runs were the longest. Fierce Japanese competition, particularly from NSK which had specialised in these market segments, hastened moves by other competitors. By 1974, SKF's 'GFSS' programme, integrating manufacturing operations throughout Europe, had improved its competitiveness in volume market segments. In the ensuing price war as SKF retaliated against low-priced Japanese competition, RHP was gradually squeezed out. The same theme was to repeat itself in the major automotive market segments, as will be discussed in the next section.

Such problems called for some decisive readjustment to this strategy. To have succeeded, such a volume-orientated strategy would have called for a much stronger international position, but some options had been ruled out by the UK government's original decision (perhaps also influenced by defence considerations) to opt for a UK-only solution. Many international options risked compromising the company's future independence and sovereignty, something not likely to have been attractive to senior executives. A major international move similar to BL's linkage with Honda might well have been another possibility.

Having decided against major international moves, RHP was nevertheless reluctant to reverse its volume-orientated stance. RHP was already deeply committed, and any trimming back in volume market segments would have meant painful surgery, cutting out substantial capacity. This was later forced on RHP but at this time rather than grapple with critical competitive problems, RHP was distracted by a third alternative.

Whilst maintaining its original strategy in bearings, it simply diversified through a rapid acquisition programme into the unrelated but attractive area of electronics. This can be seen in Table 4.9 above. Presumably RHP hoped by this means to bolster a weakening position in bearings, and ultimately reduce its dependence. It is too early to evaluate the success of these new electronics activities, though competition is likely to intensify here also; but by diverting scarce investment funds and senior executives' attention (particularly after the retirement of their original chairman in 1976) this further weakened RHP's competitive position in bearings.

Whilst imports were continuing to penetrate RHP's home market, its export strategy lay in ruins: by 1980 export volume was no higher than in 1971, and between 1980 and 1983 it fell by 43%. Sales volume fell from £150m in 1970 (at 1980 prices) to £120m in 1980 and then £80m in 1983. This was despite other new activities, which rose from 4% of total sales in 1975 to 23% in 1980 and 29% in 1983.

RHP's Strategies in Automotive Bearing's

Table 4.10 gives some introduction to the main automotive market segments now to be discussed.

The market for popular metric sizes of bearings, from which RHP had been forced to retreat, had involved order runs up to as much as 10,000,000 units p.a.. The only automotive applications in this class are for starter motors and alternators. Most automotive bearing orders are smaller.

Yet the fierce competitive battles in the popular metric segment heralded a similar increase in competition in other volume segments. Current manufacturing developments are also likely to raise competitive stakes still further. RHP has been better protected against this competition on imperial size ranges since international competitors, with the exception of US rivals, are orientated to metric ranges; but even BL, with whom RHP fortunately enjoys a close relationship, must be under some pressure to move to metrification, especially in view of its Honda

Table 4.10: Main market segments taking the example of a British conventional rear wheel drive car

	32%	25%	20%	10%	5%
Rear wheel, differential and prop' shaft bearings	Wheel bearings	Gearbox bearings	Clutch release bearings	Water pump spindle bearings,	Electric motor bearings, steering, related and others
Mostly tapered roller bearings but other options possible	May be tapered roller or ball bearings or integrated hub units	Mainly cylindrical or needle bearings	Specialist fabrications incorporating ball bearings. Higher 'value added' but needing innovative applied engineering	Double row deep grooved ball bearings, either supplied separately or as part of a complete fabrication	Starter motors and alternators require standardised small diameter radial ball bearings
Timken, SKF, RHP and others	RHP, SKF, Timken, Koyo, SNR	RHP, SKF, INA, Torrington	INA, RHP, SKF	RHP, SKF, FAG	NSK;SKF in electrical, Torrington in steering applications

link. On Ford's volume business, which is metric, RHP no longer seems cost competitive against SKF.

Wheel bearings

The more international pattern of competition has raised the stakes' in wheel bearings, one of the largest automotive markets. SKF have developed an 'integrated wheel hub bearing', a logical move from a component company's viewpoint, since the new product provides increased added value, utilises engineering expertise and so provides one direction for growth in an otherwise static market. This corresponds well with vehicle company needs for more engineering support and simplifies their own assembly operation. However, even for the world leader SKF this represents a very bold investment ($25m), recoverable only through exploiting the larger international market.

General Motors-owned US subsidiary New Departure Hyatt has followed suit. Timken have been developing their own variant on the integrated wheel hub bearing for 12 years now (illustrating the time scales involved in such major product developments).

RHP has not been able to keep up with such moves. It appears to have neither the financial resources nor the worldwide marketing capability to respond to such technical developments, even in this core area of the automotive bearings business. In the future its competitive position may become even more vulnerable if, as some predict, further product integration takes place with component suppliers perhaps collaborating and producing an integrated unit incorporating constant velocity joints.

Water pump spindle bearings

One strategy open to RHP was to concentrate on a particular segment of the automotive market, in the hope of becoming the major European specialist. Accordingly, RHP focused onto the water pump bearings segment and dedicated one of its factories onto this product. New markets were captured through aggressive pricing; but powerful German and Japanese competition forced punishingly low prices. RHP did not seem able to exploit potential volume advantages (such as 'experience' effects) sufficiently. Accumulating losses and cash flow difficulties, exacerbated by more difficult business conditions in the UK, ultimately forced RHP to close its Northampton plant specialising in this product. Much of this business has been transferred elsewhere in the group, but any momentum has been lost and RHP are no longer rated as one of the key competitors in this product area.

With hindsight, this failure seems unsurprising: even

Koyo Seiko, who were active in water pump bearings, have been forced by the strength of German competition to retrench dramatically in the German market. The high price of failure though is recorded in the high level of RHP's recent 'extraordinary' costs.

Clutch release bearings

If RHP has found itself increasingly squeezed in the volume segments, another alternative might have been to develop a role in terms of customer applications. This strategy has been successfully pursued by INA as a way of extending its base beyond needle bearings.

An important example is clutch release bearings. Like integrated wheel hub bearings, clutch release bearings represent higher value added as the product encompasses bearings as part of a complete assembly. This business segment is more closely customer-orientated and profits are earned through engineering innovation, aimed at solving particular customer design problems. For a good problem solving design, the price can reflect not so much manufacturing cost, but how much it is worth to the customer to have his problem solved (e.g. in avoiding warranty costs). Profit mark-ups can for a time at least be considerably higher than on established bearings products, and the key to competitiveness is technical innovation and good applications engineers working closely with customer design teams. Patenting can also be important.

This area is perhaps better suited to RHP's technical strengths, given its relative weakness on the manufacturing side. In the event, however, it was INA that 'stole a march' on both RHP and SKF, with the development and introduction of the self-aligning clutch release bearing, one of the few major recent developments in this market.

Although RHP later responded with its own self-aligning clutch release bearing, the product's technical reputation does not appear to be as high. SKF has responded with new product programmes and is reported to have a 'string of patents' coming out. The battle between SKF and INA is expected to intensify.

In this type of application, RHP's competitiveness seems also to have slipped back in the face of international competitors' more substantial engineering resources.

Also although RHP's technical reputation seems high in some respects (e.g. aero), Germany appears particularly strong on basic applications engineering. One reason cited for Japanese retrenchment in the German market was their inability to match German application engineers. The emphasis on, and pace of basic technical innovation (e.g. on CAD/CAM developments) seems higher in Germany than in either Britain, America, or Japan.

Appraisal of RHP's Strategies

In addition to difficulties arising from a broadly volume-orientated approach, RHP seems to have extended itself over too many fronts, particularly given its weak base. One by one its strategic thrusts have petered out, forcing it finally to retrench onto what is now a coherent (if much smaller) role as a supplier of 'specials'.

Yet the wastage resulting from not having attained a more cogent strategy at an earlier stage, and the price ultimately paid due to competitive decline have been considerable both in human terms and financially.

In spite of its weak market performance, RHP's cautious financial policies might seem on first inspection to have paid off in terms of profitability. Table 4.7 indicated that RHP's profitability, though lower than US competitors, has been better in relation to other international competitors such as Japanese companies. Its pre-tax return on capital employed averaged 8.2% during 1970-80 and 5.1% during 1980-83. Yet this performance is less satisfactory if Britain's rate of inflation and high cost of finance is taken into account.

Table 4.11 shows RHP's recent profit performance, both on a historical and on a current cost basis, and also highlights 'extraordinary items' not included in profit figures. RHP's performance on a current cost accounting basis (arguably more relevant when assessing a company's overall strategic situation) reveals a much worse position. Even on a historical cost basis virtually all £16m of profits accumulated between 1980 and 1983 were eaten up by 'extraordinary items' associated with plant closures and redundancies.

Table 4.11: RHP's profit performance (£m)

Year to 30 Sept	1980	1981	1982	1983	1984
Pre-tax profit on historical cost basis	11.02	0.75	3.93	0.66	6.23
Pre-tax profit on current cost basis	2.1	(4.1)	(2.8)	na	na
Extraord. items (pre-tax) associated with closure/ redundancy	(8.17)	(4.05)	(1.24)	(2.32)	-
Exceptional costs associated with retrenchment on continuing operations	0.0	2.21	0.61	0.34	0.61
Total costs associated with retrenchment	(8.17)	(6.26)	(1.85)	(2.66)	(0.61)

Source: company accounts

Total costs associated with such cutbacks were in fact £3m having been included as 'exceptional items' in the calculation of profit figures. Most of these costs were attributable to the closure of RHP Automotive Division's Annfield Plain factory (involving about 1,250 redundancies) and its other automotive plant at Northampton, making water pumps and associated spindle bearings. These largely reflect the price paid for allowing competitive decline, and must be borne in mind in assessing the company's strategic situation in automotive bearings.

Table 4.12 shows the proportion of RHP's overall sales and profits (unadjusted) represented by bearings. Profitability in bearings has been lower than for RHP as a whole. Sales volume in bearings has also fallen more sharply than for the company as a whole: in 1980 prices, bearing sales fell from £120m in 1975 to £95m in 1980 and £58m in 1983.

Employment has also suffered. For RHP as a whole

this fell from 14,800 in 1970 to 9,600 in 1980 and 6,300 in 1983. Employment in bearings activities only fell even more sharply from 14,800 in 1970 to 4,700 in 1983.

Table 4.12: RHP bearings' activities as a percentage of total sales and profits

Average for years:	1975-79	1980-83	1984
% of total sales	88	75	73
% of total profits (pre-interest)	64	36	53

Source: company accounts

To summarise, RHP's performance has been poor in terms of both market and financial performance, and the situation has deteriorated markedly in more recent years. The level of productivity remains well below that of key competitors and competitive decline has extracted a high price both financially and in terms of employment.

RHP's problem in dealing with a more European pattern of competition was daunting. Despite a high export ratio its share was little more than about 1% even in its strongest markets in continental Europe. Table 4.4 showed this was marginal in comparison with key competitors. These markets were already highly integrated by the time Britain entered the EEC so that the competitive situation was asymmetrical. It was difficult for UK companies to break into continental markets where the pattern of competition was already consolidated and highly oligopolistic; continental companies, on the other hand, perceived the UK as the one remaining market 'up for grabs'. One UK marketing subsidiary explained how this factor had increased their parent company's support: 'Just tell us what you need and you can have it!'. RHP's difficulty has been compounded by having to operate from a UK base that other companies too have found uncompetitive.

Nevertheless, I believe RHP would have fared better

had it been more sensitive to strategic context. Its sequence of strategies can be expressed in fairly general terms: merging to achieve consolidation of domestically owned industry, rationalisation aimed at improving financial performance, increased volume-orientation, market retreat, retrenchment and further rationalisation as the company closed its two automotive orientated factories and finally found a new if much smaller role as a specials manufacturer.

In contrast more successful strategies in this sector appear coherent and sensitive to contextual issues. Some companies (particularly the most powerful, e.g. SKF, Timken and NSK) do seem to have benefited from bold fairly simple strategic designs; but others such as INA seem to have succeeded through responsiveness to subtler opportunities. RHP too would have probably fared better had it opted for a more flexible customer-orientated approach, aimed at strengthening its relationships with vehicle companies. There have been important opportunities arising out of customers' needs for a new type of service. Rubery Owen's collapse in wheels, after BL changed its sourcing policy, demonstrates that even long-established suppliers cannot afford to take their position for granted.

Further no company seems to be able to afford to ignore sometimes quite basic issues, which are nevertheless critical to success in the context of its particular industry and circumstances. In this case, issues in the production area seem particularly important. RHP and indeed other UK manufacturers simply could not afford to get behind on issues such as manning levels. Senior executives needed to recognise the strategic significance of this and other specific issues in the production area, such as quality and more recently flexible manufacturing methods.

Progress in such matters would also seem to depend on policies designed to enhance the morale and commitment of those in the production area, particularly lower level production management; a longer-term and more constructive partnership with employee representatives than has been achieved by both sides in the past also seems necessary.

Conclusion

This sector has been directly affected by internationalisation more rapidly than other automotive component sectors. This is only partly due to the product's price sensitivity and low transport costs. The more critical factor has been market opportunities opened up by technological change, reinforced by benefits arising from volume production, which are probably higher than in many component sectors. Customer requirements have also been an important factor. In consequence the radius of competition between companies has already become Europe, and further rationalisation looks set to occur on a yet more global scale over the next ten years.

The performances of UK manufacturers in this sector have declined alarmingly and fairly comprehensively. An underlying problem has been the erosion in the UK's international competitiveness. This affects manufacturers directly and also indirectly since customers, also under international pressure, have had to insist on a more internationally competitive service.

All manufacturers have been damaged by an exceptionally unfavourable business environment in the UK, but management have also been responsible.

The only UK-owned manufacturer, RHP, exacerbated problems through insensitivity to changing competitive circumstances. Its original volume-orientated strategy, coupled with the demands from competing on too many fronts, proved unsustainable in the face of international competitors better supported to pursue similar aims. Initial financial benefits were subsequently eroded as the company was forced into costly retrenchment, and its present position appears weak in most automotive bearing markets. A more flexible customerised stance, aimed at strengthening its relationship with UK vehicle assemblers would have been preferential. The scope for offsetting a declining UK market through exports proved limited because of the company's limited international strength, close often nationalistic supplier/assembler ties on the continent, and erosion in the UK's cost position.

For most manufacturers including RHP, however, the main problem was a failure to recognise and deal with the strategic implications of fairly basic issues in production areas particularly productivity, quality and more recently approaches to improve flexibility. The effects became acute as competition intensified after about 1979.

Armed with more cogent and positive strategies, UK management needs to seek a much stronger partnership with employees, such as that so actively fostered by Japanese and German managers. Some shift in organisational emphasis will also be required to reinforce the efforts and morale of production personnel.

The UK manufacturing operations of most multinational companies are now fairly peripheral, and the market position of RHP, the only UK-owned manufacturer appears extremely weak in most automotive segments, posing a threat to this sector's future.

4.1.2 Automotive Forgings

The UK Market

As will be discussed in the next section international trade in forgings is low, so that UK manufacturers' sales figures also provide a fairly accurate indication of market trends. Sales fell 58% between 1973 and 1983 after inflation, but tonnage output figures are analysed directly in Table 4.14.

Table 4.13: Sales of forgers by value

	1973	1975	1977	1979	1981	1983
Sales £m	144	243	320	344	273	230
WPI, 1980=100	33.32	50.69	71.22	85.96	110.6	128.0
Sales £m'80	430	480	450	400	250	180

Source: Business Monitor MLH 399.5

Table 4.14 UK production of forgings
'000 tons

1965	1969	1973	1975	1977	1979	1981	1983
662	547	538	501	477	451	282	222

Source: National Association of Drop Forgers and Stampers, Economic and Statistical Review, various issues.

Over the same period 1973-1983 the tonnage reduction was 61%, suggesting that price/ton has risen marginally faster than the general wholesale price index. Total forgings production in the UK in 1973 was 0.54m tons, similar to the figure in 1969. Production gradually declined to 0.45m tons in 1979 before tumbling dramatically to 0.28m tons in 1981, and continuing down to 0.22m tons in 1983. Whilst the industry has displayed considerable decline over the longer-term, the reduction in output since 1979 to only half the previous level by 1983 is thus unprecedented on past trends.

In 1982 cars and commercial vehicles represented 53% of sales, with other mobile equipment (tractors and earth-moving equipment) representing a further 21%. Forgings for cars and vans declined particularly by 1982, to only 29% of the level in 1972.

Other major markets in 1982 were mining (5.0% by weight), pipeline equipment (4.9%), mechanical engineering (4.4%), industrial engines (1.1%), aircraft (1.0% by weight, but more important on the basis of value), agricultural machinery (0.9%), railways (0.7%) and the government (0.7%).

This can be compared with 1965: motor cars, commercial vehicles, and tractors together accounted for 80%, mechanical engineering 8%, mining 2.4%, aircraft 1.7%, railways 1.3%, shipbuilding 0.9%, others 6.4%. The fastest growing segments have been pipeline equipment, an almost negligible market 10 years ago, and mining equipment. Sectors particularly hard hit by decline have been mechanical engineering, shipbuilding and railways.

In the main, however, severe market decline between

1979 and 1981 was comprehensive, allowing little potential for offset. Despite the wide range of customers served, virtually every market segment declined over 30% in the course of one year, 1980. The best performance in this year was in the aero segment with a decline of 'only' 19%: and this segment declined further a year later.

Table 4.15: Forgings sales by customer sector, '000 tons

	1972	1977	1979	1981	1982
Total forgings	540	477	451	282	252
Cars, vans	201	122	106	71	59
Com. vehicles	123	140	149	78	74
Tractors	117	80	65	44	34
Other mobile	9	36	35	27	19
Other	90	100	97	61	66
% Cars, vans *	37.2	25.5	23.4	25.1	23.3
% Com. vehicles	22.8	29.4	33.0	27.7	29.4
% Tractors	21.7	16.7	14.4	15.7	13.5
% Other mobile	1.7	7.5	7.8	9.7	7.5
% Other	16.6	20.9	21.4	21.8	26.3

* Exports have been apportioned on basis of home production.

Source: National Association of Drop Forgers and Stampers, 'Economic and Statistical Review', various issues.

Thus if output growth is taken as an indicator of 'competitiveness', competitive decline in this sector is very much part and parcel of competitive decline of British industry generally.

This raises further questions that must be answered. Are we dealing merely with a knock-on effect of decline elsewhere? Or has the international competitiveness of this sector too been allowed to decline, contributing to problems? If so what are the key issues that must be dealt with?

International Trade in Forgings

Classification problems render trade figures unreliable and official figures tally poorly with responses received by NADFS from its members. Official Business Monitor figures shown in Table 4.16 were available only up to 1976 but give some indication of trends.

Table 4.16 International trade in forgings 1972 - 1976

	1972	1973	1974	1975	1976
Exports FOB £m	3.8	6.2	12.1	17.3	17.4
Imports CIF £m	0.45	1.1	2.6	5.3	6.6
Trade surplus £m	3.4	5.1	9.5	12.0	10.8
Exports/imports (value)	8.4	5.6	4.7	3.3	2.7
Home market £m	138	180	231	262	
Imports home market %	0.8	1.4	2.3	2.5	
Exports FOB, '000 tons	14.4	25.9	36.1	38.1	32.4
Imports CIF, '000 tons	1.2	2.8	6.5	na	na
Exports/imports (wt)	12.0	9.2	5.6	na	na
Exports value £/ton	264	239	335	454	537
Imports value £/ton	375	393	400	na	na

Source: Business Monitor MLH 399.5

Import penetration is not high but has been rising, from 0.8% in 1973 to 2.5% in 1976. This was faster than the growth in exports, and the ratio of exports/imports (by value) fell steadily from 8.4 in 1972 to 2.7 in 1976. By 1976 the trade surplus had fallen to only 4% of the value of the home market.

In terms of international trade, the sector has been competitive in the past, but there are clear signs that this competitive position has been declining with imports growing much faster than exports. Export prices per ton appear to have been lower than import prices, though there was some closing of the gap in 1974, indicating a tendency of the UK to buy in dear and sell cheap. This suggests UK manufacturers are tending to concentrate on the lower value added end of the business, at least as regards international trade.

More recent international trade ratios, compiled by the Department of Industry, are shown in Table 4.17.

Table 4.17: International trade - recent trends

	1978	1979	1980	1981
Imports/home demand	5.9%	5.5%	6.3%	6.1%
Imports/ " plus exports	5.5	5.0	5.7	5.8
Exports/manufacturers sales	8.4	9.6	9.6	4.9
Exports/ " plus imports	7.9	9.1	9.1	4.6

This suggests a generally more stable situation, with the exception of a surprisingly sharp fall in export ratios in 1981.

In fact, official figures seem to underestimate the impact of trade. NADFS export figures, which seem much closer to the mark, indicate exports have been gradually rising - from 5% of total output in 1969, to 10% in 1973, 13% in 1979, 14% in 1981, though falling back a little to 12.8% in 1982 (NADFS, Economic and Statistical Reviews). Industry sources suggest real figures for imports would also be much higher.

The direct impact of international trade is less important than in automotive bearings, affording manufacturers less scope to offset UK market decline through exports; yet it has increased significantly. There are clear signs, moreover, that this sector has become less internationally competitive than in the past.

The Structure of Competition

Introduction

Competition in forgings is extremely fragmented with over 100 companies involved. Probably over 60 of these companies are actively involved in automotive forgings of some type or another. The exact number at any one time is difficult to determine: although there is some tendency for smaller companies to specialise in particular business segments, they tend to switch segments depending on business conditions. If demand picks up in a particular market segment there is a tendency for new entrants to be sucked in.

Although there are many companies making forgings, the largest manufacturer GKN Forgings accounts for about 45% of all production and their factories number five of the top eight in the industry. In 1965, their share of all forgings was reported by the Monopolies Commission (1967)to be 44%, after adding back the output of Ambrose Shardlow and Birfield Extrusions which were subsequently taken over. GKN's general market position would thus appear to have been fairly stable.

GKN's share of the automotive market at that time was, however, considerably higher at 66%. This market was split BL 59%, GM 17%, Ford 14% and Rootes (now part of Peugeot) 9%, GKN's respective shares being 68%, 44%, 79% and 75% (Monopolies Commission, 1967).

Entry and exit barriers

Entry barriers in terms of setting up new factories are high and this has deterred new plants from being set up either in the UK or overseas, either by GKN or other advanced countries.

Exit barriers are also high. In closing plants companies have found that the effective scrap values were virtually zero. Numerous smaller companies are still family controlled and less financially orientated. It is therefore extremely difficult for capacity in the industry to adjust downwards in the face of falling demand.

A subtle factor exacerbating this, is that forgings capacity is highly 'modular'. If sales fall it is relatively easy to isolate and mothball particular items of plant (much of this equipment is anyway fully depreciated). By contrast, in the competing process of castings the process is technically highly integrated and fixed costs are higher. Falling demand here has led to many more plant closures (there have been surprisingly few in forgings), since the cost penalty entailed in running below full capacity is more serious and there comes a point where you either operate the whole plant or not.

Competition from substitute products such as castings has thus also been particularly fierce. Castings have gained ground particularly in the car market. One German car manufacturer professed little further interest in bought-in forgings because of more attractive alternative processes. Other alternatives such as fabrication or machining have also gained ground, and alternative materials such as plastics have displayed extremely rapid growth in some automotive applications. Forgings appear to have been cushioned against such competition only on highly stressed parts, such as commercial vehicle crankshafts, and some safety critical parts where their stress characteristics are more at a premium.

Within the forgings sector low utilisation, the presence of numerous fairly heterogeneous competitors, and high exit barriers have led to fierce rivalry.

Competition and competitor groupings

The major forging companies in Britain are shown in Table 4.18, for 1982.

Companies can be categorised by customer industry to some extent. This applies particularly to the aero sector, which involves quite different quality assurance systems, factory through times, price levels etc. High Duty Alloys enjoys a distinctive aero niche, though other major aero suppliers such as Daniel Doncaster are also involved in the automotive market. Cameron Iron Works is mainly involved in pipe line applications. Most companies however maintain a broad customer spread and are prepared to change this mix opportunistically.

Some categorisation derives from equipment employed and often can be stated in terms of the range of forgings weights that can be handled. For example, George Turton Platts advertises its main range as 10-300kg compared with Omes-Faulkners at 0.25 to 22.5kg. Most companies find their ranges overlap to a considerable extent.

The major distinction with regard to equipment is between those companies engaged on hammerwork, the more traditional process involving forming by means of repeated blows, and companies employing presses. The latter process attains comparative advantage particularly where longer production runs are involved. The larger companies such as GKN were particularly quick to introduce such equipment in the 1950s, as part of an attack on volume segments, particularly in the automotive market. However, even GKN would maintain a balance between presses and hammers and often the two processes are in competition, so competitors cannot be classified exclusively on this basis.

Table 4.18: Major forging companies* ranked by employees

	Employees
GKN Forgings (1)	14,401
Daniel Doncaster 2)	1,500
Cameron Iron Works	na
Firth Brown (3)	1,550
High Duty Alloys	1,800
Deritend (4)	830
Bloxwich Lock and Stamping Co	720
Burton Delingpole & Co	na
George Turton Platts & Co	530
Omes-Faulkners	500
Head Wrightson Stampings	400
Stampings Alliance Ltd	350
The Hughes-Johnson Stampings Ltd	349
T.B. Wellings	283
George Morgan	275
Chemetron	260
Perkson Forgings	250
Brockhouse Forgings	250

(1) Garringtons, Shardlow, Forgings and Presswork, Kirkstall, Smethwick Drop, Smith Clayton, Scottish Stampings, Birfield Extrusions
(2) Monk Bridge, Sheffield
(3) Firth Derihon Stampings, River Don Stampings
(4) South Wales Forgemasters, Bescot Drop Forgings

*There are also over 80 smaller forging manufacturers.

Forging applications provide for some degree of clear differentiation by product. However, firms generally also provide a flexible jobbing service. One recent trend favourable to some larger companies such as GKN has been vehicle companies wanting quotes on 'packages' of forging products, often linked to another recent trend, single sourcing, which is similarly aimed at cost reduction.

A more important distinction here applies to safety critical parts where quality control standards are higher and subject to regulation, e.g. on steering applications. A number of companies have pursued strategies based on specialist niches afforded by some of these applications (for additional details see Carr, 1985, Appendix c6).

Other sectoral characteristics affecting competition

Transport and handling costs reflect the low value of rough forgings in relation to weight and bulk. There used to be some distinction between companies originally set up mainly to serve Scotland, such as Cameron and GKN Scottish Stampings, and others set up to serve the rest of the UK. This has become less important and many Scottish companies now 'export' a high proportion of their forgings to English markets.

Steel represents half the cost of forgings and so is potentially an important feature of competition. Access to steel on favourable terms is possible to a limited extent for the largest companies, particularly GKN. Originally, GKN's access to its own steel supplies was as much an advantage in respect to quality as cost. Today, quality standards on steel are probably more homogeneous, and steel prices are in theory regulated throughout the EEC. In practice, even within the constraints of EEC bureaucracy, companies such as GKN can still gain a slight cost advantage on steel.

Britain is unique in the extent to which the forgings sector has developed independently and only about 8% of forgings are produced 'in-house', by either steel producers on the one hand or forgings customers on the other. In-house production is relatively much more important in France and Germany where it represents about 30% of the total, and also in Japan.

Overseas competition
The main threat posed by overseas competition is indirect through forgings coming into the UK as part of vehicles, for example, manufactured overseas. Although increasing, direct international trade has generally been inhibited because of limited market and technological opportunities, high transport costs, and the need for some customer liaison.

Particular markets display much higher exposure. An extreme example some years ago was the way in which forgings for the heads of golf clubs were taken over by foreign competitors. The pattern of competition in this small segment is now highly 'global' in nature, with most of these forgings being supplied from outside Europe even. Forgings which can only be done on the largest presses, or on more specialised equipment (as happened in cold extrusion), tend to be traded internationally as manufacturers in one country 'steal a march' on those in others. Longer production runs are more likely to be worthwhile sourcing overseas. Vehicle assemblers, especially in the UK, have become much more active in their international purchasing operations, so that suppliers are increasingly exposed to international competition.

An increasing number of newly industrialised countries are now developing competitive forgings industries (viz Turkey, Mexico, the Far East and Eastern bloc countries), and these pose some threat in the long-term to the UK, in view of the very low prices being offered. The main import threat is however from Europe: from German manufacturers at the top end of the market, and Italian and Spanish manufacturers at the cheaper end.

Larger companies, such as GKN Forgings, are much more affected by international competition because their comparative advantage vis a vis smaller manufacturers tends to rest on precisely the characteristics that promote international trade: an emphasis on volume, on new products and new technology. International competition, or at least the threat of it, also appears to be undermining their former advantage due to a stronger negotiating position with UK customers. This is particularly so in the automotive market.

On the continent not only is there a much higher

proportion of in-house forgings production, but supplier/customer ties are also still much stronger, Fiat in Italy being an extreme example. UK manufacturers' relative independence, which used to be advantageous in permitting better production volume, is now proving a liability because international competition is developing asymmetrically. UK forgers are being frustrated from gaining a real foothold in Continental markets because of close supplier/customer ties, whilst they themselves are increasingly under attack.

Performance Analysis of Automotive Forgers

In order to gain an understanding of the competitive situation among UK manufacturers in such a fragmented industry, 36 automotive forging manufacturers allowing continuous figures over the last 7 years have been analysed in terms of profitability (ROCE) and sales growth. The companies have also been ordered on the basis of turnover in 1976/77 at the start of the period, and then classified into 6 size groups in order to check for any performance/scale relationships. These will be examined in the next section, after first using the analysis to examine the collective performances of automotive forgers.

Market performances

Growth rates have been calculated in Table 4.19 by first taking out inflation, based on the wholesale price index, and then calculating percentage growth per annum on a simple arithmetic basis. For forging companies collectively, the decline in sales volume which had been about 2.5% p.a. in 1976-80, had sharply accelerated to just under 10% p.a. during the last three years examined. Decline has been comprehensive as in the case of automotive bearings manufacturers.

Table 4.19: Company sales growth performances by size groups

Company Groups	Sales growth 1976-1980 % p.a.	Sales growth 1980-1982 % p.a.	Sales growth 1976-1982 % p.a.
Av. group I	-4.9	-12.0	-6.8
Av. group II	-4.5	-12.3	-6.3
Av. group III	-1.0	-15.1	-5.2
Av. group IV	-2.5	-12.4	-5.5
Av. group V	-0.1	1.8	-1.9
Av. group VI	-1.8	-8.2	-2.1
Av. all groups	-2.5	-9.7	-4.6

Note: wholesale price indices for 1976, 1980 and 1982 were 59.45, 100 and 120.1

Financial performances - returns on capital employed

Table 4.20: Overall performances by size groupings

Size Group	80/83 ROCE 3 yr	76/79 ROCE 4 yr	76/83 ROCE 7yr	76/83 ROCE + growth
I	0.5	19.4	11.3	4.5
II	3.8	16.2	10.9	4.6
III	-3.5	15.5	7.4	2.2
IV	-20.1	17.0	1.1	-4.4
V	4.2	22.9	14.9	13.0
VI	-15.2	17.4	3.4	0.13
All	-5.0	18.1	8.2	3.6

The collective performance of these companies has undergone a dramatic and comprehensive decline in the last three years, with average (unweighted) ROCE for all 36 companies falling to -5.0% compared with just over 18% during the previous four years. Examination of companies with longer runs of financial figures, suggests that results during this earlier period are similar to results going back to 1963. The picture, therefore, over the last three years has been one of an unprecedented decline in financial performance. Dramatically, 58% of all companies averaged losses during the most recent 3 years, whereas only one of these 36 companies averaged losses during the previous four years.

The aero sector has generally been much more profitable, which may partly explain Hughes-Johnson as the best performer since it is also highly involved in this sector. It also seems a factor in Firth Derihon's good performance. Oil industry applications have also proved profitable for some companies, notably Cameron Iron. However, such sectors are clearly no panacea. Another large company specialising in the aero sector, George Turton Platts, has had one of the most disastrous performances, with ROCE averaging losses of 44% during the three year period 1980-83.

Thus the comprehensive and precipitous performance decline since 1979 is borne out even more starkly than in automotive bearings.

Relationship Between Scale and Performance

Sales growth

Table 4.19 showed that over the longer period 1976-82, Group V performed best in terms of sales growth, and there has been a general tendency for smaller companies to perform better in terms of market performance. In the most recent three years, whilst companies in the smallest two groups V and VI have performed better (particularly Group V), there has been little difference in sales performances in the top four groups and Group III companies who had been doing well have fallen back.

Smaller companies have perhaps more scope, through improvements in market share, for weathering market decline, and companies below sales of about £1.7m in 1976-77 have indeed consistently outperformed larger companies. (This has probably also improved their profitability.)

Financial performances
Figures on profitability shown in Table 4.20 are not susceptible to over-simplistic analysis. General notions, such as the idea that size or market share is likely to lead to superior performance clearly need to be treated with considerable caution in this particular context.

Group V, comprising the second smallest group of companies, with sales between £0.9m and £1.7m in 1976-77, again appears to have performed best over the full seven year period. ROCE's for this group averaged 14.9% compared with 8.2% for the 36 companies as a whole. The final performance indicator in the table is a composite formed by adding average ROCE and average annual sales growth after inflation. On the basis of this composite performance indicator, Group V companies averaged 13.0% compared with only 3.6% for all 36 companies.

For companies above this size range, there is some evidence that relatively smaller companies are being squeezed. The largest group, Group I, averages ROCE of 11.3% thus marginally outperforming the next largest group, Group II. ROCE performance in the next groups falls off substantially, however, with Group III averaging 7.4% and Group IV coming down to 1.1%. A similar pattern emerges on the basis of the composite performance indicator with Group I averaging 4.4%, Group II 4.5%, Group III 2.2% and Group IV -4.4%.

Once companies get above a certain size, (sales of more than about £1.7m in 1976-77), they appear to enter into much more direct competition with the larger companies, leading to something of a 'squeeze'. Companies in the next size groups up then seem to fare better.

Yet the advantages of scale cannot be overriding and at some point diseconomies, perhaps arising from organisational problems, seem to take over. The sample of 36 companies excludes the GKN group of companies, with the exception of Birfield. If any group holds advantages of scale it is certainly this group, and GKN Forgings have rationalised to exploit such advantages, yet it has not performed well. Although it has weathered recent conditions a little better than average, with ROCE during 1980-83 at 2.6% compared with an average of -5.0% for all 36 companies, its performance over the full 7-year period is less good, at 0.3% compared with the sample average of 8.2%. Similarly, although due to amalgamation continuous figures were not available for Firth Derihon's equally large sister company River Don Stampings, the latter's financial performance up to that date was well below average.

With these reservations (and the sample size is quite small), the general tendency of middle-sized companies to find their performances squeezed would appear to raise strategic questions for the companies involved. Many of these companies appear to be neither large enough to extract the advantages of scale on the one hand or small enough to find alternative competitive niches. They should therefore consider, perhaps quite bold, changes in direction if they are to escape a situation of being 'caught in the middle'. The larger ones here could consider for example amalgamation and rationalisation with other companies, moving up a rank; others might consider focusing their activities to attain greater specialisation, even if it is necessary to slim down operations. The degree of overcapacity, which must now be expected to persist even in the longer-term, suggests that fairly radical changes in direction will be needed for this group of companies, if they are to resume acceptable levels of financial performance.

The issue of scale may therefore raise strategically important questions for some companies, but such issues must be analysed in the light of circumstances and contextual evidence. The key to successful performance cannot be related simplistically to size for automotive forgers. They must be wary of relying on fairly general notions such as supposed advantages from market share, particularly if the market is interpreted on a parochial UK only basis. On average it is smaller companies who have performed best, and even in size categories where conditions do appear more difficult, some companies have still managed performances well above average. Volume-orientated strategies such as GKN Forgings' based on acquisition, integration and rationalisation to gain maximum advantage from possible scale advantages do not appear to have been successful in recent years, though they may have been more appropriate in the growth conditions of the 1950s and 1960s.

General Issues Related to Success

This section is based on an analysis of the principle strategies pursued by the 36 companies already referred to, after ranking them in terms of performance (based on average ROCE plus inflation adjusted growth). More complete details can be found in Carr (1985) Appendix C6.

A number of successful companies identified distinctive niches quite early on (e.g. on specialist safety critical applications); but they also displayed considerable commitment over many years in their investments and by focusing resources accordingly.

Not all specialists, though, have been so successful. Many companies, including some of the specialists, have fallen into what appears to have been something of a trap, that of simply going for volume-orientated equipment. Declining business volume, and disruption in order patterns resulting in a sharp reduction in production runs, have in more recent years placed flexibility in manufacturing methods at a premium. A common progression in the past was for automotive forgers to move from traditional hammers onto presses, but in economic terms these tend to be less flexible. Ironically, recent market changes have rendered many more modern presses, even entire press shops, uneconomic. In the UK, though not in fact overseas where business conditions have been less unfavourable, there has been a drift back towards older technology, and in particular back towards hammers.

In practice however, increased focus tends to involve some sacrifice in flexibility in a more general sense and also the use of more dedicated equipment. To be successful companies have to balance the advantages of specialisation against the need to retain as much flexibility as possible in their manufacturing operations. It is possible to improve flexibility through careful attention to engineering and production matters. However the days of success just through investing in the latest type of production equipment have passed by.

It is surprising how many companies have opted for

broadly similar strategies, and companies which have specialised more have often gone for similar niches. This has contributed to greater rivalry and even more intense competition. There would seem to be scope for some companies to further focus their operations, and to do so in more distinctive ways, so as to avoid quite such head on competition with other manufacturers.

It would, however, be wrong to place too much emphasis on such broad strategies being pursued by manufacturers. There is considerable overlap, with companies proving more or less successful in spite of quite different broad strategies.

Managerial commitment and attention to basics still seem to be more vital factors for success. For example, the Hill and Smith Group's two forging companies, Criterion Stampings and British and Midlands, ranked respectively 3 and 7 on performance out of 36 companies, yet their market strategies have not been particularly distinctive.

International competition has made far less direct impact on forgers than on automotive bearing manufacturers, but the subtler indirect effect has been dramatic. Profitability remained reasonable up until almost 1979 and it seemed suppliers could almost afford to ignore the problems of their UK automotive customers. At this point, as discussed in Chapter 3, the vehicle manufacturers had to insist on a more internationally competitive service, simply to survive themselves. Larger companies, particularly those operating in volume market segments, are perhaps most exposed to such demands, since the threat of international sourcing is much more credible than for small jobbing orders. This partly explains the relatively poor performance of such companies. Yet the change has crucially increased the importance of matching international rivals on key issues such as productivity, cost reduction, quality and flexible manufacturing systems. Manufacturers complacent in such matters have since paid a high price.

The Erosion of Forgers' International Competitiveness

Productivity differentials

Table 4.21 shows productivity estimates, obtained from visiting automotive forging plants, in which data seemed more reliable. The best UK data were from UKF1. This plant was chosen as a particular focus for overseas comparisons, partly for this reason and partly because of its similarity to the German plant. Figures for other UK companies are segregated.

Table 4.21: Productivity estimates for automotive forgers

Country	Company	Employees	Tons p.a. per man	Sales p.a. £'000/man*
Japan	JF1	300	129	99
Japan	JF2	340	78	48
USA	USF1	370	86	80
Germany	GF1	900	28	
Britain	UK1	460	19	23
Britain	UKF2		23	
Britain	UKF3		34	
Britain	UKF4		34	28
Britain	UKF5		9	

* currency conversions at following rates of sterling: $1.5, 4DM, 400 yen.

Differences in output mix and differences in the degree of work done in-house are discussed in Carr (1985) Appendix C5, but do not explain such substantial productivity differentials between Britain and the USA and Japan.

These situations are less comparable than those discussed in automotive bearings, relating to operations of multinational companies, but they give some appreciation of the productivity gap.

Table 4.21 suggests that larger plant size is not a factor in the better performances of US and Japanese plants. Only a few years ago UKF1's plant employed over 900 people and UKF2 plants typically employed about 1,000 people, going up to about 2,000. This confirms findings already discussed that large size does not contribute greatly to success in this particular sector. Indeed, UK plants would often seem to suffer from being above the optimal size, bearing in mind organisational disadvantages as size increases. US and Japanese plants gained through greater specialisation, though even here some UKF2 plants are also quite specialised.

Both Japanese plants are much more modern than those in other countries. Although the first company JF1 was established in 1916, an analysis of the age structure of major items of equipment (weighted by tonnage capacity) produced an average age of 13.5 years in their main press shop and only 3.1 years for all their air drop hammers, producing an overall age estimate of 12.2 years. The commitment to modern technology is supported by high investment levels and also through in-house developments. This affects manning levels: e.g. as a result of introducing pedal controls all their modern air drop hammers are now manned by single operators. The plant belonging to the second company JF2 was completed in 1976.

In 1968, the first company's plant was visited by the US company's present plant manager. He was immensely impressed by the modern equipment, but found the Japanese were considerably behind in terms of production experience. Since then experience effects, supported by impressive commitment in the area of production, have enabled the Japanese to catch up and surpass Western standards. Such investments are still continuing and the Japanese seem likely to move even further ahead.

Japanese investment levels are assisted by a dynamic and competitive customer industry base, allowing them to modernise whilst increasing capacity to meet demand. Their lower cost of capital enables them to consider pay back periods as high as 10 years, which is unacceptably high for most British or American forgers, particularly given recent interest rates.

British plant is generally considerably older, with much equipment over 50 years old. Disturbingly UK conditions have penalised companies investing in more progressive processes. This is partly because modern equipment is more volume-dependent. Yet Japanese engineers and executives were astonished to hear of the general drift back towards traditional hammers in the UK. This suggested UK conditions encouraged technological regression: hammers, apart from representing a step backwards, were considered to hold very little scope for further technological development. For example, robotic arms can now be used on presses but not on hammers. Equipment such as presses did present greater problems in respect to flexibility, but was (the Japanese argued) the only way forward in the context of technological developments taking place. However, from the viewpoint of UK manufacturers facing such conditions, the fact that companies employing old-fashioned equipment frequently outperform companies such as GKN with much more modern equipment, suggests that it would be unwise to place undue emphasis on differences in plant and equipment.

Even given good equipment, progress on manning levels depends upon everyone being determined to develop and maximise its potential usefulness. I was impressed by the Japanese emphasis on targets everywhere. For example the target output for a 1,600 ton press, manned by just a single operator, was 340 pieces an hour, reflecting a more general target of 1.5 kg/hour/man. The chalked up average actual performance for the day prior to my visit was 448 pieces an hour. Similarly down time targets were also proving effective. I found down time on one 3 ton hammer, for example, had fallen from 8.5-9% in 1977 to 4.5-4.7% in 1982.

General business conditions do matter too. UK economic conditions have reduced capacity utilisation to well under 50%, and are also discouraging people's efforts in this direction. Labour productivity would also rise if capacity utilisation improved, since staff numbers in some areas are fairly invariant. The US company's productivity has also fallen, despite considerable efforts, because of falling capacity utilisation. In 1978 output per man appeared to have been almost 100 tons/man.

It should, however, be noted that there was less evidence (if any) of any productivity gap against the German manufacturer GF1, whose plant and equipment were also fairly old. It should also be appreciated that the company is reputed to be a less-formidable competitor than other German forgers, such as Gerlach, with more modern equipment.

In conclusion a very substantial productivity gap has emerged between UK forgers and those in Japan and the USA. The fact that at least one major UK forging company UKF2 once enjoyed a reputation for much better efficiency than manufacturers such as the Japanese only adds weight to concern. Part, though not all, of the problem is the UK's exceptionally unfavourable business environment. This has discouraged investment and led to stagnation, whilst rivals such as the Japanese are moving swiftly ahead.

Flexible manufacturing methods

US productivity appears to owe a great deal to longer production runs, which are now typically between 5,000 and 15,000, with most about 8,000-10,000, and going up to about 30,000 on better selling lines. As USF1's in-house facility, the US plant is in a better position than most US forgers.

Significantly, this US advantage has been sharply eroded. Two years ago, this US plant could choose a good deal of its business allowing production runs of about 30,000 or above. Orders have fallen, but production runs have fallen considerably further, because vehicle customers are now in a much stronger bargaining position and (like others) they are insisting on a much more flexible delivery service. Japanese production runs are lower, typically about 4,000, though European figures are lower still, and disruption affecting UK production runs has been quite exceptional.

Japanese forgers, however, have had to learn how to handle relatively low production runs in order to comply with just-in-time programmes instigated by their vehicle customers over 10 years ago. As a result of numerous incremental changes in production methods, they have radically reduced both changeover times and overall factory through times.

Table 4.22: Changeover times in Japanese forging plant

	Changeover 4 years ago	Changeover times now
2,500 ton forging press	30-45 min	15-20 min
2,500 ton friction press		15-20 min
1,600 ton forging press		
25 ton-M Counterblow hammer	60-90 min	30-40 min
2,000 ton upsetter	Up to 3 h	50-60 min
3 ton hammer	50 min	15-20 min

Crews involved on changeovers comprised four men on the large 2,500 ton presses, two on the 1,600 ton presses, and seven on the Counterblow hammer. Many small teams, comprising people temporarily drawn off the production line due to below capacity working, were constantly involved in timed training exercises to reduce times even further.

Output rates on lighter forgings such as conn rods were running at 690/hour (1.5 ton hammer, using two operators). With production runs now below 4,000 on many items, Japanese manufacturers understandably claim changeovers as frequent as four or five times a day on many jobs. Output rates on heavier forgings such as front axle beams are much lower, but here die life can fall as low as 700 - 800 pieces, so there is still a problem of fairly frequent changeover. Manufacturers have thus been forced to radically improve changeover times in order to avoid excessive down time.

Western manufacturers are well behind in such developments, particularly the Americans cushioned until recently by good production runs (as shown in Table 4.23). The Americans have now recognised that conditions, even for them, have changed and have plans to cut times down to 1.25 hours, using a block die concept.

Despite particularly severe problems in this respect, I found scarcely any evidence of UK forgers pursuing such programmes on any systematic basis.

Table 4.23: US changeover times on forging plant

4-5,000 ton hammers	2.1 h set up + 0.7 h out = 2.8h
1.5 - 3,000 ton hammers	1.8 h set up + 0.7 h out = 2.4 h
General hammers	1.9 h set up + 0.7 h out = 2.6 h

Other production issues

At the heart of such progress on numerous production matters seems to be a recognition by senior Japanese management of their strategic significance, and a commitment where necessary to long-term improvement programmes. Their strategic thinking places due weight on the highly specific, often quite technical issues involved.

In contrast to sophisticated financial plans, characteristic of some UK companies, one Japanese forging company's 'strategic plan' comprised a single technical drawing. Beginning with small pie charts indicating market share targets, this plan rapidly moved into highly specific technical and production targets. Their control systems reflected these targets, and relied on numerous simple performance charts, which were highly visible, readily comprehensible and ubiquitous in all production areas. Quite specific targets in the 'strategic plan', such as flash reduction, were actually implemented: from 5.25 kg to 1.87 kg in the case of one axle beam.

Implementation, in this example as in other production matters including quality improvements, relied heavily on numerous highly committed groups of production workers, often referred to as quality circles. These production groups received close attention and support from top management.

In return for flexibility and commitment, production personnel received from top management not only job security (lifetime employment surprisingly appeared to be the norm even in quite small supplier plants), but also recognition of the strategic importance of their contribution. In comparison to UK competitors, they were treated as 'king pins' and their morale was correspondingly much higher. More reliance was placed on those lower down the organisation, as compared to staff functions, and the approach was (necessarily) associated with a better industrial relations climate.

Thus to be effective, strategies need to pay commensurate attention to such production matters. Commitment to longer-term improvement programmes seems to be essential, and may have to entail improvements in the industrial relations climate and moves to a more production-centred organisational focus.

Comparative cost levels

Steel costs within Europe are largely controlled by EEC agreements. In 1981, British forging prices averaged £968/ton and steel costs were estimated by one company at almost exactly 50%, implying their steel price was approximately £480/ton. In the same year, Tokyo Drop was paying about Y 0.13m or about £325/ton, converting at the then rate of around £=400 yen. This comparison is clearly sensitive to trends in the real exchange rate. UK and other European forgers are clearly squeezed by powerful customers on the one hand, and bureaucratically established steel prices on the other.

Trends in manufacturing earnings in Britain relative to key rival countries are shown in Figure 1.2 on page 10, although more specific trends relating to the forgings for these countries, up to 1982, are detailed elsewhere (Carr, 1985, Appendix C4). UK labour costs moved sharply against the trend after 1979, seriously damaging the international cost position of UK forgers, at precisely the moment when UK vehicle customers had to insist on greater international competitiveness.

Average remuneration paid by UK forging companies was allowed to rise from £3,500 in 1977/8 to £5,000 in 1980/81 and £7,000 in 1982/83 (ICC Business Ratio Reports, 1984 and 1981). In the context of monetary restraint, this has damaged the competitiveness of UK forgers.

GKN's Strategy in Automotive Forgings

GKN's dominant historical position

About 25 years ago, GKN Forgings was highly

competitive internationally. The UK automotive forgings market was still large and dynamic. The UK forgings sector also gained greater volume through being relatively independent of vehicle customers.

GKN's forgings strategy had been built upon volume-orientation. Its acquisition strategy had culminated in a greater market share than overseas competitors enjoyed. Plant sizes were particularly large. Their largest forgings plant Garringtons produced 128,000 tons or almost 20% of total UK production and was larger than any in Europe. Production methods were geared to volume runs, and involved a high proportion of modern volume-orientated equipment. In the 1950s, Garringtons' press shop was a world showpiece, much visited and photographed by people from all over the world (not least the Japanese).

As UK market leader, GKN Forgings' product range was also the most comprehensive nationally, and probably internationally too. They maintained a strong technical capability. Between 1960 and 1965 R & D averaged 0.44% of sales, which was above the industry average, and the company played a leading role at technical conferences both nationally and internationally.

The success of this strategy owed a great deal to the entrepreneurial flair and competitive commitment of executives such as Lord Brooks. In the context of growth the approach corresponded to UK vehicle customers' requirements at that time.

Basic production matters were not neglected. Senior management were allowed considerable free rein, owing to the parent company's loose (though financially supportive) organisational structure. The philosophy of decentralisation in respect to plants (these actually competed against each other in some cases) extended to the situation within plants. Considerable authority was delegated down to production management, though they received substantial top level support, chief executives such as Lord Brooks being exponents of 'management by walking about'.

Industrial relations were handled through a combination of paternalism (e.g. better treatment for those who had served the company longer, with the idea that they in turn would pass on the benefit of their experience to others) and tough-minded attention to the importance of precedent. In a move reminiscent of the breaking of the Nissan strike in the late 1950s, Lord Brooks broke a major strike and only re-recruited those he wanted back. This secured the principle of fairly efficient manning levels (supported by piece work incentives), and in fact a more healthy industrial relations record thereafter than was common in UK industries generally.

At this time international trade, though increasing, still made little impact. GKN Forgings' direct exports accounted for 3.7% of sales in 1965, about double the proportion in 1960, having increased considerably in 1964-65 particularly to EEC and EFTA countries. The parent company's average export ratio was higher at just over 8%, but trade in forgings was inhibited by a combination of tariff barriers, high transport costs and the close liaison between forging companies and vehicle customers (especially overseas). For automotive components in general the GKN Group tended to see manufacturing overseas as the best way to compete more internationally; but in forgings technological change had opened up fewer market opportunities in comparison to constant velocity joints, in which they held powerful patents. Volume advantages were also less appreciable. GKN Forgings therefore limited its international strategy to a policy of gradually increasing exports, but its international position was no weaker than that of overseas rivals, none of whom adopted more ambitious international policies.

Seeds of complacency

Yet already by the 1960s there were incipient signs of complacency, which were later to cost the company dear. Gradually a more 'scientific' approach to management was introduced and some degree of entrepreneurial commitment which had hitherto characterised the corporate culture may perhaps have been lost.

Industrial relations was still a thorny problem. The company gradually shed paternalistic policies, which had encouraged employee loyalty; yet it ducked the issue of how to sustain employees' total commitment. Management and unions alike exploited negotiating opportunities created by the business cycle, myopic to the need for a longer-term partnership. The development of the personnel function did little to rectify this and may have reduced the authority of production supervisors at the sharp end.

Both sides then found themselves pressured into allowing important production issues to become the sacrificial lamb in this quiescent battle of attrition. With order books reasonably full, and unions in a strong negotiating position, management allowed an ultimately disastrous set of precedents to take root.

Managerial pressure on productivity eased off, just as new payment schemes, replacing piecework, reduced individual incentives. Increasing attention to work study did little to assist, since the problem was embroiled with industrial relations issues.

As competition in general increased the parent group tightened its structure, with Forgings becoming a 'Sub Group'. Staff functions such as finance increased in importance, as budgeting systems enabled the parent group to apply greater pressure for results. A new phrase, 'the bottom line', carried increased influence in strategic decisions taken at higher level.

Inflation accounting increased awareness of the need to restore profitability; but attempts to raise prices foundered. Competitors, many with less sophisticated financial approaches and depreciated plant, benefitted from some alleviation in competitive pressure but felt no necessity to follow suit on prices. Having not first addressed fundamental competitive issues, such attempts did not succeed in raising profitability.

The extension of GKN's acquisition strategy, with the takeover of Ambrose Shardlow and Birfield Extrusions, had increased market domination; but any gains in negotiating power that might have been hoped for (e.g. monopolistic pricing) were eroded when vehicle companies' bargaining positions later strengthened substantially. Indeed, the strategy may have diverted attention and resources from the production area.

Momentum was sustained in R&D, redesignated as 'Process and Product Development' to preserve the emphasis on 'development'. This produced a number of practical technical innovations, many well ahead of Japanese rivals even in 1983, but much of this effort was wasted. There was a lack of commitment by senior management and unions to getting new processes into production which was matched by many in production management.

Efforts by such staff departments were almost bound to be swamped without greater support in production areas. But as staff functions had increased in scale and importance, relationships between production staff, senior management and other staff became less continuous; morale in production management suffered as they felt by-passed, and resentment led to a backlash.

Over-manning was recognised. The relative ease with which full production levels were sustained during the three day week in 1974 was one demonstration of this. Yet fear of expensive strikes on the one hand and pressure for rapid improvements in annual operating results on the other, led to management being unprepared to grasp the nettle until competitive conditions got much worse. The same applied to wage awards.

The need for a change in strategy

Having inherited a competitive advantage, the company had effectively allowed this to be squandered through complacency on basic matters of critical importance. Yet there was also another strategic problem.

GKN Forgings' competitive advantage had lain in volume-orientation, but (as has been argued) such benefits were relatively small in this components sector, and any margin for complacency narrow. There was therefore always a danger in trying to dominate such an inherently fragmented sector, relying on volume benefits, technology and vertical integration back into steel (see for example the demise of Prelude described in Porter, 1980). Family firms operating with depreciated equipment created exit barriers. Competitors could also switch with ease from other forgings segments back into automotive work the moment conditions improved. As growth tailed off and overcapacity grew, volume-orientation became a liability.

Second, GKN Forgings' volume automotive markets, with better technological opportunities, became subject to increased European competition. By 1981, its own export ratio had increased to 17%, with 69% of exports going to Europe. Direct competition is still restricted to imports and any import threat is limited by the lack of attractive technological or marketing opportunities. Even so it is increasing, whilst GKN's attempts to penetrate Europe are hampered by much closer ties between forgers and vehicle customers there. Its early advantage as a result of the UK sector's relative independence from vehicle customers seems to have become a liability: as in automotive bearings international competition is asymmetrical, since UK vehicle customers are more 'open' to international suppliers than overseas customers. Virtually all GKN Forgings' 'mobile equipment' customers had by this time developed international procurement operations, and the impact on profit margins was considerable.

Squeezed by international competition on the one hand and intensified domestic competition on the other, GKN Forgings' negotiating position against vehicle customers was undercut. Like the US plant, GKN also found it could no longer rely on volume production runs. De-stocking also increased disruption in vehicle company order schedules.

Thus GKN's relatively poor performance in the sector can be ascribed to insensitivity to its changing strategic context: its over-reliance on volume-orientation, exacerbated by underestimating the effects of European competition on this strategy; a lack of sensitivity to the implications of changed customer needs and lower growth conditions; and (partly as a result) complacency it could not afford on more basic issues such as productivity and flexible manufacturing systems.

Its main adjustment strategy in recent years has been retrenchment and cutting employment back into line with output. Output almost exactly halved between 1973 and 1981. Employment in 1979 was 10,000, only slightly lower than in 1973, but was sharply reduced to 6,000 by March 1982. The company estimates it could meet an additional 50% rise in demand without the need for additional labour, so its main hope is for some restoration in demand. The full benefits of efficiency improvements will not show up until then, but the company anticipates a return to moderate levels of profitability (ROCE levels are hindered by the fact that only half their 'capital employed' is actually in use).

The cost of decline has been high in financial as well as in human terms. Apart from redundancy costs, asset write-offs were considerable.

The same closure also demonstrates a reluctance, rooted in a recipe for success more appropriate to past conditions, to move away from an undue reliance on large-scale plants. Capacity had to be cut somewhere and F & P's work was transferred to other larger plants, hungry for business; yet this analysis suggests that, given continuing overcapacity, it might have been better to transfer work away from large volume-orientated plants to smaller more flexible operations.

To summarise, GKN's volume-orientated strategy has been undermined by changing competitive circumstances, particularly the increased impact of international competition in its chosen market segments. It has also suffered through neglecting matters in production, an area of strength in the past.

Conclusions

As in automotive bearings, UK manufacturers in this sector have undergone a remakably severe and comprehensive performance decline in terms of sales and profits. Again this appears to reflect an underlying problem of UK competitiveness.

A problem affecting UK forgers particularly has been the comprehensive phenomenon of decline in so many customer industries. This UK sector has been part of, but has also contributed to, this phenomenon since its own international competitiveness has been allowed to decline. From a position well ahead of rivals such as the Japanese 30 years ago, it is now well behind on issues such as productivity. Despite some improvements, it is still falling back in relative terms. Had this sector been able to provide the more internationally competitive service which vehicle and other customer industries (themselves under international pressure) can now insist upon, performance decline would have been less severe and prospects brighter.

The UK's exceptionally unfavourable business environment has however been partly to blame. Wage cost pressures have damaged competitiveness. Investment in more progressive technology has been discouraged, and massive underutilisation has led to stagnation. The direct impact of overseas competition has been less important than in automotive bearings. Trade, though increasing, has been inhibited by the product's higher transport costs and the need for fairly close customer links. More importantly, there has been less scope for technological and marketing opportunities and benefits associated with volume production are also much lower for this product. Even so, the trade position has declined and direct competition (particularly from Europe) is now significant strategically in volume market segments.

UK manufacturers have exacerbated their difficulties through not being sufficiently sensitive to their changing strategic context. Many appear to have overestimated benefits associated with volume-orientated production methods, particularly given the customer needs and the general business climate. Even in market segments where volume benefits are more pronounced, these have been offset by the increased impact of direct international competition.

UK manufacturers need to establish a closer relationship with UK customers. In the past the sector may have benefitted from a relatively independent position, but surprisingly this is no longer true. There is a limit to the reliance that can be placed on export customers, especially if UK conditions do not become more favourable, and there are many areas in which it is important that UK suppliers and their UK customers support each other. However, there is substantial scope for technological transfer agreements especially with Japanese manufacturers.

UK manufacturers need to be more sensitive to the strategic implications (in their particular situation) of fairly basic production issues, such as manning levels and flexible manufacturing systems. They also need to be prepared to change organisational and industrial relations approaches to support efforts by production personnel.

Decline in this sector is likely to be less dramatic since international trade is relatively low; but the high price paid for decline in financial and human terms, make it in everyone's interest to coordinate their efforts, in a more committed manner, to prevent this situation recurring in the future.

4.1.3 Automotive Instrumentation

Market for Automotive Instrumentation

In comparison to other component markets, Lucas 1983 review could justifiably claim, 'Few other market sectors offer such glittering prospects'. The value of an average European car's electronic content, only £1 in 1970, had risen to £25 by 1982, and was independently forecast by the Bureau d'Information de Precisions Economiques to rise to £150-£175 by 1990 (quoted in Lucas 1983 review). Accordingly the West European market for such automotive electronics was expected to grow 30% p.a. from an estimated value of £250 million in 1982 to a projected value of £1.5 to £1.75bn by 1990. Similar arguments are expressed, from a more independent viewpoint, in *Electronics* (26 January, 1984).

Also in contrast to other component sectors, UK electronic component manufacturers generally have been consistently profitable. ICC average sector figures for the largest 60 companies for the years 1980, 1981 and 1982 for ROCE were 25%, 25% and 23%, and for profit margins 9.2%, 8.6% and 8.2%.

Other markets are even more dynamic. Citing Ford, the article noted, 'Between 1970 and 1980 the electronics content per average US vehicle increased from about $25 to $250 ... Within 10 to 15 years it should approach $1,400', and predicted a world market over $14bn by 1990. This agrees with my interview findings.

Table 4.24: US and Japanese automobile electronics markets

	1982	1983	1984	1987
	Estimates		Projections	
USA ($m, constant prices)	1,693	1,932	2,086	2,588
Japan ($m, $=Y238)	1,122	1,330	1,564	-

Source: *Electronics*, 12 January, 1984

Market segments

Historically the involvement by vehicle manufacturers in electronics (apart from radios) dates back to headlight controls in the 1950s, followed by voltage regulators and alternators in the 1960s. By the end of the 1970s about thirty different electronic items were identifiable and the major segments now recognised began to emerge. In the last few years the number of new items has mushroomed so it is important to appreciate the pace of change reshaping market segments.

Underlying such opportunities has been the development of integrated circuits in the late 1950s, followed by very large-scale integration (VLSI) and more recently by microprocessors. The market for integrated circuits and transducers alone is sizable. It is particularly important in respect of automotive instrumentation, the area that because of its potential will be the focus in this study.

Bob Schultz, Chief Engineer, Buick Motor Division at General Motors, has suggested (*Electronics*, 26 January, 1984) that a future scenario in about 1990 would have to allow for whole ranges of completely new electronic products: keyless systems, automatic seat and mirror adjustment, navigation and other information systems, trip reports, moisture activated wipers, replacement of throttle cables, radar-assisted braking systems, ride controls, energy management systems, diagnostics. Vehicle manufacturers' motivation is partly the opportunity for product differentiation presented by such developments, though Ford is a little more sceptical about 'razzmatazz applications'; but it is also founded on solid grounds such as cost reduction and reliability, particularly in the more basic areas. Quality is now so high in some areas as to eliminate the need for quality checks. Unit costs of electronic parts have already improved by a factor of about 100, according to Schultz, and their reliability by about 200.

The pace of technological progress and market development in Western Europe, though impressive, has, however, lagged behind America and Japan. Within Europe, moreover, the UK market has not escaped entirely the dramatic downturn experienced by other component manufacturers.

The UK original equipment market for instrumentation, including transducers, was worth about £13m in 1976/77. In 1982 compared with expectations of about £30m this market had slumped back to about £20m, producing quite considerable overcapacity, prior to rationalisation.

Whilst Lucas' optimistic projections for the West European market seem not unreasonable, the scale of their optimism ought to be tempered by the relatively flat performance of the domestic market to date at least. UK manufacturers' export ratios in automotive instrumentation have fallen back reflecting therefore only a small share of markets in mainland Europe.

Thus even in such an exceptionally attractive sector, there are incipient signs of UK decline.

Internationalisation of the Market and Competition

Prior to entry into the EEC, tariff barriers encouraged close links between suppliers and assemblers. There was little inter-European trade in instrumentation, and the pattern of competition was primarily national and monopolistic. In the UK, Lucas tacitly agreed not to attack Smiths' virtual monopoly, in return for Smiths holding back in other markets, and a similar stalemate in Germany kept Bosch from attacking VDO's virtual monopoly.

Ford and GM were content to use national independent

suppliers until the end of the 1960s, when they shook up the pattern of competition by introducing their own in-house suppliers. Only about 5% of Ford's business (essentially transducers) is now open to independent UK suppliers, the rest being supplied on a European basis by Autolight, 'in-house'. GM business tended to be increasingly controlled through Opel in Germany, with about half supplied by their in-house supplier AC Delco in the UK, and about half 'open' and in fact supplied mainly by VDO in Germany. With the decline of GM's UK business, AC Delco is pressing for more of VDO's business to fill its own capacity.

Table 4.25: Major European instrumentation manufacturers

Britain	Germany	France	Italy	Ford	GM
Smiths	VDO	Jaeger	Veglia	Autolight	Delco

As in other components, Europeanisation has been encouraged by trade liberalisation and customer requirements, but here even more than in the case of automotive bearings, the change in technology from electro-mechanical to electronic processes of production has transformed the pattern of competition.

This change has reduced entry barriers and attracted powerful competitors with no substantial previous instrumentation involvement. Lucas and Bosch (from Germany) and other 'systems' companies have entered, recognising the future need for integrated electronic packages involving instrumentation, such as engine management systems. The investment stakes are set to increase beyond what weaker instrumentation manufacturers can afford. Motorola (USA)'s chief executive has remarked (*Electronics*, 26 January, 1984) on the 'sky rocketing' costs on the integrated circuits side: £40m by 1981 would scarcely finance one processing bay, whereas just a few years before 'it would have put you in business'. This will lead to further industry consolidation and rationalisation, and makes the UK market base with sales of £20m p.a. look too weak to sustain manufacturers in the longer-term. Other new entrants are electronics companies such as Motorola who have now established an automotive division. The change in the pattern of competition is similar, in some respects, to that taking place in the watch industry, with experience effects likely to be important.

Automotive instruments, though, tend to be highly customerised, if not almost fashion products because they are used by vehicle manufacturers as a means of differentiating their vehicles. More standard electrical items such as alternators and starter motors have already been savaged by Far Eastern competition, but other customerised electrical products such as interior lighting have been less affected. Similarly, automotive electronics are differentiated from other consumer electronic markets because of the need for close customer liaison. Systems design involvement is considerable and component development must be matched to customers' model development programmes. Also, quality and delivery requirements dictate considerable conservatism, so that the pace of change will be slower than in other consumer electronic markets. The effect will be to encourage closer supplier/assembler relationships and to inhibit the pace of internationalisation.

Investment requirements are, however, encouraging vehicle manufacturers to rely more on independent suppliers and this is weakening the position of UK in-house manufacturers such as Autolight. Yet customer ties are still important. Jaeger is owned equally by VDO and Plafinco, which is controlled by Matra, and is closely linked into Renault. In Italy, Veglia is owned by Borleti, in turn owned by Fiat. Fiat's unions oppose imports of UK parts. Thus although competition is becoming more international, it is perhaps naive to think in terms of free market competition.

In-house production accounts for almost 100% of the US market compared with 70% or so in Europe. GM is served by AC Delco, Ford by Autolight, and Chrysler by Huntsville. The only sizable US independent is Stuart Warner which specialises exclusively on trucks. This is a major factor inhibiting European entry into the US market - only VDO has a manufacturing presence there, having established an operation in support of VW's US plant.

In Japan Toyota owns Nippon Denso, which also manufactures other electrical parts, and Nissan owns Kantoi Seiki (instrumentation only). There are a number of independents such as Hitachi, but supplier/assembler relations are extremely close.

British exports are now predominantly to Europe though there is also some involvement with India and Korea. Thus initially, from a UK standpoint, Europe will be the major battleground as international competition intensifies. UK manufacturers accept that they now have to operate on a European basis if they are to survive, but arguments expressed by some, that multi-sourcing should ensure UK manufacturers a reasonable share of the European market, are unconvincing. Even the No. 2 in the US electronic calculator business, Bowmar, filed for bankruptcy after intense competitive pressure from Texas Instruments in 1975 (Hedley, 1976). Competition in instrumentation may be less extreme for reasons already outlined, but there is little room for complacency, particularly in view of UK manufacturers' weak position in mainland Europe.

Opinions differ on the question of whether the pattern of competition may even become 'global' as has happened in motor cycles, watches and consumer electronics. Some claim Ford, whilst insisting on competitive standards against alternative European sources of supply, does not require UK manufacturers to compete with costs available from Japanese suppliers. The argument continues that European governments would protect such an important industry at some point. Yet other factors are drawing world markets closer together. Instrumentation is closely linked with vehicle engines, which are supplied on a highly international basis, particularly now that engine sizes are more similar. Model types and vehicle technologies are also more similar following the drive for fuel economy, resulting in parallel pressures on component suppliers. Also although customerisation is important, the basic systems requirements for instrumentation are quite similar worldwide.

There are already important linkages taking place.

More expensive instruments, incorporating a higher degree of technology, are the first to be affected. Electronic display systems range enormously in cost from about £8 to £125, making it worthwhile shopping around for the world's best products for luxury cars such as Jaguar, Mercedes and BMW. Much simple non-electronic instrumentation equipment will though continue to be made on a more local basis for some time to come for reasons of cost.

My interviews with Japanese companies suggest that while the immediate competitive ball game is certainly Europe, this is unlikely to be the case in the longer-term. So far, Japanese export ratios have been low because of close customer links, only about 6-7% for one company visited and fairly negligible for the other. However, one company expected its export/sales ratio might rise to 40-50% in the next five years. Technical links are already established, for example Bosch and Lucas have sent director-level delegations to Japanese companies and have numerous technical agreements. Japanese manufacturers already have European sales bases (though they have met stiff resistance in Germany). They also have overseas plants, but their major first target is undoubtedly the USA, where Nippon Denso for example already has a plant for vehicle conditioning equipment.

The Japanese do appear set to gain considerable 'experience' advantages from volume. One manufacturer, currently producing a new type of pressure sensor, projected perhaps a hundredfold increase within the next 5 years. Japanese companies did see a pattern of competition developing along similar lines to calculators and watches.

In respect to Britain the close BL/Honda link and the Nissan company coming to Britain must present an added attraction. BL does receive some emission control parts from one Japanese company but the amount is small and they have found BL difficult to penetrate, to date at least.

Both Japanese and US suppliers benefit from domestic vehicle industries with reputations for being dynamic in respect to electronics. (For example, European assemblers were much slower in introducing electronic clocks.) Both are also reputed as being more prepared to pay for additional sophistication.

Interestingly, Ford UK who are reputed to favour simplicity, have just rejected a technically advanced Japanese liquid crystal display, in favour of a cheaper European model about half the price. The Japanese are so far producing only small numbers, but are very conscious of the experience effect. As volume grew, they expected costs to have halved within three years.

The example casts an interesting light on the claim that US multinational vehicle assemblers do not require UK manufacturers to compete on price with Japanese competition! The case of bearings also casts doubts on the ability of European governments to intervene in time to adequately protect manufacturers from Japanese competition, and instrument manufacturers themselves appeared to have some doubts in this respect.

To summarise this section, the immediate competitive battleground has now become Europe with companies such as Bosch and VDO posing the major threat. In the longer-term, however, although Japanese attention is initially targeted on the US and at the upper end of the market technologically, it seems highly optimistic for any British supplier to believe they will remain sheltered from a more global struggle.

Performance of UK Manufacturers

Smiths held over 90% of the free UK market for instrumentation until it joined forces with Lucas in 1983. The company's overall performance between 1970 and 1982 was well above average for the sector at 18.6% ROCE. Sales grew at 7% p.a., after inflation, between 1975 and 1981, also well above average. Yet its good performance is largely due to non-automotive activities such as aerospace. These represent more attractive opportunities than automotive work, which has shrunk proportionately. Its automotive electronics activities generally are very small in relation to Lucas and international competitors.

In the context of factors discussed in the last section, Smiths has been wary of investment levels needed to maintain its position, given the demands associated with growth and the change in technology. From a strategic point of view something had to happen. Smiths (like Lucas) recognised that competition was set to intensify on a European, if not global, basis. Joint operations with Lucas on instrumentation have emerged as a possible answer. Sceptics might see this move by the two companies as primarily defensive, and designed to stem an otherwise inevitable outbreak of fierce domestic competition.

Instrumentation has proved more attractive than other automotive component sectors. Smiths have been assisted by a rise in content per vehicle since 1972 and by exports then negligible and now 25%. However, sales of instrumentation have declined in volume terms. Disturbingly, from the viewpoint of the UK's competitive position in this sector, Smiths' export ratio in automotive instrumentation, having climbed steadily up to 35% in 1979, has slumped back to 25% following the rise in the real exchange rate. Closures and rationalisation, following the establishment of a joint operation with Lucas in 1983, do not merely represent elimination of duplicated resources, since in instrumentation there has been limited overlap. They also reflect a recognition of over-capacity and retrenchment brought about by the UK's weak international position.

Lucas, like Smiths, can call on substantial, relevant technical expertise from other activities such as aerospace. Like Bosch though, its main strength lies in being able to offer the wide range of automotive electronics, necessary on systems such as those required for engine/transmission management. For Lucas, instruments therefore became attractive complementary products to their own. Also since their scale of involvement in automotive electronics was much larger than Smiths', they could feasibly contemplate the level of investment and resources that would ultimately be involved.

Yet although benefits associated with volume are particularly high for this product, scale on its own is no guarantee of competitive success in the fast moving world of electronics. Lucas' general performance is not encouraging. Following two years of expensive retrenchment, the company has commendably turned around financial performance in 1984. However, over the longer period 1970-1982, ROCE averaged 5.7%, below average for the automotive components industry and well behind Smiths. In the context of inflation and interest rates prevailing, investors could have done far better elsewhere. Sales growth between 1975 and 1982 was also poor, both absolutely (after inflation) and relative to other component firms. Indeed, as one of the five largest component companies Lucas is a reminder that sheer size correlates badly with performance in this sector.

The company is strong in some key technological areas, such as brake systems, harnessing and fuel injection systems. Its advanced microjector was sufficiently ahead to penetrate the US market, although even here unexpected set-backs in the diesel engine market have forced Lucas to retrench, closing down their Sunbury factory.

Lucas Electrical Division's performance has been particularly poor, squeezed between powerful European competitors such as Bosch and low-priced Far Eastern competition. More standard 'finished' electrical products, such as alternator starter motors appear to have somewhat buckled under the full weight of global competition, leading to heavy retrenchment - a disturbing indication given increasing internationalisation in automotive electronics.

Lucas utilised its financial weight in attempting to establish the position of its electrical division in mainland Europe by buying a 50% share of Ducellier in France; yet Lucas has finally had to pull out, surrendering an important manufacturing base on the mainland. Given the 'ties' that still exist, this will prove a very serious weakness in Lucas' attempt to establish a competitive position in European automotive electronics.

One electronic product that has already become exposed to more global competition, the car radio, suggests room for concern over the UK's competitiveness. As the exchange rate soared in 1980, Smiths finally abandoned this price-sensitive market in the face of Japanese competition. Lucas fared little better in this product. Ford switched to Germany's Blaupunkt, whose radios, as Beynon (1984) has pointed out, are substantially manufactured in Korea.

Thus whilst Smiths performance has been extremely

good as a whole, its position in automotive instrumentation was too weak to cope with such a fundamental change in the pattern of competition. Lucas' overall performance has been poor, but in automotive electronics it is extremely powerful and has a great deal to contribute in any joint venture, in the context of changes which have taken place. There are signs of weakness in terms of international competitiveness and a critical problem appears to be the lack of overseas support.

The Lucas/Smiths Joint Operation

The Lucas/Smiths joint venture does offer real and immediate opportunities for synergy, but will probably create only a temporary respite unless accompanied by substantial strategic moves in the future. Cynically, the main immediate advantage for both companies is avoiding otherwise inevitable head-on competition in the home market. Yet as with tariff barriers, reducing domestic competition can provide only temporary cushioning against the effects of international competition. Britain's preoccupation with domestic mergers in the face of strategic problems, has generally not proven highly successful, as was illustrated in the case of automotive bearings, where internationalisation occurred earlier.

In the past, Smiths avoided such precedent and resisted linking up with Lucas. Instead, its links with Bosch and other overseas companies offered an alternative route. Even if future competition were to remain essentially Europe, some would have argued that linking with Bosch, who had a similar interest in acquiring instrumentation expertise, would have offered the more important advantage of a strong manufacturing base in mainland Europe.

Others, taking a yet more global view, suspected that Europe was now sufficiently integrated for an export-only policy to be sufficient within Europe, but pointed to the need for a competitive grouping strong enough to survive US and Japanese competition. This scenario called for a powerful European grouping, ultimately to be supported by a major foothold in at least one of the other two major markets. As global competition increased, other weaker participants, would be more likely to be squeezed out.

Evidence, discussed in the last section, veers towards the latter view, at least in the longer-term. Yet, on either scenario, a merely nationalistic and defensive merger will not be enough to sustain a credible future competitive position. The real potential for this particular venture may, however, be realised if it is used as a springboard for aggressive international moves in the future.

The UK Business Environment

On recognising the need for major structural change in 1980, both companies approached the government for assistance to support a new strategy for the industry, but felt they 'came up against a brick wall'. At the same time, the French government responded to the opportunity presented by automotive electronics. Displaying understanding of the problem's international dimension, they provided funding support but on the basis of international integration, Matra being encouraged to link up with Germany's VDO to form Jaeger. Timeliness, in such a fast moving business situation, is important and in Britain almost three valuable years were lost before any strategic response was forthcoming, and even this appears nationalistic and defensive rather than any final long-term answer. The Ministry for International Trade and Industry in Japan appears to have close long-established involvement with component manufacturers and a good reputation with these companies.

Subtle pressure applied by the French government, who are not so naive as to imagine that international competition is totally open and free in this business, effectively neutralised Lucas' Ducellier foothold in France. This move, drawing little British response, has substantially weakened the competitive position of UK manufacturers. In Germany, GKN was similarly frustrated by the legal system from acquiring Sachs which would have given it some foothold on clutches.

Both Lucas and Smiths found their competitive position damaged by the rise in the real exchange rate in 1980, and as mentioned this has done permanent damage in the case of more exposed products. Both though see their competitive position as part and parcel of a more general collapse of manufacturing in Britain. A strong and steadily growing domestic market base will be important if they are to keep up with technological change and experience effects enjoyed by more dynamic competitors overseas. UK business conditions have not been favourable either to themselves or domestic customers, either in terms of the market or relative costs.

Finally, there is concern that the education system is not supplying enough electronics engineers. By contrast Japanese automotive electronics manufacturers enjoy strength in depth in this area: 100 of 512 employees at one Japanese plant visited were engineering graduates and of these 50 had graduated in electronics.

The government is primarily responsible for action on such matters, but the crucial issue of cost pressures depends also on cooperation from employees and their representatives.

Relations with Vehicle Manufacturers

Manufacturers in this sector tend to feel that political factors will prevent any further disappearance of major vehicle customers, just as some, perhaps over- optimistically, put their faith in the view that European governments will be forced to act at some point even in the case of automotive electronics components. They also recognise that, in spite of their own increasing exposure to international competition, overseas customer/supplier relationships are still highly 'tied', and are understandably concerned about the danger of the UK market opening up more rapidly than overseas markets.

However, relationships between assemblers and suppliers are changing. Given their own heavy funding demands, most vehicle customers are reluctant to take on the heavy investments required in the automotive electronics field. On the other hand, electronic developments dictate even closer design and systems coordination than was the case with electro-mechanical systems, so that customers must anyway retain a substantial expertise and involvement. Engineers at VW have suggested this might lead to a much closer relationship between assemblers and electronic companies directly, which could tend to squeeze out 'systems' companies such as Smiths and Lucas. In fact, the task of systems companies is getting more difficult as vehicle systems are rapidly becoming more sophisticated and complex. Opportunities for systems companies, in my view, will therefore continue to develop, though the presence of new entrants will further intensify competition. On balance these developments will probably loosen ties between systems companies and assemblers.

To date Japanese suppliers such as Nippon Denso and Mitsubishi Electric benefited considerably from extremely close customer relationships. Their levels of R & D expenditure are fairly high, but they receive considerable support from assemblers. Similar support also applies to investment in plant and the rate of modernisation of Japanese plants is highly impressive. So far this close relationship has inhibited their ability to attack more global markets.

Suppliers now, however, recognise that to recover substantial investment outlays looming, and to exploit experience effects, there may be some advantage in slightly loosening traditional customer ties. Suppliers such as Nippon Denso already display more independence than typical Japanese automotive component suppliers. Shimokawa (1982b) believes there will be some decoupling in Japanese customer/supplier relationships; though even in this sector where the pressures for change are greater, he is probably correct in indicating only a limited shift. Traditional business relationships appear very strong in Japan.

To summarise, volume benefits are sufficiently high to encourage slightly looser relationships between suppliers and assemblers. One effect may be much sharper Japanese competition in the future. As mentioned, there are already some signs of this. Nevertheless, close supplier/assembler relationships will continue to be important. Therefore given the importance of volume, any further tendency for UK vehicle assemblers to 'open up' to overseas procurement in advance of reciprocal developments overseas would damage this sector.

Technological and Manufacturing Developments

Manufacturing processes have undergone a total transformation in the move from electro-mechanical to electronic systems. Such a fluid situation makes international productivity comparisons dangerous, yet the commitment demonstrated by the Japanese in the manufacturing area appears to reflect closely what is happening in other automotive component cases discussed.

Sophisticated modern equipment is much more evident as a competitive weapon in this component area than in the others. The Japanese are making a major push here towards high productivity, highly automated integrated manufacturing systems. New manufacturing systems and equipment are being 'turned over' at an extremely rapid rate.

Even in a situation characterised by such rapid strategic change, Japanese manufacturers tend not to see grand stratagems such as internationalisation, moves towards industry consolidation or diversification as the key strategic issues; again, they point instead towards progress achieved on much more specific targets affecting manufacturing areas – key priorities such as productivity, 'zero defects', value analysis, design developments aimed at materials savings, and 'worker based' morale programmes. Nippon Denso for example claims 20 to 30 suggestions per employee per year from its quality circles. Production areas still abound with the same highly visible charts noted in other component factories, showing targets and achievements on fairly basic issues. Their commitment to detail is perhaps illustrated by the seriousness attached to the many signs exhorting all employees not to use the lifts so that the company can save energy.

Japanese manufacturers in this sector have resisted manufacturing approaches such as standardisation. Close customer ties have dictated customer responsiveness even given the difficulty of having to learn to handle large numbers of product variations efficiently. This has been incorporated in key manufacturing targets.

This approach is particularly evident in the case of Nippon Denso's more established electrical products such as alternators. Pointing to impressive achievements on changeover times on one such line a Japanese engineer grinned, 'Our target production is one'. Also product life cycles have been shortened to allow a new and comprehensive series of alternators every two years, through comprehensive and well integrated future product development programmes, as illustrated in Table 4.26.

Table 4.26: New alternator product line programmes

ModelType/ outside diameter	Series 1	Series 2	Series 3
142mm	90 amps	100 amps	120 amps
135mm	75 amps	90 amps	100 amps
128mm	60 amps	75 amps	90 amps
124mm	50 amps	60 amps	75 amps
114mm	40 amps	60 amps	60 amps
107mm	40 amps	50 amps	

Source: Japanese company

Such an integrated product development programme enables individual product offerings to be continuously updated, with each new series coming out every two years, whilst making the maximum usage of investment. This approach is continuously eliminating older lines.

Japanese manufacturers' approaches were thus not based on crude standardisation programmes, such as elimination of marginal customer accounts for example, but were subtle and aimed at ensuring considerable flexibility both in terms of the number of products handled (this manufacturer was handling 400 different types of starter motor and 200 types of alternator) and also in the extent of product innovation that they could handle.

In general, through continuous and dedicated attention to detail, Japanese manufacturers such as Nippon Denso appear to have not only improved levels of efficiency but, more importantly in their own eyes, they have managed to enhance the overall effectiveness of their service. They felt this enabled them to assist customers to optimise performance over a wide range of models and engine types. The subtler issue of effectiveness, though, is of course more difficult to quantify than that of efficiency, but it is nevertheless extremely important from the point of view of competitiveness.

Thus although issues arising from volume and internationalisation will I believe be important in this sector, management cannot afford to neglect these more detailed and perhaps subtler matters.

Conclusion

There are already signs of decline even in this sector, where opportunities are exceptionally attractive; but the real threat lies at a later stage in the life cycle of these new electronic products when competition is likely to increase.

Tacit collusion under which major automotive electrical companies held off serious attack on each other's instrumentation markets, has broken down in the last five years as a result of technological and market opportunities created by electronics. Such opportunities, together with economies of scale and experience effects which are particularly important in this sector, are attracting new entrants and changing the essential structure of competition.

However, though transport costs are low, traditionally close, often nationalistic customer relationships and the need for close coordination and market sensitivity may inhibit this process. Yet the immediate competitive arena has already moved to Europe and Japanese (and possibly US) manufacturers are expected to represent more serious competition in about five years time. Pressure is likely to intensify for rationalisation within Europe, leading to the elimination of some competitors within the next ten years. By this time some rationalisation on a more global scale (including the USA and Japan) will probably have begun.

Just as direct international competition is beginning to

increase, there are signs that the international competitiveness of this sector has weakened. Changes in the UK's relative international cost position appear to have damaged the position. The sector is heavily dependent on the UK's weak vehicle industry base, which is particularly important because of volume benefits and the need to keep up technologically. The UK's lack of strength in depth in electronics expertise (and in management in this area) is also a problem. Late government recognition (in comparison with France and Japan) of the need for some strategic initiative may also have already damaged competitive prospects.

Manufacturers need to be sensitive to changes noted in the pattern of competition. Whilst the UK industry's recent strategy of domestic consolidation would certainly be attractive were competition to remain predominantly UK only, a similar danger to that already manifest in automotive bearings is evident. Given rapid internationalisation, such a strategy is likely to encounter, head-on, powerful overseas competition. Unless this strategy is followed up by major international linkages, the UK position would seem to be weakly supported in Europe. Whilst a stronger base in continental Europe represents the immediate priority, within the next ten years there will be a need for linkages to improve the industry's position with at least one of the other major world markets, Japan or the USA.

Despite internationalisation, manufacturers must be wary of any loosening in their relationship with UK vehicle customers. Overseas vehicle companies are still closely involved with, and supportive of, their local suppliers and they are likely to 'open up' more slowly than UK vehicle companies. This means UK suppliers must remain highly orientated to the needs of UK vehicle customers, and to do so they must strive to remain as flexible as possible.

More basic issues cannot be ignored. The pace of technological change in this sector will increase the importance of research and development. Although the UK record here is relatively good, the ability of UK manufacturers to match levels of funding support evident in competitor countries such as Japan is more in question, particularly in terms of investment that will ultimately be needed to translate developments into new processes. The ability to develop and market new product lines is also likely to be important. At this stage in the 'product life cycle' more incremental production improvements are less significant for this sector than for other automotive components discussed. However, they are important for more mature automotive electrical products and are likely to be so for this sector in the future. The need to keep up with such a rapid pace of change will require manufacturers to foster employees' wholehearted participation and commitment.

Decline in this attractive, 'star' component sector has so far been less severe than in others, but future threats demand immediate attention, particularly in view of the high investment levels that are likely to be needed.

4.1.4 Automotive Exhaust Systems

The UK Market

Exhaust systems, comprising silencers and associated piping, are frequently replaced, so that the after market is relatively much more important than for other products discussed. The after market (AM) has traditionally been considered more profitable than the original equipment (OE) market. Eurofinance (1980) cited Smiths' AM profit margins as having averaged 11.3% between 1974 and 1978, compared with only 6.1% for OE. Exhaust systems are regarded as a particularly 'lucrative market'.

AM sales depend on the size of the 'car parc'. Whilst foreign vehicles have penetrated UK markets quite rapidly (depleting domestic OE component markets), foreign penetration of the domestic 'car parc' has occurred more slowly. This has cushioned AM manufacturers against declining UK vehicle production levels. There has also been the opportunity to attack the AM for foreign-made vehicles, especially after the government's legislation against franchising.

A survey by Marplan suggested that the DIY market has been growing particularly rapidly. This comprises about 25-30% of the UK market, and a slightly higher percentage on the Continent. Some component manufacturers, such as GKN, have also used the AM as a means of vertically integrating operations into distribution, an attractive opportunity for growth in a declining market.

High transport costs in relation to value added, and the relatively low level of technology involved have insulated UK manufacturers from international trade. Direct trade in exhaust systems is still low, partly because of their bulk in relation to value and official trade figures are not even produced. Official figures for UK manufacturers' sales, shown in Table 4.27, ought therefore to reflect UK market trends.

Table 4.27: Sales of exhaust systems and parts

	1973	1975	1977	1979	1981	1983
Mfrs' sales, £m	26.6	39.1	58.8	74.5	38.1	42.2
Coverage, %	98	98	94	94	77	77
Adjusted sales, £m	27.2	39.9	62.6	79.2	49.5	54.8
WPI, 1980=100	33.3	50.7	71.2	86.0	110.6	126.5
Sales, £m 1980	81.5	78.7	87.9	92.1	44.7	43.3

Source: Business Monitors PQ 381.1 and PQ 3530

My interviews suggest, however, that these official figures reflect AM trends rather poorly, and that the real decline here may be only 20-25%, though OE sales may have fallen further than this. Yet even in this component market, enhanced by the existence of an attractive after market, decline since 1979 has been very severe.

Company Performances

To gain some indication of company performance levels in this sector I analysed the performances of a sample of five companies for which continuous figures were available: together their sales in 1975 amounted to 42% of the market suggested by official figures. Financial reports of other major participants such as Armstrong, Automotive Products and Quinton Hazell were not included since exhaust systems manufacture represents a low proportion of their activities. Results are shown in Table 4.28, Tenneco Walker figures being segregated because losses equivalent to -191% and -95% in 1975 and 1976 would otherwise be unduly distorting.

Table 4.28: Exhaust systems company ROCE and growth performances after adjusting for inflation

	ROCE 75-79 %	ROCE 80-81 %	ROCE 75-81 %	Growth 75-79 % p.a.	Growth 79-81 % p.a.	Growth 75-81 % p.a.
TI Cheswick	47.7	8.1	36.4	11.4	(22.1)	(3.1)
TI Nicholson	55.8	29.0	48.2	4.3	(2.3)	2.0
Burgess	16.2	7.4	13.7	8.9	(19.2)	(2.7)
Chilcotts	21.8	15.0	13.9	8.1	(21.6)	(4.1)
Average	35.4	14.9	28.0	8.2	(16.3)	(2.0)
Tenneco W.	(42.1)	2.3	(29.4)	14.8	(6.5)	6.4

Source: ICC Business Ratio Report

Table 4.28 reinforces the sales picture just discussed. The sharp reversal of trends after 1979 suggests a fall in volume of 29% (taking all five companies) over the two years to 1981.

Average return on capital employed (taking the first four companies), 35% between 1975 and 1979, fell back to 15% between 1980 and 1981. After early losses, Tenneco Walker had recovered to reasonable levels of profitability by 1978, but then it too fell sharply. (AM orientated companies such as TI Nicholson have indeed done noticeably better than OE orientated companies such as TI Cheswick and Tenneco Walker.)

Profit and sales performances have thus been better than in other component sectors, yet here too there has been a sharp reversal following 1979. Accounts of exhaust system companies visited in Japan and the USA do not indicate such substantial decline in either sales or financial performance.

The Changing Pattern of Competition

The general situation

Major companies felt competition in OE and AM markets could not be differentiated. TI Silencers and Tenneco Walker both appear to accept lower profitability on OE operations, because in the long run a strong OE position is critical to remaining competitive in their more profitable AM operations. The distinction is of more significance to smaller manufacturers, but should generally be treated cautiously.

In the OE market the main competitors are TI (particularly Bainbridge and Cheswick), Tenneco Walker and Gillet. Armstrong, previously quite heavily involved, has more recently been largely squeezed out. Other major companies involved maintain more limited manufacturing facilities, rely much more on factoring, and generally focus more on AM and distribution operations. Chilcotts, a rather smaller company focuses on OE commercial vehicle business.

Given such a variety of products still in use in the AM, even the largest manufacturers are prepared to factor marginal orders, and some smaller companies find further scope for their activities by concentrating on particularly lucrative product types or on lower order runs. Grundy and Eminox specialise on stainless-steel applications and opportunities are provided by the need for more customerised products or services. Table 4.29 gives details of major AM competitors. Although international trade is small, the impact of other European companies using local manufacturing operations is considerable. The AM is a lucrative opportunity and overseas manufacturers are involved in the UK AM for vehicles imported from their own countries; the relatively poor opportunities for scale benefits further discourage exports but facilitate a network of local manufacturing operations. The OE in its own right is probably a less attractive market opportunity, but the opportunities provided by technology and by scale advantages are probably greater; though here the driving force for change has been requests from multinational vehicle companies such as Ford.

Table 4.29: Shares in the after market and comments

Tenneco (Harmo)	German No 1, No 2 in French AM
TI (e.g. Nicholson)	UK. Mfr ops in Holland and Spain
Burgess	UK
Quinton Hazell	UK. No 3 in French AM
Armstrong	UK
SU-Butec	BL Unipart's subsidiary
Automotive Products	UK
Bosal	Belgium MNC. No 1 in French AM
Peco Silencers	UK

Source: Company interviews

Germany's Tenneco is represented in the domestic OE market by its UK subsidiary company Tenneco Walker, and in the AM by another subsidiary Harmo. The group is probably the most powerful in Europe, being further supported by manufacturing operations in Germany (Mannheim for OE, Langor and Ernst for the AM), in France (Ballinger), Denmark (Stalla), and an operation in Holland. With an aggressive pricing reputation, their impact on the UK AM has been immense. In recent years, they have increased their share in the AM at TI Silencers' expense.

Likewise a Belgium company Bosal, supported by a number of European plants and now a manufacturing presence in the UK, has entered the market. The market leader in the French AM, they too have integrated operations within Europe. They even have their own shipping operation, which reduces the cost of bringing exhaust systems into the UK. They have taken only a few years to build up to an AM share of about 5%, and their target is reputed to be 10%.

Low price imports have been noted from Ansa in Italy, and from Spanish manufacturers who enjoy a tariff advantage, facing only a 4% tariff in the UK whereas UK manufacturers face a tariff of about 37% in Spain. Volume has so far been low, but the impact on margins has been more substantial.

Thus despite factors unconducive to trade, opportunities presented by AM and OE markets have led to a predominantly European radius of competition between companies, though many compete on the basis of local plants. The impact of this change has increased recently, as overcapacity has contributed to pressures for some rationalisation within Europe. The strategic implications are already evident in the crucial OE market, as will now be discussed in more detail.

The competitive situation in the OE market

Transport costs have not in fact been a major problem within Europe: they can be reduced by expeditious shipping arrangements. In respect to their OE business, companies such as SU-Butec, BL Unipart's subsidiary, have found considerable scope for raising the level of technology and so justifying exports to the continent.

Costs to the UK or Japan would be higher, but these markets have also been distinguished by different pollution and noise controls. These factors may be changing and BL's increasing involvement with Honda might raise the question of tooling economies through joint production arrangements at some point. Japan, however, is committed to just-in-time arrangements which involve local exhaust system production and the USA is following suit, so there is unlikely to be significant trade with either of these markets in the immediate future.

Within Europe increasing interest in just-in-time operations has led Ford, GM and also VW to require local manufacturing support from suppliers. Faced with increasing international competition, these vehicle companies have also been under pressure to rationalise their European supplier networks so as to reduce costs. Ford's wish to reduce tooling costs was suggested as one of the key reasons for its decision to reduce the number of its European exhaust systems suppliers. These start up tooling costs are increased by homologation in Europe (which will probably hit smaller UK suppliers particularly hard). The effect of Ford's decision is to squeeze out manufacturers only marginally competitive in European terms. Significantly, its three major surviving exhaust system suppliers are all supported by international manufacturing operations, and can support both Ford UK and Ford Germany.

Like Tenneco, the leading UK manufacturer TI Silencers has established operations on the continent - a manufacturing and warehousing operation in Holland close to the German border, established in 1969, and a manufacturing operation in Spain, established in 1981.

Even this may not prove enough. To take full advantage of international operations, companies such as TI Silencers are now having to review organisational structures with a view to obtaining greater integration (just as happened in bearings). Scale economies are considered to be low and plants have to handle an enormous variety of products. In the past industrial relations (and security of supply) was also a key problem, so the policy was to have a number of fairly small plants, allowing management as much autonomy as possible. This is changing and to compete the group is having to consider tightening its structure, not only nationally but internationally.

Gillet, a German company, has been in a strong position, having responded earlier to Ford Europe's request to establish a modern factory close to their engine plant at Bridgend in Wales. Ironically Gillet received considerable financial support for this from the British government. In doing so they cemented their strong relationship with Ford. It is feared that Gillet's investment in the UK also reflects longer-term objectives in the AM. Gillet has also extended its manufacturing operations, into France in 1975, and into Spain in 1977 to support Ford's Fiesta.

Armstrong's problems in the OE market illustrate the strategic implications for UK manufacturers of rationalisation taking place within Europe. The weakest of participants, with full product ranges and full vehicle customer support facilities such as test rigs, Armstrong has been largely squeezed out at very considerable cost.

Armstrong saw their main problem as costs rather than non-price aspects such as quality. Their position was weakened by rising relative UK labour costs after 1980 (labour costs are roughly 25% of sales value, but the cost of other major items such as steel is fairly similar for European competitors). Overseas competitors benefited from less severe financial conditions elsewhere and from the ability to spread fixed costs, R&D etc. over a wider market base. The Tenneco Group, for example, was financially strong enough to sustain low UK prices over a long period, and so was able to squeeze out weaker UK competitors.

However, because of changes in the pattern of competition, Armstrong also suffered from a more strategic problem. Although the parent company is one of the top automotive component performers and financially relatively strong, it has other more attractive and closely related market opportunities. Its Cheadle and Blackburn exhaust systems plants had only been acquired in 1975 as part of Huntsville and its commitment to this sector has not matched that of competitors. The company was seduced by an extremely attractive deal from GKN into surrendering the core of a strong AM distribution network it had carefully built up, and without this support its AM position in exhaust systems must have been weakened.

Its major mistake was in committing major new investments into volume-orientated plant directed at the OE market. As in the case of RHP, this led to a head-on competitive collision with more powerful internationally based companies. Its demise was far more dramatic, since in Armstrong's context the importance of preserving flexibility was even greater. For exhaust systems volume benefits are lower than for bearings, and customer order sizes have fallen even more sharply.

In June 1978 the company invested heavily in a modern, volume-orientated new plant at Hull. Geared specifically to the OE market, operations were integrated from the point where pipe entered at one end of the factory, to where completed exhaust systems emerged from the other end. This involved automated assembly lines, automatic transfer equipment and key items of equipment, which were also volume-orientated.

With changeover times on such lines of the order of two days, they became highly inefficient as order runs, with only a few exceptions, fell below about 2,000. At a factory level, fixed costs were anyway higher, so that falling overall volumes rapidly fell below break-even. In January 1981 this modern plant was closed and work transferred to Armstrong's original exhaust system base at York. Much modern equipment was salvaged but remained volume orientated. As business conditions continued to deteriorate further competitive retreat was inevitable as the company retrenched onto Cheadle and Blackburn.

A continuing reduction in batch sizes was made even more difficult by an increased number of product programmes. During 1981 and 1982 batch quantities halved. Faced with setting up times now almost equal to operating times on some equipment, the company made desperate attempts to improve flexibility. Set up times on some machines were improved. They have succeeded in reducing factory through time to improve responsiveness to order variations and to reduce investments in stocks and work-in-progress. Such efforts helped regain some of the flexibility of more traditional, modular processes.

Despite such efforts and heavy investments, total output halved between 1975 and 1981/82. Employment has halved. This implies productivity was unchanged between 1975 and 1979, but had improved by about 7.5% by 1981/82 as the company strove vigorously to cut costs. Staff departments have been reduced particularly. At the time of visiting the two remaining plants were down to three and four day operating weeks respectively, despite the transfer of business from Hull and York. Such low utilisation frustrated further efficiency improvements.

Armstrong's position was further 'wedged in' by intensifying competition from medium-sized companies also desperate for business, particularly for anything resembling volume. One such company, with a reputation for 'maverick' pricing policies, in fact declined to participate in this study, as with jobs at stake competitive issues had become so highly sensitive. Automotive Products and Quinton Hazell, though mainly AM, were vulnerable also and were having to compete fiercely. Smaller UK manufacturers, such as Peco Silencers and Burgess, better adapted to poor order sizes, were also fighting to survive. Burgess for example was reputed to have called in consultants to help with its difficulties.

Like many manufacturers, Armstrong also found its position damaged by BL's determination to get a better deal from the UK components sector, in order to sustain its own competitive position. Through Unipart, BL extended its operations into areas such as exhaust systems, which were seen as particularly lucrative, this being handled through its in-house manufacturer SU-Butec. In the OE market SU-Butec could take advantage of BL's own 'cream' volume business, sufficient to justify modern integrated volume line production methods.

BL used its copyright position on exhaust systems to sue Armstrong successfully for infringement (*Engineer*, 8-15 April 1982, p.11). Other exhaust manufacturers were reported as having been forced to pay 7% royalties, a substantial figure given the pressure already on margins.

Such moves by BL really reflect the change in the bargaining position between vehicle manufacturers and UK suppliers already discussed. BL has achieved similar gains at the expense of suppliers by increasing international procurement generally, and until UK suppliers can offer a more internationally competitive deal to their customers this type of problem is bound to continue.

Yet, despite internationalisation, close OEM/supplier links are still an important feature distorting 'free competition'. Exhaust system companies argue that much of the continental market is 'tied'. GM produces most of its own in-house and the German market is fairly nationalistic: Ford Germany buys mostly from Tenneco and Gillet. VW's supply situation is complex, but it appears to buy mainly from Gillet. Even in the AM, UK suppliers felt that only about 10 to 15% of this market was 'up for grabs'. The danger, if BL 'opens up' ahead of overseas vehicle manufacturers or applies other negotiating levers too severely, is that many UK suppliers, faced with an asymmetrical competitive situation in Europe, will collapse. The UK may be 'divided and ruled' by overseas competition.

Some suppliers alert to the situation in factoring point to the demise of UK manufacturing operations in other products - Wilmot Breeden for example has largely stopped manufacturing locks and even their vehicle fittings business is reputed to be 'shaky' - Japanese suppliers coming over in the wake of Honda were rumoured to be offering British component companies attractive margins based on manufacture in Japan. Faced with such difficult UK conditions, some suppliers might be tempted, even though recognising that such expediency would signal the end of future competitiveness. Any weakening in the UK supplier base will ultimately rebound on UK vehicle customers.

Armstrong's demise highlights the need for UK manufacturers to be sensitive to changing competitive conditions, and the danger of ignoring the increasing impact of European competitors particularly in volume markets. Although its good financial performance must be qualified by the fact that it appears to have surrendered market share, especially in the AM, TI Silencers' performance has been relatively good (see Table 4.29). It has a clear picture of the competitive battle taking place in Europe.

Thus TI Silencers' better performance seems partly to reflect its alertness to the need for a stronger base in continental Europe, accompanied by some degree of reorganisation so as to extract the maximum possible synergy from its international operations.

Basic Manufacturing Issues

Productivity comparisons

British exhaust system manufacturers visited were compared with two overseas plants: JS1's plant in Japan employing 480 people and USS1's plant in the USA employing 375 people. Both were about 90% OE and so perhaps most comparable with TI Cheswick whose plant sizes were similar. The American plant in particular was able to benefit from longer production runs. Some indication of UK productivity is given in Table 4.30.

Exhaust systems prices have recently fallen behind the wholesale price index, so that UK progress on productivity is probably understated. The actual number of units/man/month produced at UKS1 remained unchanged at about 67 between 1975 and 1979, and actually rose about 7.5% by 1982. Productivity in other companies has been mixed but generally fairly stagnant, partly as a result of low utilisation levels; but TI Silencers' performance is relatively good. TI have trimmed indirect staff particularly, so that its ratio of direct/indirect staff has risen.

Table 4.30: UK exhaust companies sales/employee £'000,'82

Company	OE/AM	Recent £'000	estimate Year	Past year £'000	est Year
TI Cheswick	OE	57	1982	30	1979
Tenneco Walker	OE	19	1979	15	1975
Chilcotts	OE	26	1981	36	1973
SU-Butec	OE/AM	31	1980	na	
UKS1	AM	36	1982	44	1979
Harmo	AM	37	1976		
Burgess	AM	21	1975		
Quinton Hazell	AM	23	1976	21	1972

Source: company accounts. Figures for UKS1's exhaust systems activities supplied by company. All figures adjusted to 1982 prices.

In comparison, sales/employee at the Japanese plant JS1 was approximately £72,000 in 1982 based on that year's exchange rate of 435.2 yen/£. By 1984 sterling had fallen to 300 yen/£ so this exchange rate is probably unfavourable to the Japanese, whose domestic car prices in 1982 were well below those prevailing in Britain. This suggests an appreciable gap between the UK and Japan.

Without a value-based productivity estimate, the US plant USS1's estimated figure of 18.7 silencer boxes/man/day plus piping, at roughly twice the Japanese figure of 9.4 seems almost dubiously high. Differences in products and mixes in respect to piping may be distorting. Surprisingly, the US estimate of the proportion of sales value going on bought-in goods and services was higher at 30 to 35% than the Japanese estimate of 18 to 20%. Both

US and Japanese plants received R&D assistance not included in their figures. However, US production runs were very much higher than in both Britain and Japan.

Sales for the Japanese plant's parent company had grown 88% after inflation between 1971 and 1980, compared with a rise in employment of 13%. Historical figures were not available for the plant itself, but the productivity target was claimed to be 20% p.a. expressed in exhaust system units/man. This had fallen to about 16% p.a. between 1980 and 1982 partly because of the downturn, and this was said to have led to management being 'scolded'! Historical figures were not available for the US plant itself, but figures for the parent group (1,700 employees) perhaps give some indication. Sales/employee after inflation in 1981 fell 5% below the 1980 figure, but had recovered to 9% above by 1982, following a turnaround in their exhaust systems AM in April 1982. Both Japanese and American plants benefited from more favourable market circumstances, but productivity performances seem well ahead of the UK.

Production issues

American and Japanese plants were respectively 22 and 13 years old, with considerable evidence of plant modernisation. However, not all plant was so different: modern British plants had recently installed the same Eaton Leonard CNC pipe bending machines as US and Japanese plants.

The most striking difference lay in the flexibility of the Japanese plant, this being the result of 'just-in-time' developments. The plant had been built at Toyota's request, in close proximity. Since then they have gone from deliveries only about once a day though only on one type of exhaust system, to about eight deliveries a day involving many types.

Under guidance from specialist engineers at Toyota, they have systematically had to develop more flexible manufacturing methods. One auto-arm press, for example, now has to be changed over between 10 and 15 times a day, so they had to find ways to reduce changeover time to about 10 minutes. A machine tool company belonging to the same group has assisted with better-adapted machines: 20 recently installed Aida auto-sheet feeders have quick tool change characteristics. New more-flexible technology has been introduced, such as CNC multiform pipe benders which are well adapted to the problem of intermittent order take-offs and CAD/CAM, so as to facilitate quicker design and manufacture of new jigs and fixtures; but these developments are being pursued now in all three countries.

The sheer volume of incremental production changes is, however, remarkable. A press bending machine, converted to reduce changeover time (about 30 minutes seven years ago) to about 10 minutes, is one example; but numerous machines have had to be changed since the flexibility of the production flow rate often depends on the least flexible machine. Inherently inflexible machines have necessitated changes in factory layouts and flow routes. Pre-set tool packs are used. Though one or two 'dedicated' volume assembly lines have been segregated, most have been adapted to handling as many as ten major types of exhaust system.

Responsiveness to changing customer delivery requirements involved reducing factory through times and getting their own suppliers to respond in the same way. Just as Toyota developed a card system to inform them the moment more items were required, so they developed a similar system with their suppliers. Having reduced their own factory through time to 15 days some time ago, further progress was frustrated because material suppliers took a month to respond to the new orders. Both cooperated on the problem and they now claim each can respond in 5 days, making a total of 10.

UK and US manufacturers have had little experience of just-in-time arrangements, but TI's Cheswick plant has been substantially changed, reducing factory through time. Savings, on items such as stocks and work-in-progress costs, have also been substantial.

Japanese progress reflects sustained, patient attention to detail by numerous quality circles. These originated under the influence of Deming statistical quality control techniques, whose simplicity enabled production work groups to take responsibility for their own quality. Recognising the wider implications of such active participation, management focused attention and training resources onto these work groups. The groups were so successful on quality improvements that their role was extended to productivity improvements and other production matters such as flexible manufacturing methods. Morale and participation are high. This plant receives an average of 9.6 suggestions/employee/year.

The plant's trump card is that with rapid growth they have been able to sustain 'lifetime employment'. Employment slightly increased between 1971 and 1981 but otherwise remained extremely stable. Employees, confident that improvements such as productivity would not merely lead to themselves or their colleagues being laid off, were prepared to give 100% commitment and total flexibility. The company in return redoubled efforts to maintain competitiveness in the marketplace and was even prepared to bring in subsidiary business when necessary: steering wheel manufacture introduced to maintain stable employment represents roughly 7% of turnover. There seems to be a genuine, long-term two-way partnership.

The Americans, protected by a less exposed home market and better production runs, are nevertheless responding to such developments with greater dynamism than UK manufacturers.

Assisted by a sixfold revival in earnings in 1982 as compared with 1980, US1s' parent company's 1982 Business Report announced the key points in a new strategy, backed by a major investment programme, to rebuild their competitive position as 'the industry's lowest cost producer':

> Eight new computer programmed and controlled pipe-bending machines, capable of producing a major proportion of our total bent pipe needs. Advantages: Rapid changeover to new part numbers; scheduling flexibility for inventory balance; consistent high quality. A program to convert muffler lines to quick changeover capability, to facilitate greater scheduling flexibility, improved inventories, rapid turnover. A new high-speed shear press with quick changeover die inserts that blanks, notches, ribs and embosses

> muffler shells and wrappers in one operation. Changeover time has been cut by half.

Capital investment can only be a part of the answer to increased flexibility. Changeover time in their press shop's box making machine was still about 2 to 3 hours and was similar on other machines. Despite the annual report's natural optimism, the implementation of real flexibility will present an enormous challenge. In production areas it was admitted that set up times were still very long, and the pervading corporate culture still seemed volume-orientated. To quote: 'Our philosophy is volume' and 'For us 15,000 runs are great!'. One of the key questions is whether such American companies can really win over the total commitment of an enthusiastic but insecure workforce.

Yet the report also emphasised other 'Just in Time Preparations' and recognises the amount of 'fine tuning of production processes' necessary in addition to capital projects. It also emphasised how facilities were now being 'converted to the Deming statistical quality control system'. Their in-house magazine 'Pipeline' (Winter 1982) went on to remind employees that

> This system was developed by Dr W.E.Deming of New York University during the 1950's but generated only limited interest in the United States. The Japanese, however, seized on it, and it is now in almost universal use in Japanese industry.

The report indicated a coordinated initiative by US vehicle customers along the same lines as happened in Japan just over a decade ago.

> In addition, many of our manufacturing engineering, OEM sales and production scheduling personnel, including members of the labour union, have attended 'just in time' seminars at Ford World Headquarters in Dearborn for thorough backgrounding on the system.

The new strategy also points to:

> intensified product development and service activities by OEM sales and engineering teams working in close collaboration with automakers.

There is one final element in this American turnaround strategy which UK manufacturers should also consider. Recognising that resources necessary for investment and other 'plow-back' activities require some sacrifice in short-term living standards, this US company

> negotiated important changes in the labour contracts at the organised facilities that helped the company meet price competition in the OEM market.

Thus UK manufacturers must take more positive steps to match Japanese and US rivals on such developments taking place in production areas, and some change in organisational focus may be called for. TI Silencers' relatively good profit performance is, I believe, partly attributable to recognition at Board level of the strategic importance of such matters.

Conclusion

High transport costs, relatively low opportunities for scale advantages and a customer preference for local manufacture (particularly given increased interest in just-in-time systems) mean that most exhaust systems for UK customers will continue to be made in Britain. Nevertheless opportunities presented by AM and volume OE markets have led increasingly to a European radius of direct competition from the viewpoint of UK companies. Pressure for rationalisation in Europe increased markedly after 1979. The effect was first felt in volume OE market segments, but the after market is also coming under increasing pressure and smaller companies will also be affected in the longer-term. Such pressures will intensify further in Europe, but the effect of competition from further afield will remain merely indirect for many years.

The sharp performance decline, even in a sector made

more lucrative by the existence of an attractive AM, reflects declining UK competitiveness. This has been exacerbated by sharp decline in the UK cost position, and by a business climate so discouraging that some of the most modern assembly lines have had to be literally broken up. It is also worrying to see government support for overseas companies establishing UK plants, in situations where UK manufacturers are likely to be squeezed out.

Yet some UK manufacturers have worsened their problems through being insensitive to the strategic implications of European competition, especially in the volume OE market. Armstrong has suffered particularly in this respect. TI Silencers' relatively good performance reflects in part a recognition of the need, in this situation, to harness the advantages of a strong manufacturing base in continental Europe. It also reflects Board level recognition of the need to match international standards on key issues such as productivity and flexible manufacturing methods. Had UK manufacturers generally demonstrated the commitment displayed by Japanese and US rivals to ensuring an internationally competitive supplier service, their performance decline and the threat hanging over them would both have been less severe.

Though there is some scope for new technology to increase the flexibility of manufacturing operations, the Japanese experience indicates that more incremental improvements to production processes will play a critical role, both in respect to FMS and other important issues such as productivity and quality. Thus more positive participation and involvement of those in the production area will prove particularly important in this sector (as also in automotive forgings). This may call for a fresh approach to industrial relations and a more production-centred organisational approach.

Restoring this potentially lucrative sector's future would probably demand a coordinated approach: it requires economic choices by Britain more favourable to business development, the active involvement of UK vehicle companies (particularly in respect of just-in-time developments), greater managerial sensitivity to key issues and total support from employees in securing a competitive industry.

4.2 The Vehicle Components Industry as a Whole

The Impact of Internationalisation and of the UK's Declining Trade Position

Table 4.31 shows total production and trade figures (adjusted to 1980 prices) for motor vehicle parts and accessories from 1938 to 1982. Business Monitor production figures have been adjusted to exclude tyres, inner tubes and identifiable agricultural parts, to bring them more closely into line with trade figures taken from SMMT.

Table 4.31: Production and trade performance of UK motor vehicle parts manufacturers

4.31A.

	Exports surplus £m'80(1)	Imports prodn £m'80	Trade surplus £m'80	UK production £m'80	UK market £m'80	WPI 1980=100
1938	50	30	20	770	750	6.16(2)
1948	170	15	35	1,270	1,115	12.32
1953	330	35	295	1,840(3)	1,545	17.39(3)
1958	580	45	535	2,470	1,935	19.30
1963	740	60	680	3,250	2,570	20.81
1968	980	230	750	3,620	2,870	24.32
1973	1,510	470	1,040	3,980	2,940	33.32
1974	1,530	520	1,010	3,550	2,540	41.47
1975	1,610	530	1,080	3,380	2,300	50.69
1976	1,780	740	1,040	3,650	2,610	59.45
1977	1,610	740	870	3,600	2,730	71.22
1978	1,590	790	800	3,730	2,930	77.66
1979	1,610	950	660	3,710	3,050	85.96
1980	1,440	690	750	3,190	2,440	100.00
1981(4)	na	780	na	na	na	110.60
1982	1,160	890	270	2,530	2,260	120.10

(1) converted to 1980 prices using WPI
(2) 1937
(3) 1954
(4) import fig's unavailable due to Customs and Excise strike

4.31B.

	Exports/ production %	Imports/ UK market %	Trade surplus/ market %	Imports/ exports %
1938	6.5	4	3	58
1948	13	1	14	9
1953	18	2	19	10
1958	24	2	28	8
1963	23	2	26	8
1968	27	8	26	24
1973	38	16	35	31
1974	43	20	40	34
1975	48	23	47	33
1976	49	28	40	42
1977	45	28	32	46
1978	43	27	27	50
1979	43	39	22	59
1980	45	28	30	48
1981				
1982	46	39	12	77

Source: Production figures from Business Monitor; trade figures from SMMT yearbooks

Excluding inflation, the volume of imports more than trebled between 1970 and 1982, so that the impact of direct international competition is now substantial; the volume of exports, however, had by 1982 fallen back below the level in 1970.

Correspondingly, the strong surplus on overseas trade during most of the period has been cut dramatically. Although there has been a clear long-term trend, with imports steadily rising as a percentage of exports from 22% in 1970 to 77% in 1982, the sharpest decline has been since 1980. Taking out inflation, the favourable balance of trade fell by 60% between 1980 and 1982 as the ratio of imports to exports rose from 48% to 77%. The most recent figures, for the first quarter of 1983, suggest imports have now risen to just over 90% of exports, depleting any remaining trade surplus.

Thus UK parts manufacturers' sales have fallen partly because of a declining home market (due to the position of UK assemblers) and partly because, in the context of increasing international trade, their own international position has declined.

Decline has affected component sectors comprehensively (see Carr 1985, Appendicies D1 and D2 for detailed analysis of the international trade position of all component products for which official figures are available). Just as in case studies discussed, it should however be noted that aggregate trade figures often understate the seriousness of competitive decline. As international competition in wheels increased, for example, first Rubery Owen was squeezed out as BL was forced to go for single sourcing to provide Dunlop, its last major UK supplier, with adequate volume since its European competitors, such as Lemmertz and Kron-Prinz of Germany and Michelin in France and Spain, enjoy much larger markets. The *Financial Times* (19 August 1985, p.1) has now reported that Dunlop has applied for state aid on 'a £5m investment programme crucial to future competitiveness' on the grounds that although high risk, the investment is 'essential if the UK is to maintain the strategic ability to manufacture car wheels'. Ford, arguing it would require an investment of £9.5m to meet its future demand for lighter motor wheels, 'has opened negotiations with the unions to wind up wheel manufacture at its Dagenham factory by 1987'. Dunlop has been assured of Austin Rover purchases for three years, 'conditional upon the necessary measures being taken to make the product internationally competitive'. Such critical international decline would not easily be deduced from international trade figures.

Table 4.32 examines changes in the direction of trade. Britain's traditional 'Empire' markets represented 61% of parts exports in 1938 but even by 1963 had fallen to only 34%. This has been due to demands for local content and overseas competition, particularly from Japan. The European market has steadily risen in importance from 36% of all parts exports in 1954 to 53% in 1972 and 63% in 1980. Since entry into the EEC even the American market has fallen back in importance, from 24% in 1972 to 14% in 1980.

In 1938 69% of imports were American. Some were a stop-gap prior to US multinational companies establishing

UK manufacturing operations; some were parts in short supply in Europe. By 1972 American imports represented only 16% and by 1980 just 8%. By contrast European imports, which compete 'head on' with UK manufacturers, rose from 31% of imports in 1938 to 80% in 1972 and 85% in 1980. Germany and France alone accounted for 50% of all imports. Imports from the rest of the world were only 7% in 1980, but Asian competition has increased, particularly from Japan.

The radius of business competition is now Europe.

Table 4.32: Direction of UK trade in motor vehicle parts and accessories

4.32A: Destination of UK exports: %

	1938	1954	1963	1972	1980
Europe	45	36	42	53	63
America	6	10	16	24	14
Africa	13	15	11	8	10
Asia	14	20	17	9	9
Oceania	22	18	11	6	5
W. Germany	3	3.6	4	8	14
Belgium	2	3	3	8	11
Sweden	5	8	9	10	8
France	1	3	3	4	7
Italy	0.5	2	6	2	6
Netherlands	4	3	3	4	4
Eire	14	2	2	2	4
USA	1	2	7	14	9
S. Africa	8	4	4	3	3
Australia	11	14	8	5	3
India	7	5	5	1	0.6
Former British Empire	61	52	34	14	8

4.32B: Source of UK imports: %

	1938	1954	1963	1972	1980
Europe	31	42	63	80	85
America	69	53	31	16	8
Rest of World	0.2	5	6	4	7
W. Germany	14	9	22	33	32
France	6	11	12	9	18
Belgium	1	1	2	15	11
Italy	0.6	2	4	5	6
Sweden	5	3	8	5	4
Spain	0	0	4		
Netherlands	0.5	6	5	2	3
Switzerland	2	2	2	0.3	0.3
Austria	0.3	0.4	3	2	0.4
Asia	0.09	2	4	3	6
Japan	0.07	0.03	1.6	3	4

Source: SMMT yearbooks, taken from official sources

Company Performances Generally

The largest 66 automotive component companies for which Inter Company Comparison figures were available continuously from 1975 to 1982, were analysed in terms of sales growth and profitability (ROCE). For about 24 of these companies it was possible to extend figures back to 1970.

Table 4.33 demonstrates more generally the dramatic decline in company performances noted in the case studies. On average sales volumes declined by one-third between 1979 and 1982, reflecting market conditions already discussed and the inability of companies to offset decline through exports or diversification into other activities.

The decline in profitability has also been unprecedented. Between 1970 and 1979 ROCE's (unweighted) averaged about 18%, ranging from a nadir of 13% following the first oil crisis in 1975 to a peak of 25% in 1977.

Profitability remained stable, despite UK vehicle production halving between 1973 and 1979. Average (unweighted) ROCE then fell precipitously to 0.6% in 1980, -3.2% in 1981, and -4.4% in 1982.

Table 4.33: Averaged (unweighted) company performances

	1970-75	1975-79	1980-82
Growth: % p.a.	0.8	5.4	(10.9)
ROCE: %	18.0	19.4	(2.3)
Growth and ROCE: %	18.8	24.8	(13.2)

Note: Growth figures derived from sales in 1970, 1975, 1979 and 1982, adjusted for inflation using the wholesale price index. Rates represent total % change over period divided by number of years.

Source: ICC Business Ratio Reports / company accounts

Decline has been comprehensive. Companies were ranked into six size classifications, each with 11 companies, on the basis of turnover in 1975. Table 4.34 shows that in the three years 1980-82 every size category averaged both negative growth and negative ROCE.

Table 4.34: Performances by size classification 1980-82

Size groups in descending order	Growth 1979-82 % pa	ROCE average 1980-82	Growth + ROCE %
Companies 1-11	(9.1)	(3.1)	(12.2)
Companies 12-22	(10.2)	(4.6)	(14.8)
Companies 23-33	(11.6)	(5.5)	(17.1)
Companies 34-44	(12.4)	(1.1)	(13.5)
Companies 45-55	(12.3)	(4.8)	(17.1)
Companies 56-66	(9.8)	(6.6)	(16.4)
Companies 1-66	(10.9)	(4.3)	(15.2)

Source: Carr (1985) Appendicies D3 and D4, based on

ICC annual data.

After inflation only two companies, both in the smallest size category, increased sales volume between 1979 and 1982. Just under one quarter (and in fact only 2 of the largest 22 companies) managed a positive combined total of sales growth plus ROCE.

Of 66 companies, 22 avoided losses in any of these three years, 19 made losses in one year only and 9 in two years only. Of the remaining 16 companies which made losses in all three years, three had made losses in four consecutive years and another three in five consecutive years. By comparison, between 1970 and 1979 on average just under 9% of these companies were making losses in any given year, the worst figure occurring at the onset of the recent downturn in 1979 when the figure rose to 19%.

The extent and severity of decline cannot be fully explained either by the natural knock-on effect of declining UK vehicle production, which was relatively stable in this period, or by the normal business cycle, since past downturns had only a slight impact on performance figures. ICC's 1982 Business Ratio report examining the top 100 automotive component companies was forced to conclude:

> To summarise, the companies in this Report have been hit very badly by a whole list of factors beyond their control. It is far too easy to say that a reduction in capacity earlier or diversification into other markets and products should have taken place sooner, but the truth of the matter is many companies did this and yet still made losses...
>
> There is no doubt that the performance of the UK motor components sector has been horrific and has mirrored, if not led, the decline in industrial output in this country.

This suggests that Britain, and the government to the extent of its ability, must take more seriously the need to avoid economic choices creating such adverse business conditions, so unconducive even to companies pursuing more progressive strategies. Nor can the failure to do so be excused by glib thinking, showing little understanding of business conditions: one Chief Executive interviewed complained that the Minister concerned, on hearing his problems, had merely commented, 'Couldn't you make something else?'.

The lesson from a company perspective again echoes case findings, that sweeping panaceas are unlikely to prove effective strategies in such a context. Companies in this industry could not, in fact, rely on diversification or on gains in market share or exports. Those that did found their attempts at protecting sales volume frustrated, and many dangerously postponed volume adjustments. Some popular panaceas, such as market domination or industry consolidation, presuppose scale advantages. This issue receives detailed discussion later in this chapter, but in this industry there is little general indication that large companies perform better. Companies must therefore carefully examine the issue of scale in the context of their particular competitive circumstances. As emphasised in product case studies sensitivity to context, responsiveness to change, and commensurate attention to more basic issues seem the most likely paths to success.

The UK Business Environment

Prior to 1960, UK manufacturers remained fairly shielded from the full impact of international competition. Until then, vehicle manufacturers and component companies in particular were protected by a 30% tariff.

Between 1960 and 1978, UK wage rates in manufacturing relative to those of rival countries, had been gradually falling, compensating for slower productivity growth. These trends were illustrated in Figure 1.2 on page 10. Britain's 'real' (inflation-adjusted) exchange rate had moved so as to broadly maintain UK manufacturers' cost competitiveness, which would have otherwise resulted from allowing complacency in respect of productivity. For this reason the Select Committee Inquiry (1975) found no evidence of UK parts being uncompetitive on price with other European manufacturers.

It should be noted that UK relative labour costs are influenced by inflation-adjusted, not nominal exchange rate movements. From the viewpoint of competition, European rather than US rates (where the situation has recently improved) are particularly important.

Between 1978 and 1980, a gross discontinuity in such trends resulted in relative UK labour rates suddenly moving much more closely into line with those of European and other rival countries. Relative to UK earnings rates in manufacturing, US rates by 1980 had fallen to 66% of their level in 1978, comparable figures for other rival countries being Japan 64%, Germany 75%, France 84%, Italy 85% and Sweden 75%.

The situation by Autumn 1981 is given in more absolute cost terms in Table 4.35.

Table 4.35: Labour costs and productivity in the manufacturin industry of major countries, autumn 1981

	Hourly labour costs in DM	Hourly labour costs* as index	Hourly productivity** as index	Unit labour costs*** as index
Belgium	25.50	102	89	115
Sweden	25.20	101	87	116
W. Germany	25.00	100	100	100
US	24.50	98	102	96
Netherlands	24.10	96	97	99
Italy	19.90	80	68	118
France	18.40	74	83	89
Japan	16.20	65	78	83
UK	14.20	57	50	114
Spain	12.60	50	47	106

* Index of 100 based on Germany. Costs include social charges and fringe benefits

** Output per man-hour worked in terms of same currency

*** Column two divided by column three

Source: *Financial Times*, 12 January 1982, from Dresdner Bank

A contributory factor has been a rise over just a few years in the contribution of North Sea Oil to almost £10bn to the UK's international current account. Tighter monetary policy resulted in higher real interest rates and further attracted capital inflows. In the context of dampened demand conditions, inevitably something else had to give on the UK's current account. Real exchange movements noted were the mechanism by which international trade flows were brought back towards equilibrium. The manufacturing sector, representing almost 70% of the UK's current account transactions, inevitably bore the brunt of this change, so that the manufacturing sector's trade balance did indeed move by something approaching £10bn. The more internationally exposed and weaker sectors within manufacturing, such as the UK vehicle and vehicle components sectors, were in turn affected disproportionately.

As real exchange rates moved, UK vehicle manufacturers and their suppliers both found themselves fully exposed to international competition just as it was intensifying due to international recession; but they were no longer shielded by such high differentials in relative labour rates. UK manufacturers then found themselves faced with the fruits of past complacency.

Yet Britain's economic choices, in allowing such a sudden and unprecedented change in the relative cost position were also to blame. No country, not even Japan under dynamic conditions most conducive to sustainable productivity growth, has ever achieved productivity growth levels such as would have been necessary to offset such a sudden change in relative costs. To put the issue in perspective, few UK component manufacturers have achieved productivity gains of much over 10% in the last decade. Even allowing for 'slack', it was inconceivable for UK manufacturers to achieve productivity gains, over a period of less than two years, of over 30%, net of progress being made in more dynamic competitor countries.

UK vehicle assemblers and component manufacturers were likewise affected. UK vehicle prices, reflecting the cost position, jumped so far ahead even of continental Europe that the EEC considered action to try and reduce differentials to under 18%. Even by late 1984, by which time the real exchange rate surge had subsided somewhat, car prices in the UK market were still ahead. For example, the average price of models reported by the *Financial Times* (18 December 1984, p.15), comprising Citroen's GSA Pallas, Fiat's Panda 45, Ford's Escort XR3i, Peugeot's 305 GT, the Renault 5 GTL and the Volkswagen Golf GTI, was £5,909 in the Belgium market, £6,488 in Germany, £6,700 in France, £7,165 in Italy and £7,706 in the UK. The competitive gap, even against Europe, was therefore still substantial.

Internationally aware procurement departments of vehicle manufacturing companies, whilst traditionally cautious about over-reacting to cost changes brought about by exchange rates, recognised UK component manufacturers' decline in cost competitiveness. BL claimed it could purchase 80% of its components at prices 20% cheaper by going overseas, and a similar picture emerged from interviews with German and Japanese vehicle companies.

Volume adjustments were cautious, but the bargaining position had radically changed so that margins available to UK suppliers were cut dramatically. Itself under pressure, BL claimed it had to pass on competitive pressure to UK suppliers. Despite success in freezing most component prices over the four-year period since 1979, Austin Rover were nevertheless able to claim that they had effectively subsidised UK component prices to the extent of £24m during the same period (Bessant, Jones, Lamming and Pollard, 1984, pp.61-62).

Many UK suppliers had been slow to respond to declining customer orders and could take up some degree of 'slack', but this improvement merely restored former productivity levels. Some went further by just cutting out less profitable activities, representing further market retrenchment. Nevertheless, despite being dogged by poor market conditions and underutilisation, some real progress has also been made.

The problem is that this has made manufacturing in Britain even less attractive than in the past. Exposed multinationals noted that whilst the UK had been an attractive location for manufacturing components in 1973, the rise in relative labour rates had reversed the position, leading to UK business being relocated. UK suppliers, uncompetitive in costs, were driven back both in export markets and by increased import penetration.

The main problem is that UK manufacturers have been even further discouraged from pursuing strategies needed to improve their longer-term position. The decline in financial performances noted earlier in this chapter placed perhaps even the majority of UK component companies into virtually a 'turnaround' situation. This dictated an approach to strategy similar to that necessarily employed by receivers and precluded many progressive strategies which would not have met the primary requirement of a sufficiently rapid return to profitability. In consequence they have slipped further behind international rivals.

There has been one major gain: a more overriding commitment to competitiveness by UK manufacturers. If the importance of such a commitment were to become widely recognised, it could even represent a psychological turning point. Even so, improvements needed will still probably take a decade of patient progress (judging by the Japanese experience).

Efforts are probably doomed to frustration, however, unless a radically more conducive business environment is re-established and sustained. Unfortunately although US and Japanese rivals show clear recognition of the need for wage pressures to abate when international competition intensifies, so as to improve their business situations, there still appears little such recognition in Britain, particularly in the trade union movement. This could prove critical.

A more dynamic market is also needed, but this will prove unsustainable unless both customers and suppliers are allowed better levels of profit, so that they can attract the resources to support growth; if not inflation will frustrate such policy measures.

Relationship with Vehicle Companies

The competitive strength of the Japanese components sector originates from the recognition of its strategic importance, by entrepreneurs such as Honda (Honda Motors) and Toyoda (Toyota), and their determination to develop actively a supplier network to match their own needs. The close fostering relationship engineered between the two sectors, has been at the heart of the many initiatives that have transformed the competitive position of both.

Toyota's initiatives for example, detailed in Shingo (1981), began well over a decade ago though drawing little attention from UK manufacturers until recently. These gradually brought about changes in productivity, quality, delivery systems (just-in-time), and more flexible approaches to manufacturing methods. These changes were carried out systematically and comprehensively, not only within Toyota, but also within Toyota's supplier companies, and within their supplier companies too.

A Japanese executive explained that Japanese relationships between suppliers and assemblers in Japan were less contractual than in the West. Their agreements with Toyota were brief, often just a single page, and flexible, saving considerable time. Though frequently broken, this was acceptable because the customer relationship was perceived as essentially long-term, both 'sides' being highly conscious of the fact that their futures depended on each fostering the competitiveness of the other.

Superficially integration between the two sectors might appear lower, since Japanese assemblers typically buy in an even greater proportion of components (about 70% by value) than do UK assemblers. In fact the two sectors are closely integrated on a number of counts:

* Cross shareholdings
* As part of the same business groupings, linked by common banks
* Manufacturing and logistical links
* Financial support, e.g. on R&D
* Personal linkages as a result of senior executives moving between the sectors, particular as OEM executives retire

Shimokawa, a leading expert on the Japanese components industry, cites the 'business groupism' (Shimokawa, 1982a,b,c) between parts manufacturers and assemblers as one of the major factors underlying Japan's international competitiveness, since it permits 'vertical integration gains' whilst mitigating the conflict of interests characteristic of Western relationships. He also emphasises that this 'business groupism' extends also to machine tool companies and distribution outlets.

In the UK, both vehicle companies and suppliers have taken maximum advantage from opportunities presented by changing business circumstances to raise their own profitability at the expense of the other. Component manufacturers succeeded for a considerable time in achieving a rate of return on capital employed of about 18%, over twice the average for UK car assemblers. It was inevitable that as their customers' fortunes declined, the negotiating positions would change. Manufacturers such as BL had of course to restore reasonable levels of profit to meet their own short-term financial targets. They had little difficulty in the context of depressed conditions after 1979 in totally reversing this situation. By 1982 average ROCE for the top 100 automotive component companies was down to about 0%, whilst vehicle companies were recovering. Such a see-saw effect is extremely damaging to the competitive situation of both sectors in the longer-term, since reasonable levels of profitability are crucial to the provision of sufficient levels of ploughback.

Even BL's partner Honda seemed extremely cautious about BL's rapid moves to international procurement. Surely, they argued, BL should instead foster its own component base, just as Honda has done as part of its longer-term competitive strategy. By coming overseas to Japanese component suppliers, BL risked becoming dependent on suppliers whose bargaining power would increase later.

Internationalisation is though changing the situation. As Shimokawa (1982b) also noted, it could mean that in the future the close relationship which has proved such a competitive strength to Japanese manufacturers to date could become less so, perhaps affording an advantage to more competitive British component manufacturers in sectors where internationalisation is proceeding faster. Some UK suppliers have already taken advantage of their relative independence to pursue opportunities afforded by internationalisation: notably Pilkington's glass, GKN in constant velocity joints, and AE not far behind in pistons.

Such global strategies have so far depended heavily on exceptionally strong patent positions, as Japanese suppliers point out. For most UK suppliers the real fear is that internationalisation is progressing asymmetrically, with UK customers opening their doors to overseas suppliers (partly for reasons of expediency) more rapidly than other vehicle companies, such as GM in Germany, and particularly Fiat whose domestic supplier links are still extremely close. This is a justifiable fear. Williams, Williams and Thomas (1983) traced the rapid decline of British shipbuilding, to a fairly sudden 'de-coupling' in their relationship with UK shipping line customers some years earlier.

Timing is also important. The international competitiveness of the Japanese components industry was made possible, because it was protected until the moment the industry was strong enough to survive free trade. Had the Japanese agreed to free trade much earlier, both vehicle manufacturers and their suppliers would probably have been savaged by Western competition. Free trade has never been fully reciprocal, and by now UK manufacturers would in general be far too weak to take advantage of the Japanese market even if it was now, belatedly, fully opened up. Britain cannot ignore internationalisation, but it might be wise to use the EEC to ensure it proceeds on a fairer, more even-handed basis.

The real danger, meanwhile, is that any further decoupling in the relationship between UK component suppliers and vehicle manufacturers so far in advance of developments elsewhere may result in a process of divide-and-rule working to the disadvantage of both sectors.

This point may be contentious. There are disturbing indications that BL feels it could go it alone through increasing reliance on overseas parts; but I would argue that the competitive success of Japanese vehicle manufacturers has been crucially dependent on extremely close domestic supplier links. Conversely BL's Unipart OE operations depend on becoming independent of BL through an export policy. However, particularly while the UK's international cost position remains poor and while the competitive situation internationally remains asymmetrical, case studies discussed earlier in this chapter and my analysis of more successful companies discussed in the next section suggest there is a limit to the reliance that can be placed on exporting for the majority of companies.

The Relationship Between Size and Performance

Table 4.36: Performances by size classification 1970-82

Size groups (descending order)	Growth 1970-75 % pa	ROCE 1970-74 %	Growth + ROCE %	Growth 1975-82 % pa	ROCE 1975-82 %	Growth + ROCE %
1-11	3.4	12.7	16.1	(2.9)	8.3	5.4
12-22	0.1	26.5	26.6	(2.9)	11.7	8.8
23-33	2.6	19.6	22.2	(3.7)	19.8	16.1
34-44	(0.7)	21.4	20.7	(1.2)	8.0	6.8
45-55	(3.2)	5.1	1.9	(2.6)	13.2	10.6
56-66	-	-	-	(0.7)	10.2	9.5

Source: figures derived from Carr (1985) Appendices D3 and D4, based on ICC annual data.

Figures for 1970-75 are based on only 24 companies but suggest the largest class of companies (household names such as Lucas, Dunlop etc.), although displaying faster growth, were substantially outperformed by companies in the next three size classifications in respect to profitability. This suggests that some of these larger company groupings, formed from earlier consolidations, have already passed the point of optimum size; certainly market leadership, exercised by most of these companies (in their particular component sectors) merely in a UK context, has proved no guarantee of competitive success.

Figures for the eight year period 1975-82 are based on the full 66 companies. Growth rates are similar, so the issue of 'buying market share' does not arise, but the largest class of companies is outperformed by every other size classification. Indeed Table 4.37 shows how consistently this happened in every year between 1970 and 1978.

Table 4.37: Average ROCE by size classification 1970-82

	1-11	12-22	23-33	34-44	45-55	56-66	1-66
1982	(2.2)	(6.6)	(0.7)	3.0	(12.2)	(8.3)	(4.5)
1981	(3.4)	(5.5)	4.1	(1.9)	(6.5)	(6.7)	(3.3)
1980	(3.6)	(4.7)	9.3	(4.3)	4.5	2.4	0.6
1979	12.7	10.8	24.2	10.9	20.8	21.9	16.9
1978	15.1	18.7	33.3	15.2	23.1	27.0	22.1
1977	16.1	22.6	36.1	15.0	30.0	33.1	25.5
1976	14.5	29.0	25.9	15.5	22.5	13.3	20.1
1975	10.2	21.5	23.9	10.4	7.4	5.8	13.2
1974	11.8	21.3	29.3	13.3	5.4	-	15.4
1973	12.4	25.1	14.5	22.2	1.5	-	14.7
1972	12.7	24.9	25.1	24.1	(5.5)	-	16.4
1971	12.8	29.6	19.5	25.6	13.4	-	18.7
1970	13.5	34.4	11.3	23.2	10.9	-	17.1

Source: figures derived from Carr (1985) Appendices D3 and D4 based on ICC annual data.

Yet in the last few years this situation has changed and the second largest group has in fact been under more pressure than other groups including the largest. As noted particularly in the cases of automotive forgings and automotive exhaust systems, second tier companies have been squeezed between stronger larger companies as their vehicle manufacturer customers moved to fewer sources of supply (e.g. Rubery Owen in wheels), and smaller more-flexible competitors carrying very low overheads.

This highlights the need for sensitivity to circumstances. Many larger component companies suffered in the 1970s through over-reliance on strategies more appropriate to the growth conditions of the 1960s and through insufficient recognition of the changing radius of competition. In today's turbulent competitive conditions the issue of scale cannot be ignored, but it must be analysed carefully in context.

Table 4.38 gives details of best performing companies in the period 1975-82 and again confirms that size is no guarantee of competitive success. There also appears to be little correlation between growth and ROCE, implying that increasing market share is no guarantee either.

Table 4.38: Best performing companies 1975-82

	Growth %	ROCE %	Activities
1. IHW (48)*	(2.4)	67.4	Door hinges, OE
2. Motaproducts (66)	428.7	28.4	Accessories, AM
3. TI Nicholson (53)	0.1	44.8	Exhaust systems, AM
4. Britax Wingard (29)	(2.0)	44.9	Accessories, AM
5. Oldham (27)	1.5	36.1	Batteries, AM
6. Flexible Lamps (62)	5.0	32.2	Lighting, AM
7. Champion (21)	(3.0)	37.4	Spark plugs, AM
8. TI Cheswick (31)	(3.1)	34.0	Exhaust systems, OE
9. Airflow (38)	12.8	15.0	Body panels, OE
10.Concentric Pumps(33)	(1.0)	23.7	Water pumps, OE
11.Intermotor (64)	8.7	17.9	Electrical, AM
12.Cam Gears (13)	(4.3)	30.2	Misc, OE
13.Armstrong (14)	6.9	13.4	Exhaust systems, OE/AM
14.C H Industrials (40)	10.7	9.1	Exterior trim
15.BBA (7)	(2.7)	21.8	Brake linings, AM
16.BRD (17)	(2.8)	21.9	Prop shafts, OE

* size ranks, given in brackets, average 35 for this group

Source: Figures derived from Carr(1985) Appendicies D3 and D4, based on ICC data

The group includes a miscellany of products but after-market products such as exhaust systems are better represented, confirming case findings of a slightly healthier situation here.

Surprisingly, many better performing companies are involved in relatively low technology activities, which does not support the notion of low technology companies being inevitably doomed. This may be because such activities have so far been less exposed to the impact of international competition. From the viewpoint of UK competitiveness though, it is disturbing that higher technology companies are not better represented. This again seems to indicate the UK business environment is discouraging more technologically progressive strategies.

Table 4.39: Best performing companies 1980-82

	Growth %	ROCE %	Activities
1. IHW (48)*	(9.4)	67.4	Door hinges, OE
2. TI Nicholson (53)	(4.8)	44.8	Exhaust systems, AM
3. Concentric Pumps (33)	(6.2)	28.2	Water pumps, OE
4. Flexible Lamps (62)	(6.0)	22.5	Lighting, AM
5.Smiths (4)	(1.0)	17.1	Instruments and systems, OE/AM
6. Rockwell Maudsley (24)	(12.8)	21.1	Axles, OE
7. TI Cox (41)	(6.6)	10.3	Seating parts, OE
8. Oldham (27)	(10.1)	16.3	Batteries, AM
9. TRW Clifford (30)	(10.3)	15.2	Misc, OE
10.Abbey Panels (45)	(5.8)	10.3	Body panels, OE
11.Intermotor (64)	(1.1)	5.5	Electrical, AM
12.Motaproducts (66)	(8.0)	5.5	Accessories, AM
13.Chilcotts (55)	(12.4)	16.2	Exhaust systems, AM
14.Supra (42)	(7.1)	7.8	Materials, paints, sealants
15.Commercial Ignition (59)	(9.6)	10.0	Electrical parts
16.Turner (19)	(3.1)	3.2	Gearboxes, clutches, OE

* size ranks, given in brackets, average 42 for this group

Source: Figures derived from Carr (1985) Appendicies D3 and D4, based on ICC annual data

As noted, however, factors making for competitive success may be changing. Only half these companies appear in Table 4.39, which focuses on best performing companies in just the most recent three years 1980-82, and an even greater variety of activities are represented.

Basic Issues Facing UK Manufacturers

Productivity

Quantitative estimates of productivity differentials noted in product cases can be taken as a strong indication of a lack of commitment by UK manufacturers in regard to this issue, but I would not expect such differentials to reflect the situation in all product sectors. Where manning levels are largely process determined, productivity differentials are likely to be lower. Some multinationals, particularly those operating smaller UK plants below about 250 people, have not experienced such large productivity differentials. Also some UK plants perform a 'cats and dogs' role, where it is appropriate for productivity to be quite low. (In fact, UK conditions have led to some such plants being closed though in more normal circumstances they have served a useful role.) I would also expect many UK manufacturers to have made further improvements since my visits and would be surprised if much of the more obvious slack has not gone.

From this point on, I suspect improvements in productivity to match overseas rivals will involve a long haul, requiring rapid but sustained progress. Low levels of utilisation and stagnation in the UK appear seriously to inhibit further progress.

Britain cannot afford this situation in the context of such rapid advances by competitors. Evidence of this is ubiquitous throughout the Japanese automotive components sector. Japanese productivity in disc pad manufacture for example had increased from 31 pieces/man/hour in 1978 to 67 in 1982, reflecting the situation in cases discussed. In stagnating, Britain is slipping further behind.

Quality

Quality was a key factor from the viewpoint of OEM purchasing departments, particularly when buying internationally. Britain's reputation is better on particular products (e.g. brakes) where it has been better placed historically. In general, however, whilst British manufacturers enjoyed a good international reputation for quality a decade ago, today their reputation is mediocre. By contrast, Japanese component manufacturers had a shoddy reputation 25 years ago, but must now rate as leaders.

Japanese companies interviewed volunteered unsolicited comparisons between British and German component suppliers. The German sector's quality standards were considered high and ahead of Britain both by Japanese component companies which had visited and collaborated with both countries, and also by Japanese vehicle assemblers. One British supplier apparently hadn't even troubled to put the right number of parts in the box, a matter of some sensitivity in the context of Japanese 'just in time' delivery systems.

Multinational parts companies have undoubtedly done a great deal to tighten up quality standards in their British plants in recent years. Even so one quality control manager, monitoring identical parts from plants in Germany and the UK, stated that whilst his average rejection rate in the UK had averaged only 0.1% over the previous two or three years, the figure from the German plant was only half that figure. Tracing the causes, about half the UK rejections were due to faults on items the UK plant had itself bought in, pointing to the fact that British manufacturers were less thorough about passing responsibility for quality to outside suppliers.

Quality standards maintained in Germany and Japan are assisted by more modern plants, enabling more ordered work flow routes and equipment. The clinical neatness of German factories and of more modern Japanese plants (some even boasting small palm trees along the length of the assembly lines) is in contrast to most British component factories and provides a more conducive atmosphere for quality and other improvements. GKN's extremely modern constant velocity plants in the US have recently won American quality awards however.

German and Japanese manufacturers enjoyed closer relationships with machine tool suppliers whose support is evident in numerous minor technical improvements, tailored to their individual needs. Similarly, quality initiatives pursued by so many Japanese component manufacturers, could be traced back to the direct involvement of their vehicle manufacturer customers. The dynamic development of all three industry 'tiers', based on close fostered relationships, has been mutual and reinforcing.

German and Japanese approaches to quality, and indeed other manufacturing issues, were distinguished by a different control philosophy. Both UK and US manufacturers relied heavily on externally imposed systems, designed to stop production personnel getting too far out of line with regard to quality standards. There was still a tendency to believe in a quality/cost 'trade-off', and 'optimised' standards tended to be enshrined in quality control manuals, backed up by sophisticated control systems and higher levels of quality control staff. This also appeared to apply to production control systems.

German manufacturers were not averse to advanced quality control techniques. One company, for example, had installed a computerised statistical sampling system, and was pushing beyond go-no-go inspection principles common in Britain, by utilising advanced statistical methods in conjunction with specific error data, available from more accurate equipment. Generally though, German and Japanese companies objected to 'optimisation' approaches in any area of manufacturing policy, on the grounds that they reduced commitment to a more dynamic learning experience in the production area.

Responsibility was placed more firmly in the hands of production personnel whose morale and involvement was considered crucial. Japan's unique culture may have helped foster the commitment of working groups referred to as 'quality circles', but it should also be remembered that its entire cultural tradition had been associated in the 1950s with quality problems far worse than in Britain. What changed was not culture, but a willingness to adopt a new production-centred organisational approach together with specific and coordinated manufacturing programmes. As Nissan Motor Manufacturing (UK)'s Personnel Director, Peter Wickens (Wickens, 1987) reiterates, such changes are appropriate to UK manufacturers.

The ideas on statistical quality control, put forward by Deming and Juran in the late 1950s and early 1960s found a most receptive audience among Japanese manufacturers initially because of their pressing quality problems. The simplicity of their methods enabled modern techniques of quality control to be placed directly into the hands of operators, rather than becoming merely a staff function.

This caught the imagination of very large numbers of people involved in manufacturing operations, and encouraged the emergence of the 'quality circles' which were ubiquitous in the Japanese vehicle component manufacturers visited.

One example was a small brake linings plant employing only about 30 people. The section leader, a man who had left school at 15 and come up through operations, not only knew about the work of Deming (a US academic!) but also produced a small library of books on the subject, proudly admitting that he had his own personal library on statistical quality control methods at home. The area set aside for his quality circle was almost a shrine, with photographs and diagrams of all the improvements he and his men had produced over recent years: pride of place went to a series of beautifully presented colour photograph albums (one album for example showed eight of this group's major ideas during the previous year). This section leader, like many others in Japan, attended monthly lectures at quality groups outside the factory and about three or four meetings per month took place inside the company. Two 'circles' were in fact in operation, one a quality circle which also covered safety improvements and the other a productivity group concerned with other improvements to the manufacturing process. This group's numerous suggestions had generally been implemented and had contributed to a steady improvement in quality standards. The company's records indicated that rejection rates on brake pads had gradually been brought down from 0.68% five years earlier to 0.48%.

Toyota, which claimed to receive about 38 suggestions per employee per year, is a leading exponent of such schemes and has directly influenced its suppliers. Similar figures for suppliers were high but generally more modest. One brake manufacturer, with about 120 quality circles in operation, averaged just under 5 p.a. though the target was to beat 10 p.a.. This had also reduced the number of quality control staff to only 1.5% of the workforce, which is low for a safety critical product.

Given a favourable organisational context, something that began with quality in mind ultimately succeeded in harnessing the enthusiasm and commitment of enormous numbers of employees, and was extended to a range of other basic production improvements such as productivity and flexible manufacturing methods. Yet it was not the result of some accident or fortuitous circumstance; it was the result of management recognising and supporting such critical developments.

Research and development

In many component areas, UK manufacturers inherited a strong R&D capability. Often, they had in fact licensed out such know-how to Japanese companies, e.g. in constant velocity joints, brake linings, brakes and glass. British pistons and fuel injection systems are also technically advanced. In other areas, technological dominance has been allowed to wither away: e.g. Dunlop's supremacy in tyre technology was lost to competitors such as Michelin, particularly after radial tyres were developed.

UK manufacturers have suffered from a relatively undynamic market base, and a weak funding position. Most can only afford small R&D departments at best, and even large companies have often been forced to close departments completely during such difficult recent business conditions.

Despite limited organisational support, British R&D staff seem to have maintained a surprisingly good creative record. GKN Forgings' technical developments were still ahead of Japanese manufacturers. Individually, British R&D engineers are better trained and qualified than their counterparts in Japan. Even electronic companies in Japan place little emphasis on outside training or qualifications, though they do gain from strength in depth in terms of graduates with relevant degrees. They are also prepared to increase the number of their staff when necessary. Mitsubishi Electronics spends 3 to 4% of sales value on R&D in automotive electronics and also receives substantial support from its parent company Mitsubishi Motors.

Japanese culture and their managerial approaches tend to be less supportive in this area. Honda's production personnel, for example, were proud that R&D staff were often 'not allowed in' and saw their R&D department very much as a service department to develop their ideas. Nevertheless the morale and commitment of Japanese R&D engineers seemed high, sometimes almost matching the enthusiasm of kamikaze pilots. I asked one R&D engineer how they tested brake linings only to be told they were on the car we were driving! Those I interviewed habitually worked a couple of extra hours before going home.

Japanese executives still seemed to respect British technology, but one referred to a UK components manufacturer he had visited thus: 'A good product, but the business isn't so good!'.

The key problem facing British R&D engineers is that they lack support in the production area, so that many good developments never get implemented. The changes that have so transformed Japanese component manufacturing have not been associated with glamorous technical breakthroughs (I found little evidence of robotics for example), but have involved widespread incremental production improvements. In areas where R&D will be more important, such as automotive electronics, the Japanese ensure funding and staffing that UK companies will find difficult to match.

There is powerful European competition in R&D. German R&D engineers are even better trained and educated than in Britain. They are supported by enormous strength in depth, extending upwards to Board level and to managers and production operatives. The pace-setters in technological change in automotive bearings seemed to be Germany (process developments and applications engineering) and Italy, e.g. integrated wheel bearing developments. There is a danger that continental Europe is becoming the main hub of technological development, whilst Britain is becoming stagnant and geographically peripheral. Another example cited recently by the Rt Hon Edward Heath was a new automatic transmission. Its developers reportedly complained that no UK company was in a position to manufacture, partly because of weak funding support from British banks. It is now being manufactured in Italy. I asked an R&D manager from one vehicle manufacturer about the technological position of UK suppliers. His main worry seemed to be, not that they were technically poor, but that they did not any longer have 'developments already in the pipeline' in the same way as German counterparts. This probably reflects a weak funding situation.

Flexible manufacturing methods

Japanese vehicle companies and their suppliers have worked concertedly together over the last decade to create an overall system, more flexible in handling variability in order patterns, and in dealing with an increasing variety of new products. Whilst Japanese vehicle companies have achieved extremely high volumes on some models, their emphasis surprisingly is on increasing (and upgrading) the number of their models and accelerating the pace of model changes, rather than standardisation. Suppliers have been subject to the same pressure to improve flexibility. Honda's wheel supplier, for example, having built up experience in dealing with the astonishing pace of model changes in motor cycles, was having to push through similar programmes to meet similar Honda demands on the car side. They are experiencing product changes about every six months.

A total 'systems' view of the operation is required. Vehicle companies have even found it necessary to advise suppliers of changes required in their distribution and logistical arrangements to meet their needs efficiently. Car seats for example must now be delivered to a particular place next to the assembly line on an hourly basis. They have become involved in quite detailed matters such as getting suppliers to switch to smaller trucks.

After 1979, more difficult business conditions placed a premium on such flexibility. Order runs available to suppliers have been sharply reduced and subject to more frequent disruption everywhere. UK conditions have been particularly bad in this respect, and manufacturers have paid a high price for their failure to pay the same degree of attention to the issue of flexibility.

From an engineering stance, FMS developments that

have transformed the Japanese automotive components sector, cannot in general be equated to the more sophisticated robotic systems which now capture the public's imagination. To date, at least, robotics appear to have played a very minor role.

Investment and R&D have played a limited role in these developments. FMS improvements have required changes throughout the entire process route and have been heavily dependent on incremental developments pursued by work groups in production areas. As in the case of quality and productivity improvements such progress has in turn depended on a better partnership with employees and production-orientated organisational approaches, together with numerous detailed engineering improvements. Specific changes involved have been discussed in detail in the two product cases in which they were particularly important: automotive forgings and automotive exhaust systems.

Such progress appears to have been fairly comprehensive across all components however, reflecting coordination by their vehicle manufacturer customers. The importance of such developments and progress made by Japanese component manufacturers does vary though. Production methods for components such as volume automotive bearings and to some extent spark plugs are inherently more process determined. It is harder (and perhaps a little less worthwhile) to gain flexibility without incurring too great a cost penalty. Even here there is evidence of similar progress. An extreme example is glass, a process inherently inflexible. Japanese manufacturers had dealt with this problem by adopting a different approach to planning and control. This company was considering selling such expertise to US glass manufacturers who are now facing the problem of supplying Japanese vehicle plants in the USA.

After over a decade of progress, almost ignored in Britain, Japanese commitment to such developments appears unrelenting. As one manufacturer of electric motors put it 'Our target production run is one!'. Their relevance to UK suppliers was again highlighted by Dunlop's request for state aid reported in the *Financial Times* (19 August 1985, p.1). Investment was required because Dunlop saw new flexible manufacturing systems as the way to deal with Britain's small production runs. The new investment is intended to give the flexibility to change from production of one type of wheel to another within an hour. The normal change-over among volume manufacturers can be 10 to 20 hours.'

Industrial Relations

Strikes are merely an extreme manifestation of poor industrial relations, a symptom of a more fundamental degeneration (sometimes for understandable reasons) in employees' commitment to ensuring an organisation's continued competitiveness. The power of precedent is such that 90% of the time changes can be disrupted merely through the unspoken threat of such problems. More importantly, though, faced with such dynamic international competitors, an ambivalent or merely passive attitude to change is no longer likely to be adequate to ensure business survival.

My interviews with German and Japanese manufacturers confirmed more general research findings that their strike problems were of a totally different order of magnitude. Asked to remember back as far as possible (10 or 20 years if they could) the eight German component plants visited were unable to produce a total of hours involved in strikes much above 10 hours, with some claiming no hours lost at all. The absence of strikes in the Japanese vehicle industry has been noted by Shimokawa (1982b, p.275) as a major factor in the rise of its competitiveness and my interviews confirmed a similar picture in the case of vehicle component manufacturers.

With delivery reliability now more important the wider industrial relations scene is also relevant. The international purchasing department in one German vehicle company pointed out that UK component suppliers were also damaged by fears of disruption in UK ports and transport communications. As a result they tended to either restrict shares of business going to UK suppliers or insist on high levels of stocks held locally, placing an additional financial burden on UK suppliers.

By 1982, US component manufacturers appeared to be experiencing more industrial disputes than UK manufacturers, whose situation had improved. However, employee attitudes seemed enthusiastic and dynamic in comparison with Britain where morale sometimes seemed at a low ebb. Japanese multinationals were able to negotiate US labour contracts as long as three years, and apart from pressure at such times, few problems arose and the industrial relations atmosphere was considered quite positive. Their main problem was in harnessing employees' longer-term commitment and loyalty. US labour turnover figures were high. Often employees, repressed any feelings of discontent and would merely leave the moment a better job opportunity arose.

NSK (as discussed earlier in this chapter) had a high regard for UK employees and did not feel industrial relations was a problem. Their UK plant had though been set up on a green field site basis, top managers were Japanese, and they had only employed people under the age of 28, whose attitudes were felt to have had less opportunity to become encrusted by past conflicts. Japanese ideas on employee participation were generally transferable, though progress on quality circles could only be gradual anywhere and UK employees lacked experience.

German executives in one multinational had deliberately trained some UK production workers in Germany. There was no difficulty in achieving German performance standards, but when these operators returned to the UK plant, their performance (which was monitored) slumped back to UK norms. NSK also stated UK production workers matched Japanese standards on training, but they did not experience this problem.

Prais (1981) has argued that British industrial relations problems escalate mainly as plant size rises above about 250 employees and NSK's UK plant was a little below this size. One German executive made the same point. Industrial relations were not a problem in his company's UK plant, but they were conscious of the need to keep down plant size in Britain below about 500 employees, after which problems escalated.

Both German and Japanese executives who had dealt with British companies were critical of British managerial attitudes towards employees. These were felt to be divisive and myopically exploitational. Executives in both countries emphasised their responsibility to safeguard the interests of employees, particularly in terms of continued employment; in the absence of such a commitment by management, they believed it was impossible to secure consensus and employee commitment on any long-term basis.

In Germany, this commitment was in part formalised, through works councils and worker representatives on higher tier boards in larger companies, but the attitudes of German managers seemed very different. One German superintendent was an active campaigner on behalf of employee interests and also had formal duties in this capacity. In terms of any 'them and us' it was clear that his identification appeared to lie more with employees than the company. Neither he nor senior management considered this in any sense unusual or out of order. One chief executive reminded me that even before the last war the attitude had been 'we are all workers, even if some of us work with our brains rather than our hands'. Any residual class differences he felt had been levelled in the common experience of reconstruction from almost nothing after the War. Another executive commented on the rapid turnover of British executives he dealt with compared to the situation in mainland Europe generally. He had the impression that British employees were judged more on whether 'their faces fitted' than on their ability to do a job. The perceived divisiveness of British boardrooms, and in particular separate dining facilities, was criticised by German and Japanese executives alike.

Japanese executives criticised the shorter-term, more contractual, relationships between companies and employees in Britain and America, and the tendency for employees to be laid off the moment it was convenient. As with assembler/supplier relationships, such an exploitational relationship would inevitably cause employees to hit back and exploit the situation when conditions improved. Such conflict damaged consensus and undermined employees' commitment, their training and career development.

Though I visited only a few small Japanese plants and their 'tertiary supplier sector' was not fully represented, virtually all suppliers visited appeared to operate lifetime employment schemes. To safeguard employment companies were prepared to bring back work in-house or even, sometimes, to take on work outside their normal ambit (as in the case of the Japanese exhaust systems manufacturer discussed on page 178). Market targets were fought for tenaciously. When work was slack, employees were taken off production lines and recruited into improvement groups. One factory visited had almost 60 people in such groups. 'We can use their brains not their hands for a time', they said, 'but when demand rises they will return to the lines.'

Such policies were financially viable because the partnership with employees was two-way. Wage bonuses, which were high, could as in Germany be reduced in difficult conditions. With such commitment the supply side of the Japanese economy was clearly in shape to sustain higher non-inflationary growth rates, mitigating unemployment problems more generally.

Greater commitment by UK management and employees to a genuine two-way partnership will be essential in restoring competitiveness in the longer-term. NSK's experience in the UK and Nissan's agreement with the AUEW suggests that this is feasible.

Organisational Issues

Japanese executives also attributed their success to an organisational approach which contrasted with that of many Western companies. The president of one component company appeared to confirm the popular view of decisions frequently being 'bottom up' rather than 'top down'. 'Yes', he said, 'it makes my job very easy!'. Other executives, however, clarified that it was very much a two-way process. Senior management is anything but passive, as illustrated by the entrepreneurial influence obvious at Toyota and Honda.

Surprisingly career appraisal systems were also two-way. An accountant from a large Japanese component company, seconded to the British operation, compared the situation in Britain and Japan. Company policies were similar to those of other large Japanese companies. In the context of lifetime employment, career development was regarded as very important and appraisals occurred twice a year. Though his salary is little affected, assessments make the difference later between advancement and being shifted into a backwater. Like most of his Japanese colleagues he works an extra couple of hours most evenings. 'No one wants to get left behind.'

Such appraisal systems are fairly common in larger UK companies, but he was puzzled to find no equivalent of the second part of his company's assessment system. For he, in turn, is required to complete a standard form for his personnel department, the first questions after standard entries being broadly:

* How good are communications between you and your boss?
* How good are communications between you and other colleagues?
* Do you have any problems with your present work?

He felt the British system was perhaps unfair, since without this system there was no feedback coming from those lower down the organisation. Any comments were bound to be a little veiled, but his personnel department carried considerable weight because they influenced his manager's next career move.

The Chief Executive of Allied Steel and Wire, a UK steel supplier which has worked closely with the Japanese, also emphasises the vast number of reports Japanese personnel departments received on even low level managers, from bosses, colleagues and subordinates. He feels that British managers compare unfavourably with those in Japan, but that critical managerial qualities can only be assessed on the job. The Japanese system, he says, ensures poor managerial ability gets spotted early on. Even large companies really know their staff over years of career development and can ensure that only those with the right qualities rise to take responsibility for others.

Academics in Japan such as Shimokawa and Ballon distinguish 'groupism' rather than individualism as lying at the heart of Japanese approaches to organisation, education and training. Ballon acknowledged Japanese businesses displayed little interest in the content of university courses. Such courses were not even particularly intense, since at this level they wanted to encourage group cohesion rather than pushing individual competitiveness too far. Japanese companies took little interest in outside training courses and rejected the concept of professions such as engineering and accountancy. This was felt to encourage identification with individual goals, rather than identification with the working group and with the goals of the company. This was perceived as creating divisiveness and damaging to consensus, a luxury companies felt they could not afford. (This may explain why Japanese engineers interviewed were generally less well educated and trained than those in Britain.)

The personnel manager of a major Japanese supplier illustrated the change in orientation required. Some years earlier they had identified a technological gap emerging between themselves and another Japanese competitor. Having determined that their own technical staff differed very little in either background or ability from those of the competitor, they traced their problem to a lack of support from production personnel. They found their professional staff were so 'swamped' with resulting problems, that they had little time to carry out the numerous minor changes which were putting their competitor ahead. The solution had involved a radical reorientation, making production operators themselves the focus of attention, and training resources had been accordingly redirected.

Their changed orientation, in fact, closely mirrored the fairly extreme production-centred organisational approaches advocated by vehicle companies visited, particularly Honda, Toyota and Mitsubishi. The same approach had been adopted by suppliers visited. It was reflected in the status given to production workers and also pay. Engineers working in production were paid on precisely the same scales as accountants or salesmen. (Age and length of service were the main determinants of pay and status, with billboards outside factories proclaiming the names not of directors but of long service workers.)

The organisational contrast in both UK and US plants

of one multinational company was marked. It was more advanced, particularly in the USA, than its key Japanese competitor, which I also visited, on 'systems' operated by staff functions. Financial, production and quality control systems were sophisticated, highly detailed and utilised advanced computerised information systems; by contrast Japanese 'systems' mainly comprised extensive simple control systems of the type discussed earlier in this chapter.

This multinational's performance was in many respects impressive. Financial performance was well above average, its international strategies had been aggressive and timely, and it was technologically well advanced. Nevertheless they were concerned with the strides their Japanese competitors were making in the area of production.

Self confidence and morale in Japanese production areas were high and there was indeed ubiquitous evidence of progress (similar to that discussed in other cases in earlier in this chapter). By contrast morale in the UK plant's production areas was poor and production management seemed swamped by externally imposed systems. I asked supervisory staff what happened to voluminous computer printouts of quality records after filing. 'It's pretty rare that anyone comes down here to use them,' they explained, 'so eventually they just get thrown out to make room for more recent printouts.'

Authority for handling industrial relations had largely been transferred to the personnel department. Supervisors complained they could 'never get an answer' from such distant staff departments. Left with resultant problems, they themselves felt undermined.

Production management felt excluded from the chief executive's full support. They could not help noticing they said, that on his visits to the shop floor he would walk straight past them without even greeting them; instead he would regularly seek out the shop steward asking solicitously after his health condition. Junior production management felt hurt and excluded by the staff/hourly paid class divide in their organisation, which left them despite their considerable responsibilities on the wrong side of the fence. Whilst they were not invited to the plush yearly staff dinner dance, the seventeen-year-old girl student who served their tea was. Such stories are not rare in British factories, but here there were also signs from the staff side of the same divide.

Senior staff did not seem to recognise that production personnel needed greater support and authority so that they could be rebuilt as a strong team. This alternative approach appears to have assisted Japanese manufacturers to transform their competitive position over the last twenty years.

The point echoes fears that Western management philosophies may have downgraded the contribution made by production personnel (Garvin, 1983). One US car worker was said to have understood that he had been laid off because the Japanese had got ahead on quality, but was left perplexed by the fact that in twenty years no one had sought his opinion as to how it could be improved.

Organisational changes, similar to those implemented in Japan, must be taken more seriously by UK component manufacturers.

The Approach to Strategy

The UK planning environment

The UK business environment, discussed earlier in this chapter, has been so severe that planning horizons were necessarily shortened to preserve financial control. It has also been subject to more extreme fluctuations than Germany, Japan and America. German executives with experience of Britain pointed out that, whilst production forecasts from German vehicle companies provided an accurate basis for planning, such information in the UK was unreliable even a few months ahead. The German sales office in one company claimed to have been within 1% of sales budget forecasts in each of the previous five years. Close customer relationships in Japan and to some extent Germany encourage an almost logistical approach to business planning.

The lack of analysis of strategic issues in the UK

Although remaining competitive was a matter of survival

for many UK manufacturers, few outside the very largest companies seemed to have much idea of who their main competitors were (even in the UK). Fewer had the data which might logically have highlighted key competitive issues. In smaller companies, sales and financial records over five years old were often not stored in any accessible manner. Very few companies had had much time to draw conclusions from any competitive data they did have. Often the only people with much knowledge of the competitive position were marketing or sales staff, and many chief executives seemed preoccupied with day-to-day operating matters.

Yet since it is largely competition which holds down profit margins, unless such issues are analysed more effectively, manufacturers seem destined to remain 'fire fighting' and at the mercy of competition which will continue to intensify relentlessly. UK manufacturers generally need more knowledge of key UK competitors and increasingly (particularly for larger manufacturers) a knowledge of key European competitors. Information sources available on continental Europe are a handicap: this most critical area is much more poorly documented not only than the UK, but also than other trade blocs such as the USA and Japan. Manufacturers also need to know more about Japanese manufacturing methods. Since competition with Japan is mainly indirect, there would seem scope for technological transfer agreements.

Generalist approaches to strategy in Britain

Mant (1979, pp.95-100) has criticised what he regards as the 'generalist' predilection characteristic of British management. In comparison with the Continent, British boardrooms are too dominated by those with accountancy backgrounds, 'as if the primary task of industry was laundering money, with production as an irksome constraint rather than vice versa'. He argues that functions such as accountancy, personnel, and those of other head office specialists and even marketing are frequently peripheral to the key problems of British industry. These are seen as being in the production area, and in the tendency for production to be treated as a 'Cinderella' function.

In the context of the UK vehicle components industry,

the previous section found some evidence to support the organisational implication that there is a need for a more production-centred approach. Mant's argument that 'breadth of vision' must be complemented by 'a meticulous eye for detail' is also applicable to effective strategy thinking. It implies that UK managers need to achieve a better balance between general concepts of analysis and more specific issues of key contextual importance (particularly in respect to basic issues such as production). To take an analogy, there has been increasing recognition that for British 'Research and Development' to be more effective, the emphasis needs to be as much on the more 'applied' Development as on the purer Research. The latter may be of more general interest but is often of less contextual significance.

Case studies discussed earlier in this chapter indicate a similar need for analysis of more general issues to be balanced against more specific issues, often in the production area. A characteristic of UK component manufacturers' strategies appears to be their generality.

The most common strategic theme among UK component manufacturers has been retrenchment and rationalisation. Traditional accounting policies were cited for example by Automotive Products' chief executive as having become the top priority. Other manufacturers faced with such a severe decline in profitability have shared similar priorities - control of fixed and working capital, particularly cash flow and a quick resumption of ROCE, if necessary by cutting out marginal activities. This general emphasis on retrenchment and rationalisation has been reflected in a widespread tendency towards unprecedented charges on extraordinary and exceptional items taken 'below the line', e.g. RHP, GKN and Lucas.

Such strategies may be necessary given the UK's situation but they are essentially defensive and by no means sufficient, if manufacturers are to regain competitiveness internationally. Such retrenchment is less characteristic of better performing overseas rivals such as the Japanese, though some US component companies have also suffered.

UK manufacturers have also displayed a greater dependence on general strategies such as diversification, acquisition and mergers than their counterparts in Japan and

Germany. Frequently these strategies have been defensive. They have perhaps helped manufacturers cope with competitive decline; but so far they have not represented effective countermoves against overseas competitors.

UK manufacturers often seem overstretched in the context of increasing international competition. Yet diversification, weakening core business areas further, seems of greater interest to UK than to overseas manufacturers. Such strategies often seem to have done little to restore international competitiveness. For Dunlop, once pre-eminent in vehicle tyres, diversification may have produced some new activities, but at the inordinate cost of surrendering its core business area of tyres. Its wheel production (discussed on page 188) also seems on the brink of collapse unless government money is forthcoming. These automotive activities took years to build up; the value of its smaller new activities cannot be judged until they have withstood the test of competition. Such a loss of world leadership in automotive component sectors cannot be rated as an effective strategy approach.

This is not to suggest such general strategy issues are never important, only that effective strategy thinking involves their being interpreted sensitively in context. Scale for example raises important strategic issues for many UK component manufacturers, particularly as business competition becomes more international; but those who have relied unduly on volume-orientated approaches without adequately taking into account their competitive context and circumstances appear to have suffered disproportionately.

What many UK manufacturers have failed to do, in comparison to overseas competitors, is to recognise the strategic significance (in their particular context) of many basic issues, particularly in the production area (as indeed suggested by Mant).

Overseas competitors' emphasis on more specific matters

Despite the popularisation of their strategies in more dramatic terms (such as 'laser beam marketing'), Japanese competitors in this sector shared with German manufacturers an aversion to general strategy concepts, such as portfolio approaches. This was partly because their business environment and the structure of Japanese business discouraged major moves such as diversification and acquisitions. They therefore seemed to find it more profitable to focus instead on basic issues and on creatively developing their 'own patch of grass', with a longer-term orientation. Their close relationships with vehicle manufacturers encouraged this and also induced an almost engineering approach to planning.

Whereas strategic planning in UK companies tended to be heavily financially orientated, in Japan the emphasis seemed to be on key market targets, expressed in quite simple terms. Attention then focused on fairly numerous 'physical targets' aimed at bringing about improvements necessary to attain these market targets. One Japanese manufacturer's approach was discussed on pages 180-184. Financial targets (such as ROCE) and budgets were not ignored, but cost reduction and profit projections appeared mainly derivative and could be summed up fairly simply.

The contrasting situation in one UK company seemed to epitomise the danger of applying the general approach to strategy suggested by Argenti (1980) superficially. Here the process worked the opposite way round. Financial targets were set and translated into more detailed (though still largely financial) targets. Fairly minor amendments were made to existing operating plans. For example, if the general view at the top was that cost levels would have to be lower (to meet targets), this was translated into more optimistic productivity assumptions, with an accompanying budget amendment for increased capital investment to pay for more equipment, creating the impression at the end of the planning cycle of a coherent overall plan. Production issues inevitably received superficial treatment, whilst detailed financial projections produced an illusory sense of control; real control requires that competitors are matched on key developments.

Asked to comment on their strategies, German executives emphasised specific developments but were reluctant to make general assertions. Like the Japanese they tended to avoid standardisation, preferring to maintain a customised service even where this involved additional costs (such as for applications engineers).

German companies were distinguished by the

importance attributed to technological developments - process design and development, product developments and applications engineering and also 'know-how'. Some companies felt their slim top tier of executive officers (often only about three people) produced better communications with engineering staff in design, development and production. One chief executive felt cosy British boardrooms tended to lose touch with technical developments critical in his industry: 'Your Boards don't have any designers on them at all, do they?'. The managerial structure also helped German chief executives maintain tight communications with others such as salesmen.

One German chief executive held strong views against over-theoretical approaches to business strategy. These he felt often involved misleading notions of optimisation. This was illustrated by his company's rejection of optimisation ideas based on supposed trade-offs such as between cost minimisation and quality. His philosophy which extended to business strategy was based on the '80% rule'. By focusing on specific practical proposals and pushing ahead as fast as possible, even if he eventually proved not to be quite on the right lines, he maintained crucial advantages in decisiveness, implementation and flexibility. The attitude seemed to reflect Ackoff's (1981) view that companies should prepare for a future that is anyway uncertain by maintaining a flexible stance strategically. It also seemed to reflect some of the paradoxes noted in successful strategies by Peters and Waterman (1984). Resources could possibly be wasted though. German brake linings companies interviewed held varying and quite contradictory views on how to organise international operations in the face of recent developments.

US companies were distinguished by a more 'scientific' approach to planning, and by an emphasis on top down control systems monitoring progress against such plans. There was much greater interest in broader strategic issues such as how to play the more global competitive game.

Yet their style appeared dynamic, positive, highly competitive and refreshingly open. Many executives had noted advances made by Japanese manufacturers and acknowledged they had perhaps neglected developments in the production area, where traditionally they had been strong. They recognised the importance of developing employees' potential. Employees too were prepared to make sacrifices and US manufacturers seemed determined to fight their way back to the number one position in the world.

Any generalisation is dangerous. Yet the approaches taken to strategy by UK component manufacturers broadly seem to reflect the weakest feature in US approaches - their tendency (in comparison with German and Japanese manufacturers) to neglect critical production developments. This is paralleled by a tendency to down-value the strategic contribution of production personnel. UK manufacturers would do better to imitate the real strengths of US companies, their positiveness, their openness, their willingness to make sacrifices when necessary, and their decisive commitment to fighting their way back to the number one position in the world. In the absence of such competitive commitment, American management techniques such as financial analysis, seem to have merely taught UK manufacturers how to control a steady process of decline, the costs of which are already being reaped.

5

The Vehicle Components Industry Today: Seeds of Recovery?

Is Britain's International Position Recovering?

Table 5.1: Trade in motor vehicle parts and accessories 1970-86 (£ million at 1980 prices using the producer price index for vehicles and parts)

Year	Exports	Imports	Balance	Imports/Exports
1970	1,900	460	1,440	0.24
1975	2,360	810	1,550	0.34
1980	2,040	990	1,050	0.49
1982	1,700	1,280	420	0.75
1983	1,690	1,580	110	0.93
1984	1,830	1,620	210	0.89
1985	1,910	1,850	60	0.97
1986	1,890	2,130	-240	1.13

Source: Memorandum submitted by the Society of Motor Manufacturers and Traders Ltd (M76) to Britain's House of Commons Trade Committee (1987, p. 330)

Despite internationalisation and the pressing need to offset a declining home market, there has still been no real improvement in exports. Any slight suggestion of a recovery in the real level of exports during the last four years is contradicted by the longer-term trend. Exports in real terms fell between 1975 and 1980 and by 1986 they have again fallen, to a level just below those achieved in 1970 when internationalisation was only just beginning to take effect.. The rise in imports has in contrast continued relentlessly: indeed since 1982 there has been some acceleration even in real terms. In 1970 imports were only a quarter of exports. By 1980 this ratio had risen to one half. In 1986 imports are actually 10% higher than exports and the trade position for the first time is in deficit.

Thus the longer-term decline in UK vehicle component manufacturers' output and sales still reflects not merely knock on effects from the upstream domestic vehicle assembly industry, but a more fundamental and continuing decline in the international position. Impressive trade surpluses, which so contributed to sales and output levels in the early 1970s, have now entirely vanished.

Has Corporate Performance Now Improved?

Following severe contraction in the years 1979 to 1982, vehicle component companies have staged some hesitant recovery in terms of sales growth: the average growth figure (unweighted) for those 45 companies (out of the original 66 companies in the last chapter), for which there is still continuous data, being 7.1% p.a after adjusting for inflation. Larger companies, falling in the top half of size rankings, have 'survived' better than smaller companies - 27 compared with 18 - but their growth rates have been lower at only 3.5% p.a compared with 12.4%. Thus any sales recovery has been much more hesitant than that in UK vehicle production levels, presumably reflecting the continuing decline in the international trade balance discussed in the last section.

Figure 5.1 shows the average (again unweighted) rate of return on capital employed for all these companies between 1970 and 1986. Any apparent recovery more recently looks fragile and hesitant when viewed in a longer-term perspective. Further improvement in market conditions seems likely and this will probably lead to some further recovery in profitability, but sooner or later competitive conditions will again intensify. Three years averaging an actual loss, followed by four years in which return on capital employed has averaged just over 5% (pre-tax) places UK manufacturers in a weak financial position particularly from the view point of funding investment and research and development. In the context of vehicle companies' stated plans for reducing supplier numbers (worldwide) still further, this could prove a serious weakness. The profitability of UK companies, which dropped back from 8.4% in 1985 to 5.8% in 1986, must therefore be viewed as somewhat precarious.

Figure 5.1: Profitability of UK vehicle component companies - ROCE %

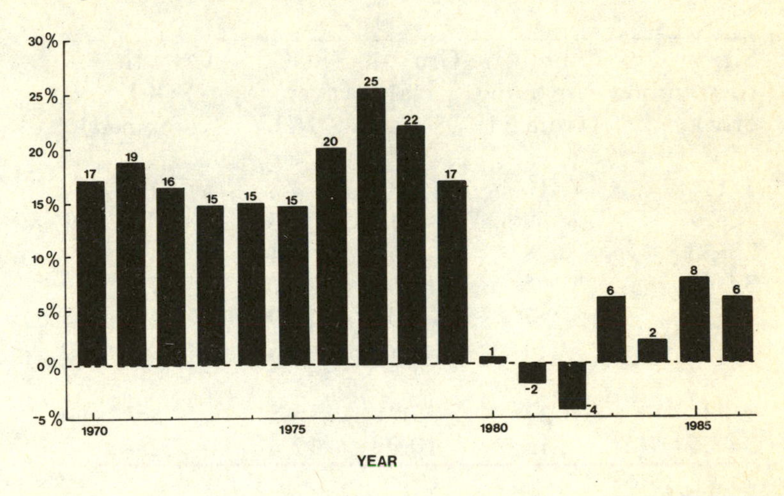

Is the Relationship between Size and Performance Changing?

More recent figures in Table 5.2 again refute any notion of sheer size necessarily leading to better performance. Small/medium sized companies have generally performed better both in respect to sales growth and also return on capital employed.

Table 5.2: Performance by size classification 1983-1986

Size groups (descending order)	Numbers surviving (from 11)	Growth real %p.a.	ROCE (average) %	Growth % +ROCE % (combined)
1-11	10	7.4	4.3	11.7
12-22	9	-1.1	1.3	0.2
23-33	8	9.5	5.1	14.6
34-44	5	16.6	21.0	37.6
45-55	7	9.9	12.9	22.8
55-66	6	4.7	4.6	9.3
1-33	27	5.2	3.5	8.7
34-66	18	10.0	12.4	22.4

Source: Analysis of ICC Business Ratio Report. Size rankings based on 1975 sales as in earlier analysis

On the other hand the adverse relationship between size and performance, which was notably consistent in the past, has been less so more recently and there are signs of some changes. First, for the first time companies in the very largest size group have outperformed those in the second largest. Part of the reason may be the effect of assemblers changed sourcing policies and the effect of reductions in the number of their suppliers. This may be causing further polarisation, leaving suppliers in the second size group in something of a squeeze. Also although surviving smaller companies are generally performing better, depletion rates are higher though mainly as a result of take-overs. Reductions in suppliers are affecting smaller companies particularly and may also explain why again for the first time the smallest size group has performed relatively much worse than in the past. Small companies are again well represented, though it should be noted that GKN Kent Alloys and Hardy Spicer are both part of the large grouping GKN. TI Cox and TI Nicholson are part of TI. A small number of larger companies have recently performed better, though significantly all of these are extremely well supported overseas.

Table 5.3: Best performing companies 1983-1986

	ROCE % av.	Growth % p.a.	Activities
1. BBA (7)	8.85	61.94	Brake linings etc, OE/AM
2. C.H. Industrials (40)	13.73	48.25	Exterior trim & misc'
3. GKN Kent Alloys (46)	25.18	31.15	Light alloy wheels, OE/AM
4. Britax Wingard (29)	39.20	15.68	Accessories, AM
5. Concentric Prods (49)	23.28	28.34	Metal products
6. Hardy Spicer (12)	44.73	6.21	C.V. joints, OE
7. T.I. Cox (41)	27.23	16.55	Suspension parts, OE
8. Motaproducts (66)	31.40	11.21	Accessories, AM
9. Eaton (11)	22.55	12.94	Transmission, OE
10. Airflow Streamline (38)	16.18	18.72	Body panels, OE
11. Supra (42)	17.73	14.63	Sealants etc, OE
12. Flexible Lamps (62)	22.33	6.65	Lighting, AM
13. I.H.W. (48)	24.08	2.94	Hinges & mechanisms
14. T.I. Nicholson (53)	19.40	5.66	Silencers, AM

Order based on combined performances. Size ranks, given in brackets, average 39 for this group.

Source: Analysis of ICC data

If sheer size is no guarantee of performance, then neither is market growth. Table 5.3 contains a miscellany of product areas and higher profitability still shows no particular correlation with sales growth. Interestingly many relatively successful UK manufacturers would be classic 'dogs' in terms of strategic portfolio position. Even low technology and fairly mundane, low technology products are well represented, again giving the lie to any notion that such areas are inevitably doomed by the advent of competition from low cost countries : it is well to remember the real competition is still predominantly European.

If sheer size or even market growth are still no guarantee of competitive success, specialisation directed towards international product leadership, has however become even more important. During this last decade GKN has turned round the fortunes of its Kent Alloys subsidiary by reorganising its entire factory around the concept of an upmarket light alloy wheel designed to appeal to more specialist producers, and by contributing finance and marketing support. GKN's Hardy Spicer's success is built around constant velocity joints, a product where GKN commands worldwide dominance, assisted by its manufacturing operation in Germany, two extremely modern, purpose built US factories and licence agreements with NTN of Japan.

Thus success depends more than ever first on having an internationally coherent strategy, with adequate overseas support particularly in the case of larger companies and second upon matters of basic operational efficiency; over-reliance should not be placed on simplistic strategic rules of thumb.

Has Productivity Now Improved?

Data on sales per employee for the period 1975 to 1986 were available for 22 UK supplier companies. Since component price increases were felt to have lagged behind increases in the general wholesale price index, adjustments were then made for inflation using the more specialised index for 'motor vehicles and their engines' produced by the Business Statistics Office. For 1970 it was necessary to revert to the more general WPI, but since 1970 data were available for only very few of these companies, 1970 figures here should be interpreted as merely a rough indication.

Productivity was unusually low in 1980 because of the lag as manufacturers sought to bring employment levels back into line with sharply reduced output. Now that such adjustments have taken place and output is again picking up, it is clear that there has been some real improvement in the productivity position. Leaving aside the exceptional decline in 1980, productivity during the 1970s had clearly stagnated at just under £28,000 sales/man in 1985 prices. The subsequent improvement to just under £32,000, representing about 14%, is probably understated as I suspect that most component prices have risen more slowly since 1979 than even the motor vehicles and parts index would imply.

Table 5.4: Average sales/employee £000'85

1970	1975	1978	1979	1980	1984	1985	1986
27.8	28.4	26.4	27.9	25.7	31.7	32.6	31.6

Source: Analysis of ICC data

This is a substantial achievement in relation to historical trends and even bringing manning levels back into line with reduced output levels is no easy task. Yet given the degree of market retrenchment, this is still some way off the sort of 'productivity miracle' that is needed if the UK is to catch up with its overseas rivals. 14% is not high in comparison to the international productivity differentials found to exist between 1981 and 1983, as discussed in the last chapter. Nor would the implied average improvement of only some 2% p.a. since 1979 compare with the pace of productivity growth found in Japan at that time. Why furthermore is it that productivity seems to have once stagnated during the last three years? Or has the shock effect of deep recession already begun to subside?

What has been achieved so far could even prove to have been the easier part of the problem. Closing the residual gap will involve a much longer haul. Apart from further investment, this will require extensive incremental improvements, calling in turn for employee participation, and commitment sustained over many years. More positive programmes in this direction (quality circles are just one example) are not problem free. As even the Japanese have discovered, they take years and even decades, to get right and many UK manufacturers have yet to travel down such a road. Few have even taken the first essential step, that of securing the sort of positive and longer-term relationship with employees enjoyed by rivals in Germany and Japan.

British Manufacturers' Relative International Cost Position

In 1978 British component manufacturers were, despite their lower productivity, nevertheless internationally competitive in terms of cost levels thanks to a substantial decline in the real exchange rate. The precariousness of their position only became manifest in 1980 with the sudden, steep rise in this real exchange rate: as already discussed the cost position became quite uncompetitive internationally and this in the context of international procurement operations contributed substantially to dramatic declines in profitability. Evidence by several vehicle companies to the House of Commons, Trade and Industry Committee (1987) suggests that British manufacturers are once again internationally competitive at least in terms of cost levels, a fact which has undoubtedly contributed to the modest recovery in company performances.

Although productivity movements discussed in the last section have contributed to the improved cost position, Figure 1.2, discussed in Chapter 1, would suggest that real exchange rate movements have been the main underlying factor. That there is now greater recognition of the danger to competitiveness of allowing a soaring real exchange rate such as occurred after 1979 is to be welcomed, but UK component manufacturers cannot afford to assume a low exchange rate has now become the order of the day. First, although official policy may now be more wary of allowing extreme fluctuations in real exchange rates, the general desire would seem to be maintaining sterling at a fairly high level so as to dampen inflation. (Interventions by the Bank of England seem generally to be in the direction of supporting sterling's level.) Second, the more fundamental factor behind relative real wage movements is direct pressure on consumption and real wage levels. Whilst inflation has fallen, it has not fallen as far as in rival countries such as Germany and Japan. Pay deals in British manufacturing at the end of 1987 were still running at 8.5%, higher than at any time during the year, and the Bank of England's most recent figures show that UK industrial competitiveness had again worsened by 7% during last year (*Financial Times*, 14 November 1987). The immediate outlook is that higher interest rates, driven by the requirement to control inflation, will help prop up the real exchange rate. If a low exchange rate has not in consequence become the order of the day, UK component manufacturers could once again find their relative international cost position undermined. This would have severe performance implications for any companies that may have been tempted (once again) into over-reliance upon a more favourable exchange rate position.

Non-price Aspects of Competitiveness

Perhaps the most critical question is whether UK suppliers, in more recent years, have succeeded in closing the gap already identified and discussed, in respect to non-price aspects of competitiveness. Up to date evidence is provided by the House of Commons Trade and Industry Committee Report (1987), based on extensive hearings involving several vehicle customers both in Britain and continental Europe, suppliers and industry experts. From 12 vehicle customers questioned as to their purchasing criteria, the following rankings emerge with a considerable degree of consistency:

1. Quality
2. Cost

3a. Technical excellence, including developmental capability
3b. Delivery, including flexibility as well as reliability
4. Marketing commitment, expressed in terms of pricing policy, willingness to provide local plants; (particularly in

the case of French customers), language ability; and more specifically, the time taken in demonstrating new products required
5. Credibility, in respect to financial resources and managerial capability

Whilst factors affecting the cost position of UK suppliers have been discussed, other non-price issues such as quality are also critical to competitiveness and will now be discussed in order of importance.

Quality

GKN is perhaps typical of other UK suppliers in being prepared to acknowledge that quality 'had not been sufficient' around 1979/80, but also in feeling that they were now fully internationally competitive in this respect (House of Commons, Trade and Industry Committee, 1987, p.92). Certainly there has been progress in absolute terms, as suppliers have become more aware of the strategic importance of such mundane issues.

Substantial improvements were noted not only by vehicle customers such as Austin Rover, Jaguar, Ford, GM, Peugeot Citroen but also by overseas customers such as Opel and Daimler-Benz in Germany, many being highly critical of quality in the past. However, customers also pointed out that quality standards in rival countries were also rising rapidly: in relative terms UK performance was still patchy, at a time when they were still cutting out suppliers on the basis of quality audits conducted internationally.

There are some areas where UK suppliers are now achieving international quality standards. Nissan for example stated it was satisfied with the quality of parts such as soft trim components, rubber mouldings, some electrical components and glass, but they also pointed out that 'The UK seems to display a very broad range of supplier capability with the best companies as capable as any in the world automotive industry, whilst others are significantly uncompetitive in terms of quality systems, productivity, investment and development capability'.

(ibid., p.75).

Jaguar cited the following product areas where UK quality was weak (ibid., p.66) - plastic components for radiator grilles and headlamp surrounds; damped lids; ashtrays; blow moulded plastics for fuel tanks and hydraulic control reservoirs; door seals; fuel hoses.

Porsche cited the example of a UK manufacturer, with an excellent test product for which they were ready to give a 30 per cent sourcing share, but which failed to get through their test line: out of 1,250 parts supplied some 800 were returned as of inadequate quality, due to failures in machining and inspection (ibid., pp.308/9). Likewise Opel pointed out 'UK quality is improving but they would prefer the quality to be right the first time (ibid., p.308). Forgings (already discussed) where GKN has been dominant in the UK, were again specifically singled out for criticism by continental customers.

Relentlessly rising quality standards are thus still a key problem for many UK suppliers. Bill Hayden, Vice President, Manufacturing Ford of Europe expressed the issue starkly 'The quality of the British supplier base has improved dramatically but so has the quality of their competition; and they have never closed the gap (ibid., p.63)'.

A critical remaining problem is that supplier quality improvement programmes coordinated by UK assemblers, such as Ford's Q.101 system utilising statistical process control, whilst now underway, have yet to be pushed through to their conclusion. Such programmes have yet to fully involve many smaller manufacturers. Many UK suppliers still rely too heavily on ex-post inspection procedures in contrast to Germany and Japan; yet 'built in' quality approaches rely in turn on strength in depth in terms of production skills and on participative approaches, which take many years and substantial commitment to develop effectively.

Technical Excellence

From an engineering perspective, issues such as quality and technical excellence cannot in practice always be disentangled: quality is not merely a matter of surface finish and it is inherently affected by both product and process technical specifications. The entangled issues of quality, technical excellence and also delivery seem to be at the heart of why UK suppliers are still being bested by German manufacturers in their battles to win business from Volvo Cars in Sweden. Volvo is one of the most independent vehicle customers: it relies heavily on bought-in components and about 70% of these are purchased abroad. West Germany supplies 35.2% of the total, UK suppliers contribute 6.3%. Volvo stated that the German dominance is a consequence only of the excellence of its product and delivery. Because of the high value of the DM they were actively searching for alternatives to West German suppliers, and were anxious to find component suppliers who could develop quality products. However, they felt that some UK firms were inadequately capitalised to provide the quality of research they sought. Volvo itself devoted 10% of its turnover to development (ibid., p.307).

Similar problems explain why UK suppliers only account for 8% of car components for Saab of Sweden, and only 2.5% in the case of Scania, their truck operation. As with Volvo, the company language is English. Saab complained, however, that UK components often failed to keep pace with developments, and particularly in the area of electronics (ibid., p.308). Daimler-Benz also complained that many UK suppliers had inadequate research resources and that their products took too long to come in stream. Saab likewise pointed out that typically a German company took a fortnight to demonstrate a new product, whereas a British company would take 6 months (ibid., p.308).

Research and development in UK companies has probably been hampered by poor financial performance and by such severe declines in profitability. It is therefore disturbing that UK profitability has remained at unsatisfactory levels. Peugeot-Citroen stated that UK suppliers were often inadequately capitalised to carry out the R&D they demanded, and Renault underlined the importance of this point by commenting that what they wanted were suppliers who could offer high technology backed by substantial financial resources (ibid., p.309).

Delivery

Delivery performance has improved very substantially: in particular the problem of disruptions, due to strikes and industrial relations problems, has improved immeasurably in more recent years. Nevertheless there are still areas where performance is patchy: in terms of service GM still felt UK suppliers had some way to go (ibid., p.85). Once again although UK suppliers have improved, Saab pointed out (ibid., p.308) that in order to compete with Japan its standards are rising even faster: they were seeking further improvements in manufacturing lead times of 25% over the next four years. Nissan also pointed out that UK inventory levels were higher than in Japan (ibid., p.75). With the introduction of just-in-time inventory management, disruption anywhere down the chain of direct suppliers - their subcontractors - and raw material suppliers had a disproportionate effect. There is still a tendency according to Jaguar for example for suppliers to double guess assemblers in terms of detailed scheduling: they noted that their overseas suppliers were very much more reliable to programme, though this was achieved in return for negotiated schedules firm for 6-18 months ahead (ibid., p.65). Tragically, the improvement in Britain's strike reputation over recent years, could be reversed at a stroke by recent strikes at Ford and also by the Shipping strike, which has visibly demonstrated the vulnerability of supply.

Marketing Issues

Some specific marketing related issues, such as UK suppliers slowness in demonstrating new products, have already been touched on but appear symptomatic of a lack of marketing commitment more generally. Customers, especially in Germany, complained about pricing policies: many UK suppliers for example were still increasing DM prices despite the substantial decline in the value of sterling in relation to the DM. Daimler-Benz noted that 'UK firms demand immediate profits, they are not prepared to break even simply to gain a first-hold in the market' (ibid., p.308).

Opel stated that it had detected no real improvements in marketing techniques by UK firms despite their in-built advantage of a favourable currency and warned that if UK firms failed to act soon their chance would disappear: they noted powerful competition from French suppliers and were examining Japanese and Korean alternatives (ibid., p.308). Ford (ibid., p.363) cited the example of foundries where German suppliers paying wage rates equivalent to 19 dollars an hour were price competitive against UK suppliers paying between 8 and 9 dollars an hour (labour represents about 30% of foundry costs). Pricing policy may well reflect financial issues already discussed, but again the problem seems to reflect more fundamental business attitudes: GM and Ford both afforded UK suppliers highly convenient access to their German assemblers, yet they noted little marketing drive:

> Q. Are you telling us they are not taking flights to Cologne or trains to Dagenham?
> Mr Spencer (Ford) 'They are not'
> (ibid., p.62).

Again Austin Rover noted 'mirror suppliers advise us that neither Pilkingtons nor anybody else in the country is either interested in supplying mirror glass or has the technical capability so to do' (ibid., p.169).

The provision of marketing support, through local manufacturing operations, will become increasingly important in the future. Renault argued that 'UK manufacturers could increase their market share by establishing their presence in the French market and meeting Renault's engineers, by negotiating in French' (ibid., p.309). Porsche cited its preference for US suppliers who it claimed gave 'a better service, remained very competitive and are prepared to set up on the doorstep' (ibid., p.308). Such overseas investments, whether in terms of new factories or acquisitions, are enormously expensive yet (as has already been discussed) strategically important. For most component areas the immediate competitive priority must be continental Europe; yet overseas investments, particularly recently in America, appear to have been dictated by financially orientated portfolio considerations, rather than by any logic relating to the competitive position.

Why Rectifying the Competitive Position Still Represents a Race Against Time

Given the substantial improvements (in absolute terms) which have recently taken place in supplier performances and equally dramatic improvements in terms of the immediate market outlook for UK components, British manufacturers may once again be tempted into complacency and into playing down these remaining problems. Yet market conditions inevitably see-saw and will again intensify. The real threat arises from the continuing culling process, caused by vehicle assemblers reducing (on the basis of precisely the criteria discussed above) their supplier numbers worldwide. Austin Rovers' suppliers have been reduced from 1,200 to about 700 (ibid., p.164); Ford's have been reduced from 2,500 to about 900 in the last 5 years (ibid., p.58); Peugeot Citroen's have reduced from 2,000 in 1981 to 1,229 in June 1986 and are projected to fall to 950 by January 1989 (ibid., p.309); Renault has projected a reduction from 1,415 (December 1985) to 900 by the end of 1988 (ibid., p.309); Saab has projected further reductions from 446 in 1986 to 300 by the end of the decade (ibid., p.308); Nissan's internal target was to keep suppliers very low, not much more than 150 by 1990 including the supply of ancillary items such as greases (ibid., p.77). Supplier reductions conducted inter-nationally mean that international wars of competition are very much for real. Not all vehicles component manufacturers are going to survive in the industry; poor performers are already being weeded out; those who achieve what would once be regarded as quite satisfactory performances, albeit mediocre by today's standards, will be the next to go; in the long run excellence by international not national standards represents the only chance of survival.

To understand what is happening in terms of this underlying struggle for survival we must again turn our attention to the level of individual products, where individual companies and competitors can be identified and examined, so as to distinguish the strong from the weak. The last section analysing the reasons for competitive decline in the past examined four product sectors in particular detail, concluding in each case that the position of UK companies was fundamentally weak and precarious in terms of surviving such competitive battles. For each sector in turn, armed with the most up-to-date information we can now put this gloomy diagnosis (and indeed an important part of this whole methodology in analysing issues of competitiveness) to the test. This will also provide an up-to-date outlook.

It was argued that the strategic position of RHP, Britain's only major national ball and roller bearings producer, was fundamentally weak. Just one month ago RHP announced its decision to pull out of ball and roller bearings, the area that (with Government assistance) it was specifically set up to rescue in 1969.

One disturbing feature of Britain's competitive decline, illustrated by this situation, is that although the issue might arguably be considered as one of the most important facing the country, almost no-one at top level appears to shoulder any responsibility, or indeed to feel unduly concerned.

RHP's divestment raised not a murmur of concern from government, from any government department, from top level corporate management and certainly not from stock market commentators delighted that RHP was now quite out of an area offering poor financial performance. 18 years have passed since RHP's formation at the instigation of the 'Industrial Reorganisation Corporation', an arm of government that has long since passed away. That it has taken so long for the competitive position to reach some sort of conclusion is not surprising: the development of industrial competition has been continuous since the turn of the century. Such a time span would seem though far too long for political memories. The present Conservative government understandably feels no responsibility for the virtual collapse of an industrial strategy, instigated so long ago by a Labour government; nor does a Labour opposition today display any inclination to highlight the matter. Since 1975 RHP's top management has ceased to be dominated by staff from bearings activities, so the new team presumably feels little personal responsibility; indeed it would be quite natural for them to congratulate themselves on having finally succeeded (through the mere reshuffling of their corporate portfolio) in 'passing the parcel' of the small rump which remains of the former British bearings industry. The extreme alternative of central planning is certainly no panacea either: this year Russia's entire economic growth plan has been left in tatters as a result of supply problems in this single critical industrial sector; but should not someone, somewhere be a little concerned at the demise of what was once regarded as a strategic sector of the British economy?

A similar situation pertains at the company level to automotive forgings. Two years ago GKN finally divested their entire forgings group, comprising almost half of Britain's forgings capacity, by means of a joint venture with British Steel; divestment will not of course be finally complete until new joint operations can go it alone, but ultimately any corporate level responsibility at GKN seems set to disappear.

In exhaust systems it was argued that UK manufacturers such as Armstrong had already been squeezed out of mainstream original equipment business, leaving TI Cheswick the largest and probably most efficient UK owned manufacturer in something of a competitive squeeze against major German rivals such as Gillet and Tenneco Walker. Subsequently return on capital employed at TI Cheswick, plunged into losses of an astounding 663%, although there has been some subsequent recovery and in many respects they have performed well in relation to other UK suppliers.

Finally despite attractive opportunities at the high technology end of the industry, it was argued that the consolidation of Lucas and Smith's instruments operations was not (as indeed was the case with bearings) a satisfactory strategic response to the process of rapid internationalisation, which was expected to take place in that sector. Whilst the much smaller UK automotive electronics operation, AB Electronics, succeeded in growing thirteen fold (ibid.) in a growing market, the joint venture's output stagnated. Finally during last year the joint operation has virtually come to end with the closure of their major new dedicated factory in Wales. Ironically in announcing reasons for the closure, the company cited pressure from Japanese competition, something which during the earlier part of this study was not held to be a strategic threat.

It would, however, be wrong to over-dramatise such results, though the speed with which such prognosis of further decline have been confirmed is alarming. Many vehicle component manufacturers are still doing much better, particularly given the dramatic improvement in market conditions, and it is worthwhile gaining some idea of those areas in which Britain is relatively strong and those where it is relatively weak.

In those areas where Britain has been relatively weak, we are already seeing 'large gaps in component coverage in the UK industry' (Ford, ibid., p.51), gaps also of course reflected in the deteriorating balance of trade in vehicle components. Areas where the UK has either already virtually gone or where the position is weak are listed in Tables 5.5 and 5.6. Examples of areas where the UK is relatively strong would include soft trim, cloth, some smaller plastic components, glass and electrics (as opposed to electronics) constant velocity joints. Sadly even where UK suppliers have a relatively strong position, often monopolistic behaviour is driving multinationals to source overseas: Peugeot Citroen (ibid., p.314) cites the following examples - glass (Trapluc); heaters (Delanair), steel road wheels (Dunlop) and engine electrics (Lucas).

Conclusion

The previous sections argued that two broader issues lay at the heart of Britain's problem of competitiveness in the past - first, an exceptionally unfavourable UK business environment and second, an unduly general and superficial approach to business strategy, which resulted

Table 5.5: UK components no longer available other than on a limited basis

Foundry facilities for blocks and heads
Large aluminium die-castings
Fuel injection equipment for cars
Carburettors
Major presses and transfer lines
Entertainment systems
Bumper safety
Compression struts
Fuel rails of furnace brazing type
Gearboxes, particularly automatics
Aluminium bumper beams with wilding capacity
EPDM compression mouldings particularly for bumper beam applications
Chrome plating of plastics with self contained moulding facility
Steering wheels
Plastic rubber decoration co-extrusions
Door seals
Decorative ashtrays with clamped action
Plastic blow mouldings e.g. for petrol tanks
Fibreboard moulders
Decorative badges, second surface finished
Petrol hoses
Air-conditioning compressors and condensers
Remote controlled exterior door mirrors
Rear wash/wipe motors
Ignition coils

in many of the contextual implications of internationalisation being inadequately addressed. Their competitive position undermined, some of Britain's major companies have effectively withdrawn. The position of many others is still weak, and gaps are now beginning to appear in this UK sector's overall supply coverage.

Refreshingly, in more recent years there have, however, been major improvements in absolute terms both in respect to the UK business environment and also in

Table 5.6: UK components for which supply position is particularly weak.

Plastic mouldings and dash installations
Major castings
Areas where UK dependent on imported raw material, particularly foam and plastics
Electronics
Gas struts
Self levelling suspension units
Radio aerials
Plastic raw materials
Full electronic ABS systems
Precision forgings (suspension and gearbox)
Air flow meters
Electric seat slides
High performance tyres
Seat belt webbing
Mirror glass
Small motors

respect to the attention paid to some of the strategic issues highlighted. Nevertheless in relation to progress made overseas, there is still a long way to go and many specific areas identified in this study still call for improvements.

UK suppliers are once again broadly cost competitive due largely to the dramatic improvement in the real exchange rate since 1980, though there are signs of this once again creeping up. Yet this important exchange rate improvement seems more a reflection of somewhat arbitrary market movements than of changes in terms of economic policy or longer-term economic choices. More underlying factors such as pressure on real wage levels have yet to show any real abatement. In absolute terms inflation is certainly much lower, but it is still higher than in rival countries such as Germany, Japan and even France. Profitability in terms of return on capital is still nothing like high enough in relation to the cost of capital (reflecting economic choices) enable UK suppliers to invest adequately.

Financial markets, seem to have become even more short-term in the orientation, encouraging component companies to place a similar and undue emphasis on manipulating business portfolios and financial policies to extract short-term gains, rather than on directing attention to longer-term issues affecting competitiveness. Asked why it felt many UK suppliers were not keeping up with technological developments abroad, GM commented (ibid., p.86) that German companies were supported by cheaper finance and often by supportive arrangements with banks at the supervisory board level, whereas this was not the case in Britain.

Those larger UK companies which are better backed up in terms of financial resources, particularly those which have grown through acquisition tend often to be highly financially orientated and this itself can lead to a shorter time perspective. BTR for example claims that although in a formal corporate planning sense they are only looking three years ahead for each of its companies, it can nevertheless cope with the long lead times typical for new product developments in this industry (ibid., p.194). Volvo's lead time for new suppliers varies between 1 and 7 years (ibid., p.307), and to this must be added the time taken to achieve a satisfactory return. Major international moves necessary to penetrate overseas markets can take many years before the benefits are reaped. It would seem difficult to reconcile BTR's claim that this strategic approach is not unduly short-term - a charge recently levelled against BTR (though contested) by accountants Coopers and Lybrand. What really matters though is not so much the formal planning horizon, but the sort of long-term vision underpinning business strategy. It is from this viewpoint that the contrast between such attitudes and those encountered among German and Japanese executives, is so disturbing. Japanese manufacturing initiatives such as just-in-time, quality circles etc. have in many cases taken over a decade to get sorted out.

General Motors, who like Ford are heavy purchasers of components from both Britain and Germany, was asked specifically whether UK firms were successful in pursuing technological developments and replied 'Not necessarily as well as some of our German companies. We tend to find the UK companies taking shorter-term views. That may be because they are part of major conglomerates, public quoted companies, who are looking for a short-term return whereas the German companies seem to take a longer view and therefore are more willing to make a long-term investment without necessarily an up-front commitment.' (ibid., p.86). Replying to the same question, Ford Europe's Vice President Supply, Mr Spencer expressed similar reservations but felt that the prime responsibility rested with managerial approach adopted by companies:

'Britain has a remarkable ability to come up with very interesting technical inventions. Our engineers are presented with these. What is lacking is the follow-through. What is lacking is somebody who can put down a new product with total reliability so that we feel we can put this into our new model and that the customers will not have the reliability and servicing concerns which your colleague was mentioning. Unfortunately, such a new product is rare. There are many examples of small, medium and indeed leading companies who do a lot of development work with us and who, at the end of the day, disappoint because they cannot bring through the reliable delivery of mass production. That is something where the German suppliers tend to have an edge'.

> Q. 'Can you say why you believe the German suppliers have that edge?'
> Mr Spencer 'It is consistency and the detailed planning that they do before their production.'
> Q. 'It is not their financial backing?'
> Mr Spencer 'No. It is due to attitude of mind, I think'.
> (Ibid., pp. 62-63)

Thus what is really of concern is whether an undue emphasis by British management on financial manipulation (albeit encouraged by an unconducive financial environment) has at the strategic level eclipsed attention from those more detailed contextual issues, in areas such as technology and production, which may be both so intractable yet also so critical from a longer-term point of view. The previous section concluded that, until the approach to strategic thinking became less generalist and more penetrating in this regard, British management were effectively managing merely a controlled process of competitive retreat in world markets. In more recent years, great strides have been taken in a more positive direction, but there is still a long way to go and many specific issues to attend to, if large areas of this industry are to survive and flourish.

6
Britain's Competitiveness Today

Recent events have understandably led most commentators to become much more optimistic about Britain's competitive prospects. Sales are almost booming, reflecting real GNP growth in 1987 of 5.2%, higher than the USA and even Japan, and considerably higher than European rivals such as France and Germany (*Sunday Times*, 1988). Growth in manufacturing output has increased to an annual rate of 6.5% 1987a) and manufacturers generally are operating close to capacity limits.

At a company level, the financial position is now much stronger. Hoare Govett estimates the average return on capital in 1987 has risen to 23% (and this in the context of lower inflation) and that gearing is set to fall below 10%, compared with 30% in 1981 (*Financial Times*, 1988a). British manufacturers are generally much more cost competitive thanks, partly to a more favourable exchange rate, but also to productivity rising at an annual rate of 4% (*Financial Times*, 1987b). Non-price aspects of competitiveness have also improved. Strikes for example are at their lowest level for fifty years (*Financial Times*, 1988a). It is little wonder that Government ministers talk in terms of a 'British cure' and suggest that we are looking at 'the early stages of what could become an economic miracle of the type achieved in the Federal Republic of Germany in the 1960s' (*Financial Times*, 1988a). It is tempting to believe that the problem has been resolved and that comparatively little remains to be done.

Closer inspection however reveals that, despite

substantial progress, UK manufacturers in general still have a long way to go if they are to close the gap with international rivals.

Despite recent growth, manufacturing output in September 1987 is still only about 1% above the level in 1979; this contrasts with gains of 32% in Japan and 23% in the US (*Financial Times*, 1987b). Taking a longer-term perspective the UK figure is about 2% lower than in the 1973 boom; again, this contrasts with gains of 49% in Japan, 46% in the USA, 18% in Italy and 16% in West Germany (*Financial Times*, 1987b), though more recently performances elsewhere in Europe have been less buoyant.

Looking to UK sectors other than vehicle components most have also improved productivity substantially in absolute terms. Productivity growth in the shoe industry has averaged 5.75% p.a. in real terms since 1982; in chemicals, it has averaged a little over 4% p.a. since 1979; in the food processing industry it has averaged about 3% p.a. since 1980 (*Financial Times*, 1988a).

Yet there appear to be few areas in which UK manufacturers have succeeded in substantially closing the gap which exists relative to international rivals. An exception perhaps is steel. Output per man year at British Steel in 1980 was 150 tonnes; by 1983 it was 230 tonnes which was claimed to be 15 tonnes ahead of the Germans (*The Times*, 1983a); the figure most recently was 300, though total output is only 10.3m tonnes compared with 17.4m tonnes in 1977-78 (*Financial Times*, 1987c). The relative position elsewhere in the metals processing industry is however less healthy. A recent report comparing French, German and UK engineering sectors (defined broadly to include car-building, aerospace, computer and other office equipment, in addition to machinery and other forms of mechanical engineering) showed that in 1984 the UK's productivity was only 56% of that of Germany, the figure for France being 79% (Paribus Quilter Securities, 1987). UK output had also been declining at some 2 to 3% p.a., and concessions in market share had accelerated since 1980 as companies had sought to restore profitability. Britain is the only major machine tool manufacturing country (with the exception of France) not to have seen output recover to 1979 levels, and productivity continues to be half that of Germany, with Switzerland being even further ahead (*Financial Times*, 1987d).

In the relatively low technology area of furniture manufacture a detailed recent study found that West German productivity was 66% higher than the UK: in the production of cabinet panels output per man was twice as high (*Financial Times*, 1987e, f). In higher technology areas, British Telecom's productivity levels in 1985 were found to be among the lowest recorded among Western telephone service operators, reflecting investment levels also among the lowest in 13 countries studied (*Financial Times*, 1987g). For example, the number of lines run per employee rose from 52 in 1975 to 89 in 1985; in France the number per employee was about the same in 1974 but rose to 138 in 1985, whilst in the US over the same period the number jumped from 89 to 169. Sales per employee in 1986 at Rolls Royce, a rather more successful British company, were $69,000 compared with $148,000 at General Electric and $115,000 at Pratt and Witney, its two key rivals in the USA (*Financial Times*, 1987h).

For manufacturing in general Table 1.10 in chapter 1 showed that the UK productivity gap with rival countries overseas has narrowed only slightly in recent years, and still remains substantial.

With much of the obvious slack in terms of overmanning now taken up, and with manufacturers up to full capacity, further improvements in productivity relative to those competitors is likely to represent a tougher challenge.

The impact of such productivity differentials on relative cost levels is of course modified by relative wage rates. Although the latter position has improved, Table 1.12 in chapter 1 showed that British cost levels are frequently still higher than those of rival countries. An example of the effect of productivity on cost levels is provided by the building industry. Output per employee is about a third higher in France than in Britain and their building costs in 1986 were estimated to be some 34% lower (*Sunday Times*, 1986a).

Real wage pressure moreover shows little sign of abating and UK industrial earnings are still rising much faster than elsewhere, as shown in Table 6.1. As a result the rate of inflation, though much improved, is still above that of most rival countries.

Table 6.1: Rises in industrial earnings and inflation rates in 1987

	Increases in industrial earnings % p.a.	Increases in consumer prices % p.a.
UK	8.7	4.1
Japan	3.5	1.2
France	3.0	3.2
W. Germany	3.3	1.0
USA	3.3	4.5

Source: Credit Swisse First Boston, quoted in *Sunday Times*, 3 January 1988

As UK manufacturers again approach full capacity further progress will depend upon positive business development activities. Whilst per capita levels of investment remain low by international standards improving profits and cash surpluses have been substantially channelled into financial rather than productive assets. Companies have also diverted expenditure from organic growth into takeover activities, which reached a record of £13.5 bn in 1986 almost double the figure in 1985 (*Financial Times*, 1987i). Short-termism is still a problem. In spite of increased demand manufacturing investment in 1986 (including leased assets) was still 13% lower than in 1979 (*Financial Times*, 1987b), a concern also highlighted in the latest Financial Times Survey of UK industrial prospects (*Financial Times*, 1988a). 'One of the most glaring weaknesses in British companies at present lies in the low level of expenditure on plant and equipment over the recent past'. And although some sectors such as chemicals, pharmaceuticals and aerospace were doing relatively better: 'In many areas, therefore, it is difficult to escape the conclusion that the rising sales of British goods derive less from investment in new products than from competitive prices, stemming from relatively low wages, and a currency, which until recently at least, has been competitively priced.'

UK industry also still appears to be reluctant, compared with the USA or Japan, about investing in research and development (*Financial Times*, 1986a). UK industry's share of US patents fell from 4.2% to 3.5% between 1975 and 1984, whilst Japan's rose over the same period from 8.9% to 16.6%, Germany's share also increased to 9.5% (Department of Trade and Industry, 1987). The UK's share of US patents declined in all but 5 of 20 industrial areas covered by this report - notable exceptions being pharmaceuticals and chemicals, Lucas being the only UK company to score highly in the vehicle component sector.

Yet in general the real technological strength of Japan and Germany arises not from research in isolation, but from the way in which research and development (with an emphasis on incremental development) is closely integrated with strategic priorities in the market place on the one hand, and with the efforts of other engineers and production personnel on the other (*Financial Times*, 1987j, k, l). This may also explain why many UK manufacturers have failed to derive much real benefit even from promising advances, such as computer integrated manufacture (*Financial Times*, 1985a, 1986b), a matter even more significant than their failure to keep up in terms of the number of robots installed.

UK manufacturers' shortcomings in respect to detailed planning and other operational issues may reflect the same lack of coordination and integration. Whilst disruption due to strikes is now less of a problem, half of UK plants recently surveyed (British Institute of Management, 1986) were still unable to achieve a target of having only one order in four late. Although there have been some improvements (for example in manufacturing lead times), the same survey noted UK-owned sites performed significantly worse than 87 foreign-owned plants on operational issues, and concluded senior UK management spent relatively little time on manufacturing efficiency.

Again vehicle component suppliers are not the only manufacturers to have paid the price for falling behind on critical issues such as quality. A recent report by the National Economic Development Council (NEDO, 1985) estimated the potential for further cost savings amounting to at least £6 bn a year, particularly in respect to scrap, re-working, inspection and the costs of dealing with customer complaints - but in addition the sales value of UK goods could rise by as much as 20%. Whilst the benefits of quality circles (so long as they are pursued thoroughly and consistently) have also been demonstrated in a wide range of industries (Crosby, 1979), it would appear that UK management in industries other than the vehicles sector has often been even slower in responding to such developments. Whilst in Japan such programmes are ubiquitous and have generally been on-going for over a decade, in the UK such programmes are still fairly rare and over 71% over those programmes that have now been instituted have been running for 3 years or less (Industrial Society, 1987). Furthermore, whereas coverage is estimated to have reached some 48% for the engineering and vehicles sectors, coverage for other sectors such as construction, distribution, hotels, transport, communications, banking, finance and services appears to average only about 4%. Employee involvement though was cited as the main benefit to derive from quality circles by over five times the number of respondents citing quality itself.

The main impediments to the successful implementation of such improvement programmes were found to be first, the attitudes of those involved in operational areas, particularly those of managers themselves, and second, (though actually slightly less important) their skills and training. Whilst UK managers have successfully utilised their much stronger negotiating position to end strikes and to re-assert their right to manage, there are few signs of their entering into the more positive longer-term employee relationship, characteristic of countries such as Germany and Japan. A recent survey of the construction industry for example noted that managers generally felt less personal loyalty towards employees than that felt by employees towards their companies. This situation has inevitably undermined the morale and motivation of those who work in operational areas. Anecdotal evidence suggests that UK managerial styles have even toughened.

The attitude of UK management to training was described in one recent study (*Sunday Times*, 1986b) as frequently 'ramboesque', and even positively antipathetic by stark contrast with Germany, Japan and also America. More than half of British companies made no provision for management training, a figure rising to 75% for smaller firms (NEDO, 1987). A recent British Institute of Management survey of production managers revealed (*Sunday Times*, 1987a):

* Just over half (50.5%) of respondents started work at the age of 17 or younger
* Less than half (40.3%) had a degree
* Some 36.6% started work on the shop floor
* About one quarter (24.6%) had served in the production function for 20 years. Most had very limited experience of working in other functions.
* Considerable dissatisfaction was expressed with relations between sales and marketing, costing, research and development, and design.

Poor performance in relation to maintenance, highlighted in recent surveys by Works Management magazine, appears to reflect a similar lack of attention to operational details. Whilst most UK companies complained about the lack of any proper planned maintenance policy, about two thirds surveyed in 1985 still operated a mend-it-when-it-breaks policy, a figure roughly the same as two years previously. About half of factory managers complained that their maintenance departments lacked the necessary spare parts. This figure is significantly worse than that revealed in 1983. Poor training and poor pay (a quarter of companies medium-sized manufacturing paid maintenance managers less than £10,000 a year) were also a problem.

At board level, UK companies would still seem to treat detailed operational and technological areas as of lesser strategic importance. With median board-level salaries of £24,100, production and engineering came bottom of the league table in a recent survey of executive pay (Monks Publications, 1987), and compared with salaries of £30,000 for finance and planning; £27,500 for administration and secretarial; and £26,900 for sales and marketing.

Many of these issues are not new, but the factors which have accentuated their impact in the case of vehicle components are also likely to have a similar effect in other industries. For vehicle component companies the rationalisation of industries on an increasingly international basis has proved to be a severe test of the effectiveness of their strategic thinking. The effect particularly after 1979 of customers' moves to exploiting the full benefits of international procurement, combined with programmes aimed at radically reducing supplier numbers, has been to cull weaker participants. At the corporate level, this has led to companies either disappearing, pulling out hurt or simply being absorbed by more powerful rivals; from the viewpoint of Britain's national competitiveness this has meant loss of market share in home and international markets, and the emergence of more or less irreversible gaps in the industry's overall supply capability, reflected in a diminishing trade position. It can be argued both at the corporate and at the national level that such a retreat out of areas of intensifying competition does not unduly matter, and that there is anyway a case for moving into more attractive activities. Yet it is clear that other markets, even those less competitive and more immediately profitable, are moving in the same direction under the influence of similar forces. Facing up directly to such intensifying competition is not something that can be indefinitely postponed: the sooner positive and necessary adjustments are made the less ground will be lost in the meantime. This has particular implications for the role of operational areas, since competing internationally would seem to call for a quantum leap in terms of the British capability in this respect.

The trend to international procurement and to sharp reductions in supplier numbers is not unique to the vehicle industry. Similar industries such as agricultural machinery and tractors followed suit rapidly after 1980. Other industries' distinctive characteristics have merely postponed similar developments. The market for railway equipment is more sheltered because of differences in national specifications and standards but by 1986 similar trends were beginning to make a real impact on suppliers. Many of the issues encountered by vehicle components companies' in the face of internationalisation particularly after 1979 will also strike chords among those in other quite different industries such as chemicals and textiles, and the process of international rationalisation is now under way in areas such as publishing and even many service sector activities previously insulated (the Big Bang in respect to financial services being a notable example).

Internationalisation has implications for companies' overall strategic positioning. Again vehicle component suppliers are not the only UK companies to have found themselves caught out of position, through over-relying on volume orientated strategies, and through failing to re-focus resources more sharply so as to have any chance against powerful international rivals. Widespread misdirection of scarce investment resources has already resulted. Other examples just after 1979 would include BSC in steel, ICI and other major UK chemical companies such as Shell, Allied Colloids, British Vita and Laporte, and Courtaulds in textiles. Most of these companies have subsequently had to shift to more customerised speciality segments, just as has happened in the case of vehicle components.

There are depressingly few sectors where UK companies have gone out to become world players in a truly competitive sense (or even full-blooded players within Europe which is generally the immediate priority). Those most notable would include aerospace (British Aerospace), aero-engines (Rolls-Royce), defence electronics (Marconi), chemicals (ICI), pharmaceuticals (Glasco, ICI, Wellcome, Beecham, Smith and Nephew, Fisons and Boots) and oil (BP). Even here there are points of vulnerability. Britain's position in commercial (as opposed to military) aircraft is relatively weak and there is concern over the future position in space activity (*Financial Times*, 1988a). Rolls Royce still looks vulnerable as against GEC, and Pratt and Witney in the USA (*Financial Times*, 1987h). The cancellation of GEC's airborne early warning project and the award of the contract to Boeing of the USA perhaps illustrates points of concern within defence electronics. Nevertheless it would be encouraging to see more

British companies positively adapting their strategies so as to achieve positions of world leadership in the way that ICI has done in paints for example, following its recent international acquisitions programme.

A comprehensive study (Stopford and Turner, 1985) of British multinationals warned that many were failing to respond to internationalisation, a phenomenon which it was argued was taking place in industry after industry. Rather than fighting aggressively to become world leaders in their industries, as was the case with most Japanese and many US companies, 'far too many of the largest British firms have been content to settle among the followers ... or to seek niches that may not be defensible'. Yet any position short of leadership, the study warned, 'promises ultimate failure'. Too many UK multinationals were small by their industries' international standards. Any aspirations towards world leadership were hindered by the diversion of scarce investment resources, away from technology, into unrelated portfolio opportunities, and by an undue emphasis on short-term financial results. Foreign investment resources in areas such as services, managed on a 'local-for-local' basis would be of less long-term benefit to Britain than they would be in technology-driven industries. UK companies such as GEC also ran risks in relying too heavily on financially orientated acquisition strategies, whilst diverting funds away from fundamental investment in better product design. In traditional sectors, UK companies were failing to utilise technology so as to achieve regeneration in the same way as German pump manufacturers for example; but their position was found to be even weaker in the newer, more highly research intensive industries. Too many British companies were still under the illusion that they were technological leaders, and even when research was successful benefits were frequently dissipated, either through business strategies lacking in international coherence or through a lack of more detailed operational planning, as exemplified by EMI and Sinclair. Moreover, having had to retreat in area after area, UK companies have found themselves further handicapped by a ruined domestic base and a consequent loss of volume.

There are still grounds for such fears. Britain has an

impressive record on overall investments overseas. Between 1980 and 1985 Britain's net assets more than doubled from about $40 bn to $90 bn, a record only surpassed by Japan whose net overseas assets soared from only $10 bn to $130 bn over the same period *(Financial Times*, 1986b). However, only part of this represents corporate investments, and even here many UK companies are opting for the portfolio attractions of unrelated acquisitions in the USA, rather than for moves reinforcing somewhat fragile competitive positions, particularly in continental Europe (confirming fears expressed by Constable, 1986). UK companies' spending on US acquisitions more than doubled during 1987 to $2.9 bn *(Financial Times*, 1988b), major purchasers being conglomerates such as Hanson Trust.

The pulp and paper industry provides a recent illustration of greater aggressiveness being displayed by overseas multinationals. Over a third of the sixty or so producers in Britain are foreign-owned, and Scandinavian and North American companies are now increasing their UK investments. Unilever for example has just sold Thames Board, its last remaining UK paper business to Iggesund of Sweden *(Financial Times*, 1988c), and, likewise, Wiggins Teape has recently sold two paper businesses to the US group James River. Such decisions reflect a reluctance to invest. Tom Wilder, Chairman of Bowater UK, argues that such foreign takeovers are at least 'better than being starved of capital', a problem he sees as endemic within the UK industry. Similar considerations also applied in TI's recent sale of its Raleigh bicycle business (representing just under half of all UK bike sales) to an American consortium *(Financial Times*, 1987n). The real problem here is that so few UK companies are balancing defensive moves with their own positive international strategies, supported by investment and acquisitions where necessary.

The financial orientation of British companies presents similar problems in the domestic appliance industry. Electrolux of Sweden's recent takeover of Thorn-EMI operations now gives it for the first time a UK manufacturing base and some 20 to 25% of the domestic market *(Financial Times*, 1987o) and there is no British company than can remotely match it in international terms. UK domestic appliance manufacturers have emphasised short-term profitability, by concentrating on niche markets whilst retreating from fast-growing sectors such as microwave ovens. GEC Hotpoint, the only indigenous full range appliance manufacturer, has been consistently among the most profitable in Europe (*Financial Times*, 1987p); but whilst it has performed well in more traditional domestic market segments, it still hesitates to venture in force across the channel. Geoff Steven, their Managing Director, takes the view that 'Exporting is fine if your products do not require service' (*Financial Times*, 1987p).

The same pattern is repeated in more research intensive sectors such as electronics, computers and information technology more generally. Sir James Blythe, until recently Plessey's Managing Director, has warned that UK electronics companies' niche strategies aimed at maximising short-run profitability have frequently relinquished any hopes of their becoming genuine world players (*Financial Times*, 1987q). In concentrating on relatively protected sectors of the domestic market, they have progressively abandoned other important areas. In the critical area of semi-conductors, in spite of some success by Ferranti and Plessey, UK production is fragmented and confined to only a few narrow market segments; not one UK company figures among the top 10 suppliers, whilst 48% of this world market in 1987 was claimed by more aggressive Japanese manufacturers (*Financial Times*, 1988d). British companies have virtually surrendered to foreign-owned companies (who are often supported by substantial local manufacturing operations) in consumer electronics areas such as televisions, sound and video, and there are none remotely comparable with say the Dutch company Philips. Philips' UK Chairman Anton Poot has put the problem squarely 'Britain is not sufficiently invested on a world scale' (*Financial Times*, 1988d).

Despite Britain's early start in the fast growing computer market, ICL Britain's only substantial world competitor has less than 20% of the large mainframe market and could be vulnerable, should an anticipated shake-out take place in the industry (*Financial Times*, 1987r);

Amstrad on the other hand has minimal UK assembly. Similarly in telecommunications, where Britain has moved from a trading surplus in the early 1980s to a deficit of £216 m in 1986 (*Financial Times*, 1987r), there is no British company to compare with Ericsson. British Telecom looks vulnerable even in the domestic market in the wake of liberalisation, as do many of its suppliers. Britain is not keeping pace with the fast growing area of information technology more generally. Taking the broader definition of information technology so as to include computers, industrial, medical and office equipment, this represents only 6.5% of UK manufactured output compared with over 16% in both Japan and the USA. The trade position which in 1970 was roughly in balance, fell to a deficit of £600m in 1980, and in 1986 it plunged yet more sharply to a deficit of some £2 bn (*Financial Times*, 1987r).

In the absence of moves by British companies to a much more international orientation, the gradual disappearance of entire sectors (noted in Chapter 1) would still appear to be continuing. UK shipbuilding, whose decline (almost to the point of disappearance) can be traced to problems similar to those experienced in the vehicle component industry (*Financial Times*, 1986c) , seems set for further decline. British Shipbuilders' position looks weak internationally, and few of the other remaining UK yards look likely to survive even in the more protected domestic defence market. The argument that decline in traditional manufacturing sectors is to an extent inevitable and will necessarily be offset if companies move towards a greater service orientation is dangerous in two respects. First, so far it is generally manufacturers which have been in the vanguard of internationalisation, but as many areas even on the services side also become exposed, it is quite possible they may encounter very similar problems of adaptation. Second, sectors are so highly interdependent (assemblers and component manufacturers being a good illustration), that decline in one sector inevitably reinforces decline in another. Internationalisation now has an equal effect on merchant shipping, which represents the service side of this business; but even moving away from the manufacturing side, UK prospects are scarcely any healthier here. Garry Runciman, President of the General Council of British Shipping has recently warned 'If nothing is done, the UK-owned and registered fleet will by 1995 have shrunk to almost total insignificance, except for one or two specialist areas' *(Financial Times*, 1986d). At some point it is essential to cut in on this reinforcing spiral of competitive decline with more positive strategies.

Faced with internationalisation UK companies must focus their strategies more tightly so as to be able to afford the overseas resources they will require to complement core operations at home. What they need, but in general now lack, is good distribution networks and local manufacturing support overseas. Even in mainland Europe it is naive to imagine that more than modest market shares can be achieved in the absence of such support, and without a reasonable share of those larger international markets UK companies remain chronically handicapped by relatively low output volumes and vulnerable, as international competition relentlessly intensifies.

So long as British companies are pursuing their own aggressive strategies and are gaining their fair share of the larger international cake, it will then not matter if overseas multinationals play an increasing role in Britain. Indeed given that such involvement is to some extent the inevitable consequence of internationalisation, it is important that the country maintain a positive strategy for ensuring that Britain remains a competitive base from the viewpoint of multinationals generally. Britain has many natural assets, not least its language and educated workforce, but it is important to maintain a broad based strategy. Retaining the more competitive real exchange rate, particularly against the deutsch mark is the first priority and it is important that the increased recognition of this problem, shown by the Government more recently in its economic policy, continue. On the other hand there is some danger that Britain's increased attractiveness as a manufacturing base recently depends too exclusively on somewhat capricious exchange rate movements. The European Management Forum's annual scoreboard, which is based more comprehensively on some 340 criteria of competitiveness, in 1986 ranked Britain at only 15 out of 22 industrially advanced OECD countries *(Financial*

Times, 1986e). We should take note of the factors underlying the competitiveness of rival countries. Japan has returned to the top of the league due particularly to lower inflation (double weighted on this scoreboard), its high proportion of profits to national income, its national savings ratio and its low real interest rates. The USA and Germany ranked second and fourth respectively. Britain's competitiveness had actually lost the small gains it had achieved a year earlier, and a particular criticism was that 'British industry was over-specialised on low-value products bringing it increasingly into competition with the Third World.'

Another answer lies in British companies radically adapting so that they become even more internationally orientated (in a broader organisational sense) than rivals, rather than less so, which is frequently still the case. A recent study (*Financial Times*, 1987s) comparing Scandinavian companies, who have long borne the same handicap of a poor domestic base, attributed their success in international markets to a more emphatic international orientation. Compared with British companies' frequently rather limited exporting mentality, Swedish companies showed greater evidence of a global perspective in their strategic thinking and their awareness of the issue at all levels of management: 'It is often the first thing that managers will raise when asked about future challenges.' In contrast, 'in most of the British organisations we have talked to the issue of internationalisation does not figure strongly in managers talk.' Other European countries, according to a recent survey by International Management were also increasing their commitment to doing business abroad. 'This includes, for example, efforts to foster a global corporate image, involvement in international alliances, sourcing more components from foreign firms, and expanding production abroad.'

Nor is the need for a greater international orientation confined to large or multinational companies. Smaller companies' more limited resources may restrict them to exporting, but even here an exhaustive survey by the British Overseas Trade Board has recently revealed huge, as yet untapped, potential (*Financial Times*, 1987t). Only half of the 12,000 firms with turnover of between £1 m and £10 m did any exporting at all, and only one third - or 2,000 - of these were 'active' exporters in the sense of having a thought-out strategy for selling abroad and having exports representing more than 15% of total sales. The report further argued that Britain could increase its exports by £5.2 bn a year, if the 4,000 'passive' exporters - which responded to foreign orders but had no strategic plan - could be persuaded to become more active. Small companies such as Railex Systems, faced with a domestic market that had declined some 40%, have found attacking continental European markets to be the only solution.

There is in conclusion a remarkable degree of congruency between the experiences of UK vehicle component manufacturers 'examined under the microscope', and the broader experiences of British businesses in respect to the specific themes explored in this study. Whilst many UK vehicle components manufacturers have found themselves in the vanguard of internationalisation, clearly the same phenomenon is spreading to other sectors and other UK businesses are increasingly having to accommodate to the same intense pressures.

As with vehicle components, although there has been a considerable improvement in Britain's overall performance recently, the competitive position in relation to rivals looks much more vulnerable on closer inspection. The three key weaknesses which remain in the case of vehicle component manufacture also seem to apply more generally: an inadequate level of investment and technological development, inadequate attention to basic operational matters, and an inadequate response to internationalism.

7
Restoring Competitiveness

Whether or not these first signs of Britain fighting back mark the beginning of a genuine recovery in world markets will depend critically upon whether lessons, so painfully wrought over the last few years, become accepted and acted upon. This final chapter reviews those principles of competitiveness more fully elaborated in Chapter 2, so as to develop the concept of competitiveness and to highlight what yet remains to be changed.

The framework outlined in Chapter 2 is shown again in Figure 7.1 though slightly amended to highlight the issue of 'generalism', which would seem to have contributed significantly to Britain's problems, particularly in the past. By generalism I am referring to the tendency to over rely on rules of thumb of general applicability without adequately taking into account the more specific context and circumstances encountered by particular economies or businesses. Such superficiality of approach has two consequences. One is that even those issues which are of more general importance (economic choices and so on) are inappropriately addressed; the other consequence is that more detailed issues (such as 'mere' operational matters) become dangerously neglected. In Britain's case this phenomenon of generalism has proved so pervasive and damaging, that it would seem necessary to advance some 'concept of competitiveness' as a reminder that any sustained performance improvement is contingent upon a *penetrative* analysis of *all* those issues outlined in Figure 7.1, including those *detailed* contextually determined issues no matter how seemingly mundane.

Figure 7.1: Principles fundamental to achieving competitiveness.

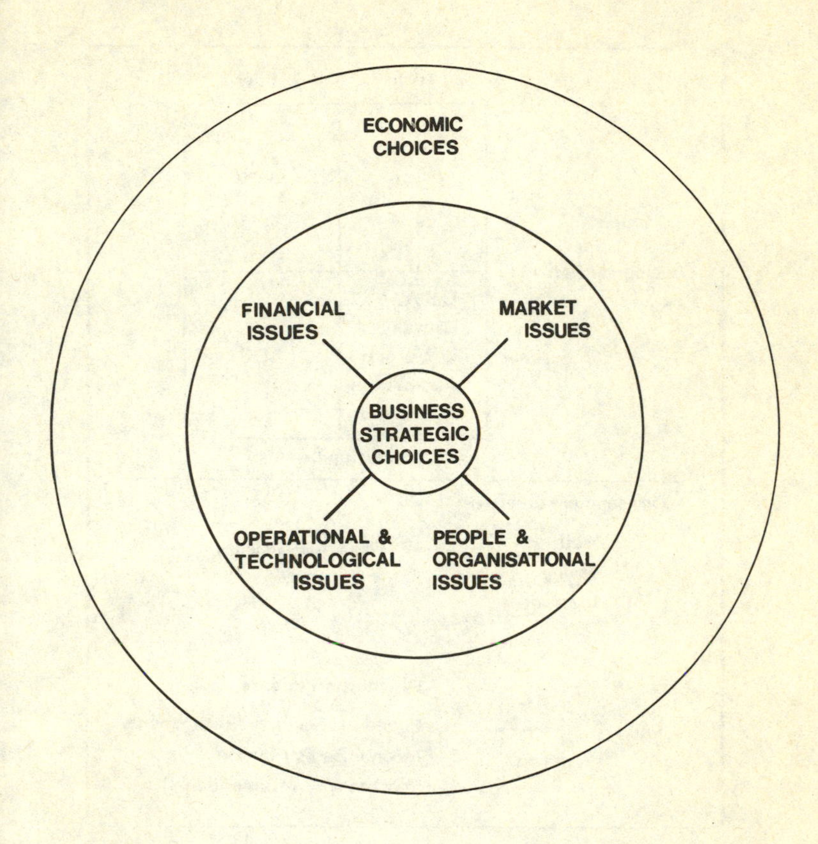

Economic Choices

It was argued in Chapter 2 that the primary economic choice affecting future competitiveness was people's willingness to forego maximum immediate opportunities for consumption so as to make room for higher profits and investment. In terms of Scott and Lodge (1985)'s classification, Britain historically has been distribution rather than development orientated, as represented by the lower left hand quadrant in Figure 7.2.

Figure 7.2: Country-strategy matrix

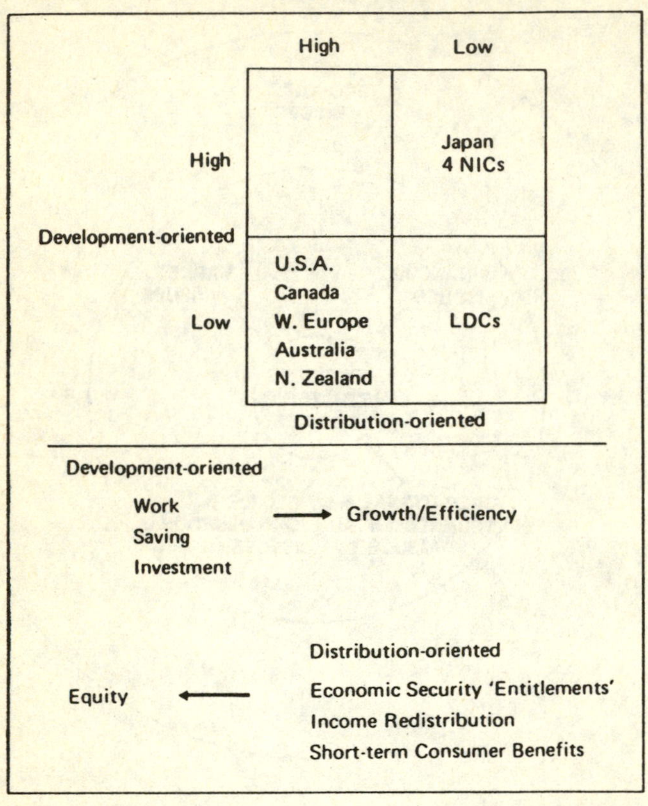

Source: Bruce Scott and George Lodge, *U.S. Competitiveness in the World Economy*, Harvard Business School Press, Boston, esp. pp. 124–127 (1985).

Since 1979 there has been some shift towards the right hand side of this diagram, reflecting less emphasis on equity, redistribution and security 'entitlements'. Yet the emphasis on short-term consumer benefits remains as strong as ever, and levels of savings and investment are still critically insufficient. If it is to match outstanding rivals such as Japan, Britain also needs to move upwards in Figure 7.2 towards the top right hand quadrant.

As discussed in Chapter 2, undue demands for immediate improvements in living standards have a number of interrelated effects all of which contribute to a loss of competitiveness. In a closed economy the direct distributional effect is lower long-term profitability, but an equally important indirect effect is that lower net savings lead to high real interest rates, increasing a company's cost of capital. These two factors taken together determine whether companies will be in a financial position to sustain future growth or whether they will be forced to trim back their activities causing reductions in output and employment. High levels of unemployment in Britain, particularly in relation to rivals such as Japan, suggest that real wage pressure is still having an unnecessarily damaging effect on competitiveness, as has indeed been evidenced in this study. In an open trading economy such as Britain an important second order effect of real wage pressure is the less obvious real exchange rate effect, determining wage levels relative to international rivals. This has critically affected the international competitiveness of internationally exposed sectors such as vehicle components, evidenced in this study, another obvious example being ICI's experience of this same phenomenon particularly in 1980. Some improvement in this situation during the 1980s has contributed to some restoration of competitiveness, but as has been argued there is still a long way to go and only limited recognition of the dangers inherent in allowing an unduly high real exchange rate.

Although the Government can and should provide a lead in warning against the danger of unduly high real wage demands, its influence has tended historically to be either marginal or temporary. The distribution of profits versus wages in total value added is primarily a matter of negotiation between employers and employees (and union representatives). Sadly this issue has become so politicised that despite enormous unemployment, few trade unions are prepared to recognise publicly any trade-off between their wage demands (expressed in real terms) and future competitiveness, which in turn determines companies' capabilities to provide employment. On the other hand, having increased its own pay substantially, UK management seems extremely reluctant certainly in comparison with the USA, to hold down real wage pressure so as to exploit the benefits of an under-utilised labour market. Management has demonstrated little leadership in this direction. UK managerial salaries during 1988 for example are expected to rise some 10% compared with inflation at approximately 4%, clearly undermining the credibility of any tougher negotiating stance. Nor are there yet signs of any broader consensus in favour of tackling this issue. Politically most opposition parties still seek to outbid the Government in terms of their electoral offerings, particularly in terms of the consumption of public sector services. At the same time the Government's own position is ambiguous when confronted with real trade offs: though it asserts the importance of lower real wage settlements, one of its over-riding objectives in practice appears to be to place more rather than less spending power in people's pockets through cuts in personal taxation - a goal seemingly shared by most of the electorate. Until there is greater recognition of the trade-offs which influence competitiveness, British businesses will not receive the support they need if they are to keep up with developments now taking place internationally.

To gain sufficient consensus the only politically feasible solution for Britain today would seem to be a massive extension of share ownership making use of tax incentives. Share ownership is still far too narrowly spread to ensure that there is a political body of interest, sufficient to counter-balance pressures for immediate consumption in favour of investing in Britain's longer-term future. Tax incentives in the case of mortgage tax relief succeeded in boosting home ownership to levels ensuring powerful political support, and it would be possible (if contentious) to use the same technique to generate a greater consensus of support for British business. Benefits from subsidising home ownership (essentially another consumption item) are by now encountering diminishing returns; could these be made more selective, some funding contribution would be available for tax incentives on share ownership, and similar powerful political effects would be likely to ensue.

It must of course be recognised that there are limits as to what can be achieved by wage restraint, for the ultimate aim in seeking to restore competitiveness is to provide an economic base capable of sustaining high rather than low living standards. It is clearly not desirable for Britain to initiate the characteristics of less-developed economies (as represented by bottom right hand quadrant of Figure 7.2). In the past over-reliance on declining wages relative to other European rivals merely served to cushion British business from the need to adapt to international competition. Yet today, so long as UK companies respond to the issues discussed later in this chapter rather than becoming complacent once again, they will need all possible support if they are to regain their position in international markets.

More widespread recognition of the necessary trade-offs could lead to more appropriate economic choices and these, though no panacea, would make a valuable contribution in restoring competitiveness. This would also provide the essential context without which policy makers, both at governmental and corporate levels, will find themselves straight-jacketed in their efforts to bring about more positive strategies for recovery; with far less room for manoeuver than is generally recognised, the danger is that policy makers at all levels will otherwise find themselves almost inevitably drawn towards shorter-term, defensive measures.

Economic Policies

Having ducked the real and difficult choices discussed in the last section, Britain has tended to place undue reliance upon broad economic policy prescriptions, which have often exacerbated problems as well as distracting attention away from more underlying issues. The crude experimentalism of British economic policy (by contrast with Germany and Japan) has by now been taken to directionally opposite extremes, but with little success.

At the one extreme excessive stimulation of demand, combined with an over-reliance on substantial devaluation of the currency in 1973, did nothing to secure the longer-term future of the UK vehicle and vehicle components industry (nor I suspect of other industries). Limitations on domestic supply merely resulted in imports almost doubling, providing importers with a firm foothold for future expansion, and the industry has really never recovered from the resultant loss of volume. On the other hand, an excessive curtailment of demand exacerbated by the tightening of monetary and fiscal targets after 1979, combined with a willingness (in the context a desire to control inflation) to allow an unprecedented rise in the real exchange rate, helped undermine the relative international cost position of UK vehicle assemblers, component suppliers and indeed UK manufacturers generally. UK performance was so severely affected, that in many cases the ground that was lost in international markets will never be recovered.

The over-riding preoccupation with targets relating to demand management has also placed heavy constraints on more specific measures aimed at supporting industry. During the 1960s and early 1970s, considerable damage to the vehicle/vehicle components industry resulted from substantial and erratic changes in tax surcharges and hire purchase controls, used as an adjunct to stop-go economic policies. Even today the industry suffers from an additional 10% consumer tax charge, for which there is no longer any justification as has been rightly argued by the House of Commons, Trade and Industry Select Committee (1987). More generally the abolition of 100% first year capital allowances has had the effect of depressing recent levels of investment, at precisely the moment that manufacturers are running up against capacity constraints, and criticisms by customers that they are not investing enough to keep up with rivals overseas.

Sustaining a favourable business environment of course calls for some sensitivity to issues (depending on their severity) such as inflation and the balance of payments, affecting the stability of the economy; yet the Japanese experience suggests that there is scope for a moderate degree of pragmatism. Control over general economic targets such as the money supply and the public sector borrowing requirement is much more relaxed than in Britain (though wild excesses have been avoided); yet paradoxically Japan has performed far better on economic goals such as growth, employment and particularly inflation.

The scope for manoeuver depends to some extent on the

degree of wage restraint, which for Britain remains more of a constraint. The critical factor though is the attention paid in Japan to the development of the supply side of their economy (and I am not referring merely to their labour market). Though reasonably sensitive to macro-economic issues, the Japanese appear to have retained some broader perspective of where their economy is going in the longer-term. This has often involved specifically rejecting the short-termism implicit in a whole range of economic notions. The vehicle and vehicle components industries are a particular example. Had the Japanese not been prepared to subsidise their lame duck industry (as it certainly was for many years after the war), providing general assistance through their Ministry for International Trade and Industry (MITI); had finance been available to the industry, only at the real rates of interest typical of Britain today; had they refused to step in to assist companies such as Mazda which would otherwise have collapsed; had they espoused a naive and doctrinaire purity on free trade (until, that is, their own industry was ready to compete): then this crucial economic sector (like many others) would have been strangled at birth by international competition.

The best that can be hoped for is that Britain will avoid the wilder excesses of demands policy and that greater sensitivity will be exercised in respect of the inflation adjusted exchange rate (particularly in relation to other major European currencies). Since the somewhat extreme situation in 1980, there has been some improvement in both respects contributing to a more favourable business environment, but undue economic dogmatism could again undermine the position. The emphasis needs to shift away from generalist economic prescriptions towards more specific longer-term industrial policies, as indicated by a movement downwards in terms of the overall perspective presented in Figure 7.1.

Industrial Policies

The extreme emphasis placed upon industrial policy by centrally planned economies has scarcely been associated with competitive success, and it would be wrong to exaggerate the scope for industrial policy in restoring competitiveness. MITI's role in assisting vehicle assemblers and suppliers has generally been subtle and catalytic, particularly in recent years. Cruder moves, such as attempts early on to mimic Western policies of industrial rationalisation, by contrast often met with little success; yet MITI has played a powerful coordinating role and has ensured that successive key industrial sectors obtained the necessary support when they most needed it. The evidence from this industry is that a consistent industrial policy, sensitively handled, can produce real benefits.

Industrial policy in Britain has not enjoyed the same degree of consistent support. Politically the voice of business interests carries less weight than in Japan. In the early 1970s one MP having attempted to put forward the interests of his motor industry-based constituency, recalled the then Prime Minister's rebuff 'What's the matter. You've only got a few tin-pot industries in your constituency.' Faced with appallingly difficult business conditions in the early 1980s, the Managing Director of one vehicle component company recalled the then Industry Minister's glib and indeed strategically quite naive response 'Why don't you just make something else?' Even a top exporter such as ICI appears to have met with little additional sympathy. More recently one leader of the Confederation of British Industry was heard lamenting that he would give his right arm to have the political lobby power of the National Union of Farmers.

British civil servants are quite aware that the Department of Trade and Industry ranks well down in the list of departments of standing, a list headed by the Treasury whose interests and expertise relate exclusively to economics and finance. In Japan, MITI carries greater weight, relative to its British counterpart, when coordinating and putting forward the interests of business.

The fact that it lacks a supportive and consistent framework in which to operate, explains in part why the Department of Trade and Industry has failed to achieve any coherent strategic overview of developments facing major British business sectors - a failure starkly revealed, under cross-examination during recent Select Committee hearings in the case of the vehicle components industry (House of Commons, Trade and Industry Committee, p.17):

> Q. 'In which components is most penetration being made, or are you not aware of that? Let us not waste each other's time. If you do not know say so.'
>
> A. 'I do not have that data.'

Such instances led, unsurprisingly, to the permanent secretary concerned being accused of complacency (ibid. p.36).

Such complacency is not confined to the vehicle components industry. Senior DTI officials questioned even more recently by another House of Commons Trade and Industry Committee investigating the UK information technology industry had to confess themselves 'at a loss to explain the UK's huge trade deficit in IT products, which last year (1987) reached £1,839m - up from £444m in 1979', *(Computer Weekly*, 18 Feb. 1988). Again under close questioning they were forced to concede that 'the UK has no strategic aim like Japan's intention that IT contributes 20% of its gross national product by the year 2000', *(Computer Weekly*, 18 Feb. 1988).

A change in attitude and approach is called for, rather than any extension of bureaucracy. The problem is not one of staff numbers: MITI has only three staff dealing exclusively with vehicle components (plus one or two others on related engineering industries), whereas the DTI by comparison employs 11. Nor does the background, training and calibre of individual MITI staff appear to be so very different from their counterparts at the DTI. The problem is that the lack of any overall sense of direction in industrial policy has, far from precluding interventions, actually spawned a whole host of piecemeal and often overlapping projects which have fragmented the efforts of staff at the DTI. Until some more pro-active approach is achieved, British industrial policy is likely to continue to veer between the two extremes of crude interventions on the one hand and negligence on the other.

In conclusion, Britain still needs to address real, albeit

difficult economic choices and it needs to shift away from an unduly generalist approach to policy, so as to become more sensitive to strategic issues facing specific business sectors.

Business Level Strategies

Approaches to business strategy adopted by British companies have been skewed, partly as a result of inappropriate economic choices, towards postures that are still unduly defensive. This has led to a similar problem of 'generalism' at a corporate level: an unwillingness (particularly in the past) to address critical yet intractable problems such as those found in the area of production, complemented by an over-reliance on broad, higher level strategies such as diversification; acquisitions, mergers and industrial consolidation; the pursuit of the economies of size and scope, rather than those of genuine specialisation; and financially orientated strategies based on retrenchment and rationalisation. Competitiveness ultimately hinges upon a more thorough analysis of specific, contextually determined issues, and calls for some sense of entrepreneurial vision, direction and determination.

Finance

The financial orientation of vehicle component suppliers, and indeed other British companies generally, does threaten their competitiveness; but it should also be acknowledged that there are also financial issues which have to be addressed. Britain's economic environment in the years immediately after 1980 placed extreme constraints on vehicle component companies, the majority of whom had no choice but to recognise that they were in a turnaround situation. At that moment it would have been sheer folly to have subsumed the immediate goal of restoring the financial position to an emphasis on market share and market orientation often advocated (see for example Doyle, Saunders and Wong, 1987). Had they done so there is no question that even some of Britain's most powerful companies, GKN for example, would have gone under. The problem was a savage decline in performance, not just for one year but for several years, and very many companies even if not actually liquidated would have found themselves sitting ducks for take-over, had they not at that time moved to a degree of financial orientation that was extreme, even in relative international terms. Companies have little choice but to be sensitive to the context in which they operate, and the importance of the financial function vis-a-vis other policy concerns depends on this context.

In seeking to improve competitiveness it is therefore first important to recognise that over-defensive strategies adopted by British companies are to some extent logical, given the unfavourable business environment which has resulted from having ignored macro-level issues discussed in the last section. Popular criticisms directed at the financial orientation of UK companies (particularly when this leads to unemployment) need to be matched by an equal measure of popular concern to ensure that companies have sufficient resources and incentives to pursue more positive strategies, and some willingness to accept the trade-off in terms of immediate consumption that this entails.

Companies are judged (at peril of being taken over) by earnings per share performances. The sad reality given the British business context is that many looser, financially orientated groupings such as BTR and Hansons have performed better during the entire period 1981-1985 than other companies who have tightened up the focus of their operations and are struggling harder to hold on to their markets (Goold and Campbell, 1987a, p.49). This is not a healthy situation. Competitiveness is determined not by the sort of 'paper growth' which results from companies merely re-shuffling their portfolios, but by organic growth genuinely achieved by the individual business units within the portfolio. On this basis it is disturbing that such profitable strategies in Britain are associated with organic growth rates that were actually negative during the period 1981-85, and much worse than for other companies (Goold and Campbell, 1987a, p.51).

Dealing with this problem requires firstly more

appropriate economic choices, and secondly a change in competition policy. A much more conservative line needs to be taken in allowing unrelated acquisitions which do little to generate organic growth, whilst a relatively more favourable view should be taken of acquisitions where demonstrable synergies exist and where such moves form part of a coherent international competitive strategy. The Monopolies Commission preoccupation with domestic monopoly power has been rendered out of date by internationalisation, though they are probably still right in taking a fairly sceptical view of synergies suggested during takeovers. Yet it seems absurd for them to have turned down GKN's bid for Associated Engineering (to take an example) on the grounds that GKN's technological contributions would be low, but then to accept the later bid from Turner and Newhall, a component company whose products and processes are far less related and whose international competitive performance has been very much weaker.

Even given the UK business environment however, the degree of financial orientation exercised by UK companies still looks unhealthy. Given their predicament in 1980 one may sympathise with the degree of financial orientation adopted, yet one must also question how this position was allowed to arise in the first place. One of the root causes of the performance decline, as has been argued, was the failure to maintain international competitiveness, but this in turn reflected an undue financial orientation sustained over the longer-term. Ironically Japanese suppliers who have consistently placed a much greater emphasis instead on the production function have ultimately come out much better financially. The full cost of undue financial orientation is of course only revealed once competition really begins to intensify, as companies who have not kept up with more positive developments begin to pay the price. Consequential costs of retrenchment through asset write offs and redundancy payments, identified in this study, have been extremely high though often quietly taken 'below the line' in the profit statements of UK companies. Undue financial orientation, if sustained, can thus prove counter-productive and ultimately can even raise questions of survival. Automotive Product's publicly stated strategy for revival (Pears, 1982),for example, was essentially an accountant's prescription for turnaround; but its failure was underlined by its subsequent takeover by BBA, a smaller yet more progressive components which Automotive Products could once have swallowed without discomfort.

British component companies have therefore been seriously handicapped by an unfavourable business environment; but beyond this, as customers such as GM and Ford rightly perceive (House of Commons, Trade and Industry Committee, 1988) is a problem of attitude and approach - mere financial planning is no substitute for an effective business strategy.

Marketing

Given Britain's unfavourable economic environment and the increased importance that this has on occasions afforded to the financial function, there is a danger in simplistically advocating more marketing-led approaches to strategy and organisation, as has sometimes been suggested (see for example Doyle, Saunders and Wong, 1985; Doyle, 1986). On the other hand, this study does bear out some of the longer-term costs associated with market retreat, and such a tendency has exacerbated the problems experienced by many UK companies in attempting to compete internationally from such a poor volume base. Marketing arguments provide a useful reminder of such problems.

Used positively and carefully related to context marketing concepts can deliver useful insights. Strategically many British companies for example have ultimately found their positions damaged as a result of trading customer orientation for the perceived benefits from volume orientation and greater independence. The British industry has been damaged by the weak and distant relationship which has existed between customers and component suppliers; this contrasts sharply with the much closer relationship which has been pivoted in so many of the developments which have led to the rise in Japanese competitiveness. Porter (1980) is right in stressing the potential significance of changing buyer-seller relationships, but this study suggests that it is dangerous to lay too much emphasis in strategy on the search for defensible positions, on the basis of market power. Many larger UK companies enjoyed such benefits for a time, at the expense of their customers, but this has ultimately backfired. Both suppliers and customers are right to move towards closer, longer-term relationships.

It is important to recognise the extent to which the customer base has now become international. Porter (1980) would appear correct in highlighting the danger of companies finding themselves caught strategically out of position. For many UK companies this problem has often come about as a result of internationalisation: competitive strategies which would have made sense had competition remained primarily domestic were rendered incoherent by the subtle transformation to a pattern of competition that is now primarily international in nature.

The level of investment required to keep pace with the competition has increased enormously as a result of internationalisation. If they are to meet the needs of internationally based customers, British companies will have to support their operations overseas to a much greater extent. This requires heavy investment in distribution arrangements and often even overseas manufacturing facilities (especially in continental Europe), and such moves in turn need to be supported by moving to a much more international orientation. Given their relatively weak funding positions, this also calls for much more focused competitive strategies.

Those few companies who have moved decisively in this direction (for example GKN particularly in relation to constant velocity joints) have seen benefits in performance and their underlying competitive positions are substantially more robust. Many on the other hand have been seduced by the more immediate portfolio attractions presented by more or less unrelated diversification moves, but the additional dilution of scarce resources has further undermined their underlying competitive positions and contributed to retreat in the market place.

Once again the UK business environment is partly to blame and there sometimes seems to be a conflict between what is good for companies wishing to restore satisfactory stock exchange ratings, and what is good for Britain's competitiveness. The performance of conglomerate diversifiers such as BTR and Hansons has already been discussed, but the number of UK companies (RHP in ball and rolling bearings for example) that have found it attractive simply to abandon core activities completely, merely to start again with something different, is highly disturbing. The structure of Japanese business by contrast is such that few vehicle component manufacturers would find diversification either an attractive or indeed a feasible option: the result has been much higher levels of competitive commitment. Again the answer, in part, depends upon more appropriate economic choices and tighter controls on unrelated acquisitions.

From this viewpoint superficial interpretation of notions associately with marketing has proved positively unhelpful. The marketing concept itself (Levitt, 1965) contains the suggestion that faced with declining markets companies should redefine their businesses more broadly, so as to reorientate towards newer faster-growing markets instead of merely dissipating further resources on activities whose prospects are perceived as limited. For most companies such a search for growth calls in practice for such a very broad definition of the business, that the obvious corollary becomes one of diversification into areas, offering better immediate growth prospects, but only tenuously related to existing operations.

Evidence from this study suggests that in the long run competitive advantage is a much more important determinant of performance than short-term market growth prospects. Popular (and somewhat 'generalist') strategic notions about the inherent unattractiveness of sunset (as opposed to sunrise) industries would appear to be highly misleading, certainly in the specific context of vehicle component manufacture. The option of unrelated diversification has proved no panacea, whilst within the components sector British companies have actually performed worse in much faster-growing market segments, such as automotive instrumentation. The decline in performance after 1979 coincided not with market decline which by then was more or less complete, but was associated with a loss of international competitiveness. An immediate causal factor was the sharp change in the real exchange rate, but such changes can also work to the benefit of the industry as has happened more recently. Rugman (1987) has argued that superficial notions as to the relative attractions of sunrise versus sunset industries ignore the effect of comparative advantage, which operates strongly via the mechanism of the exchange rate - a point which, for an internationally exposed industry such as vehicle components, has certainly proved important. Longer-term causal factors behind the performance also include a number of other strategic issues (not least in the production area) which have had little to do with market growth.

Over-reliance on strategic prescriptions such as market share (too broadly interpreted) has also proved damaging. Many UK vehicle component companies have pursued economies of scope rather than any genuine specialisation; yet sheer size has in general been negatively correlated with performance. Many have achieved dominance in terms of domestic market share (often through mergers or acquisitions), only to find any potential benefits undermined by internationalisation; and few as has been discussed have achieved any market dominance in more international terms (and this has become a more relevant measure). In fact overall the evidence is that neither growth, nor market share, nor even the absence of technological opportunities, need necessarily preclude high levels of performance provided strategies are coherent and that sufficient managerial attention is paid to their detailed implementation. Many relatively more successful UK component businesses have proved to be classic 'dogs' in strategic portfolio terms. International industry life cycle concepts, broadly interpreted, can also be misleading. Even in low technology vehicle component areas, it is generally advanced rather than low cost countries (with the possible exception of Korea) who have been winning out. Thus imagining that decline in such industries merely represents a sensible decision to pull out of areas that are inevitably doomed would seem to provide a rationalisation for competitive retreat, rather than any accurate portrayal of reality.

Why the marketing concept needs to be replaced by a more genuinely integrative concept of competitiveness

A weakness in the marketing concept, as put forward originally in Levitt (1965) and as elaborated subsequently, is that either it is interpreted so broadly as to include just about everything - can initiatives by Japanese quality groups operating in the production area really be construed as evidence of a marketing led approach? - in which case the concept becomes so general as to be almost meaningless from the viewpoint of determining the correct policy emphasis; or alternatively if it is more narrowly defined, it can actually be rather misleading. Changes in the market place can give rise to strategically critical issues, and these can become of over-riding importance in some fairly extreme circumstances (such as Levitt's (1965) classic example of manufacturers involved in the horse-drawn carriage business at the turn of the century); but strategically critical issues also arise in other functional areas, as has been well borne out in this study.

For any one functional area such as marketing to claim pride of place in respect to the overall approach to either strategy or organisation would seem just as dangerous as becoming unduly financially orientated. Doyle's (1986) argument that British companies need to become marketing-led rather than finance-led, as if we were dealing with a merely two-handed problem, has already been touched on : but it also seems to epitomise the dangerous tendency in Britain to either ignore or downgrade the strategic contribution played by production and technology, quite apart from important 'people' issues. From this viewpoint, Levitt's marketing concept is not altogether satisfactory. Profit does not arise merely from satisfying customers but from doing so on a competitive basis, and this in turn calls for a well rounded integrative approach to strategy, better portrayed by a broader conception of competitiveness as argued here.

Operations and Technology

This study has attempted to highlight in a balanced way

the main principles affecting competitiveness. The discussion so far in this chapter has centred on higher level economic and business strategic issues and has yielded important conclusions. Yet it is only really as we examine more specific operational issues (represented by a further movement downwards in Figure 7.1), that we arrive at the heart of matters which have undermined Britain's competitiveness in the past, and which even today underpin the pre-eminent competitive positions of more successful manufacturers such as the Japanese.

The quality of research and development teams in Britain seemed relatively quite good, surpassing the Japanese (though probably not the Germans) in terms of training, and also in terms of results in several instances. In areas such as automotive instrumentation, where rapid technological advances can be expected to have major competitive implications, the problem for UK suppliers is that the lack of a volume base compounded by an insufficiently international orientation, means that the scale of such R&D efforts is inadequate, given the speed at which internationalisation takes place in such circumstances, and the scale of programmes instituted by global competitors. Thus only relatively few British companies can afford to place much reliance on major R&D breakthroughs in spite of a high degree of natural aptitude. Even where important breakthroughs are achieved, and even where the patent position has been unusually clear such as GKN's position in constant velocity joints up until this year, companies have only a limited time in which to gain international dominance. Achieving this calls for a more comprehensive armoury of skills and resources than is available to all but a minority of UK manufacturers. For most components on the other hand, subtler product and process developments, involving only incremental advances in technology have anyway proven more critical to competitiveness.

After several years of financial constraint, British companies are frequently now behind rivals such as the Germans in terms of having enough new products in the pipeline, and there are many areas where there is no longer any British presence. Priority should be given to any necessary investment as profits recover, but given their position many companies would now be advised to make greater use of collaborative ventures and also of the option of licensing in technology and know-how from overseas manufacturers, not all of whom are in direct competition. Response times should also be helped by investments taking place in information technology such as on computer aided design.

Investment in process technology will also be required, particularly as utilisation levels improve, but companies must take care to avoid the traps which led to much past investment ultimately being wasted. In parallel with an emphasis at the broader strategic level on economies of scale, associated for example with industrial consolidation and rationalisation, there has been a costly tendency in the past to over-rely on the perceived benefits of volume-orientated factories and manufacturing processes.

In cases such as automotive rolling bearings where the benefits from volume are more appreciable, internationalisation of competition has taken place more quickly. As a result, several UK companies attracted by the cost reductions seemingly promised by a volume orientation, have subsequently been forced to retrench in the face of powerful competition from companies able to pursue precisely the same benefits at a more international level. In other cases such as automative forgings the potential benefits from volume are anyway lower. Whilst internationalisation has here had slightly less effect, it has been important enough at the margin, particularly in volume market segments, to cause UK manufacturers to regret such heavy commitments to volume-orientated processes. Most UK manufacturers need, therefore, to emphasise flexible rather than volume-orientated manufacturing processes.

Manufacturers also need to recognise what flexible manufacturing systems really involve; for many appear vulnerable to falling into a second trap, that of relying too heavily on investments in more glamorous technological advances labelled as flexible manufacturing systems. Strides taken by Japanese component manufacturers in terms of being able to deliver genuine flexibility, primarily reflect comprehensive programmes of incremental improvements such as machine change-over times and work flow improvements directed at cutting factory through times; more technologically sophisticated equipment such as robotics have not been in fact much in evidence. Less comprehensive approaches risk creating 'islands of flexibility' of more limited value. Modern flexibly orientated equipment is generally better suited to their needs than volume-orientated process technology, and does also play to their development skills, but unless UK companies get the balance right many will again be disappointed with the returns from their investment. There are already some signs of this.

The main problem for most British component manufacturers is their critically weak performance on the more comprehensive improvement programmes pioneered by Japanese manufacturers, these being directed not only at increased flexibility, but also at productivity and quality. Japan's substantial performance lead, evidenced in this study on all three counts, has yet to be bridged.

The quality of Britain's engineers does not appear to be the main problem. Though Britain could still learn from Germany in this respect (Carr, 1982) my comparisons suggest the formal training and professional development of individual British engineers is almost certainly more thorough than in Japan. It is though easy to underestimate the learning potential of highly motivated engineers in Japan, particularly in the context of life time employment which even in the components sector was surprisingly common: as working groups, the morale of Japanese engineers is higher than in Britain, particularly in areas such as production. A key difficulty is that without the degree of technical support from operational personnel, enjoyed by their counterparts in Japan, British engineers remain swamped by the sheer number of operational improvements needed. Britain lacks strength in depth in operational areas.

Why should this be so, particularly when many Japanese multinationals that have established UK operations have pronounced themselves satisfied with the skills available? Culturally based explanations so far advanced seem unsatisfactory. The culture is certainly distinctive and it may well have contributed to the effectiveness of Japanese working groups, but it has not changed so substantially since the 1950s when Japanese manufacturers suffered to a much greater extent from precisely the same problems as even now plague British manufacturers. The real explanation for differences today lies in the fact that a series of specific change programmes, initiated by management (notably executives such as Taiichi Ohno at Toyota) almost 20 years, ago were almost totally ignored by management in Britain. Even today many UK companies excuse their failure with initiatives such as quality circles on the grounds that after trying them for a couple of years, they found there were snags. There are; but their counterparts were still discovering snags five years after initiating such programmes, and they have continued learning ever since.

An important factor further underpinning this problem is that in Britain, as in the USA, production and quality control systems tend to have substituted control over the status quo, for more positive controls aimed at ensuring real momentum behind a dynamic, longer-term learning process. Some optimisation approaches, which seem logical when viewed from a short-term perspective, have in the longer-term proved counter-productive. Japanese quality programmes for example have hinged on a quite specific rejection of notions such as supposed quality/cost trade-offs, and the same is true of the approach in Germany; similarly their crucial just-in-time programmes reflect the rejection of optimisation techniques such as economic batch quantities. In all these cases a critical step is to recognise that progress will be limited unless there is a willingness to pay a price in terms of short-term disruption.

The distinguishing characteristic of more successful management teams is that they recognised early on that these basic production issues had to be treated as matters of critical strategic importance, requiring where necessary a longer-term perspective and commitment, rather than 'as mere operational matters' to be determined purely at an operational level, under the constraints of a relatively short-term budgetary perspective. Apart from one or two exceptional UK companies (as noted in this study), the general approach to strategy has been superficial: concerned to a far greater extent than their counterparts in Japan with higher level strategic issues, UK management has frequently failed to address with the same resolve these intractable operational issues. An Eastern proverb recalls the fate of a man travelling with his eyes so set on the heavens, that he plunged abruptly into a pool; had he kept his eyes to the ground, the proverb goes, he would have anyway seen the heavens reflected in the pool's surface. Higher level strategic issues do of course merit careful consideration; but had they kept their eyes on such real practicalities at the more basic level, many management teams in Britain would have been far more effective in achieving their higher level corporate objectives, and more defensive strategies wouldn't even need to be on their agenda.

It is not that senior management in Britain are uninterested in such operational matters, but such comprehensive programmes call for strategic vision. Without this element the natural temptation is for incremental improvements to take place on a far more piece-meal and limited basis. The fact that they have so frequently found themselves in the position of 'fire-fighting' such problems in an operational time perspective, must therefore be recognised as a deficiency in their overall strategic approach. Unless this is improved, such situations inevitably become chronic and self-perpetuating.

Top management must also recognise that this is not the sort of strategic problem that can be delegated to corporate planners. Planners can provide excellent help on high level issues such as diversification, but they simply don't possess the organisational levers or the power to make things happen further down the organisation. This calls for top level leadership, and Chief Executives who are really closely involved with what is happening on the shop floor.

People and Organisational Issues

This suggested shift in strategic emphasis raises important 'people' issues, as represented by the final quadrant in Figure 7.1. The problem in essence is that unless British manufacturers restore the morale and motivation of personnel in operational areas, they will not receive the level of support necessary if they are to match rivals such as the Japanese on those programmes identified as critical in the last section.

UK companies generally need to move towards a more production-centred organisational approach, supported by an enhancement of the role and status of the production function in relation to other functional areas such as finance and marketing. Training resources need to be directed first, to improving the quality of UK production management and supervision, which is poor particularly in relation to Germany (Carr, 1982), and second, to providing extensive rather than necessarily in-depth training so as to release the fullest potential of operational personnel more generally. Government initiatives may help, but the emphasis needs to switch so that training becomes a more continuous part of peoples' on-going work experiences: only limited use is made of outside training in Japan.

Top management must also take the initiative in moving towards the much longer-term and constructive relationship with employees, that again has been part and parcel of changes instituted by Japanese management following their own experience of strikes during the early 1950s. Manning levels in UK companies in 1980 were so out of line, that substantial redundancies formed an inevitable part of their turnaround strategies; but with much of the obvious slack now taken up it is important to achieve a positive and participative industrial relations atmosphere. Total employee commitment depends in turn on companies being prepared to place a much higher priority on job-security, and moving at least some way towards a position of life-time employment. Given their still difficult circumstances many companies will argue such moves are unrealistic, but even where this is the case a change in the attitudes of management towards their employees could go a long way in improving the situation.

Harsh circumstances have changed the balance of power. It may well have been essential for management to exploit such a change so as to restore their right to manage. Yet the evidence suggests that many managers have exploited the change, to the extent of adopting even more 'macho' styles, in stark contrast to their more successful counterparts in Germany and Japan. Competitiveness is a long-term problem. Many of the worst features of British work practices in the 1950s, 1960s and 1970s can be traced to the trade union backlash, resulting from unemployment and harsh managerial practices during the 1930s. Managers must recognise that the balance of power will shift back substantially as utilisation levels rise, and as the present imbalance of supply and demand in the labour market begins to moderate. Already skills shortages are beginning to make themselves felt. Just-in-time delivery systems and the greater reliance today on component single sourcing will increase the vulnerability of the vehicle industry to stoppages, as the Ford Strike in January 1988 amply demonstrated. Management must move pre-emptively before the bargaining power shifts to establish more positive relationships and to ward off a potentially more volatile industrial relations atmosphere.

Britain's historically and culturally established class divide was a factor here, noted by both German and Japanese executives. The Japanese to some extent accepted the stereotyping of their employees as workaholics, but countered by pointing out that Britain has much the same expectations of those in managerial and professional classes; the difference is that in Britain a similar degree of workaholism is neither expected nor unsurprisingly always achieved so extensively. Class divisiveness still saps Britain's potential strengths on the shop floor and we must remember that it is in general group consensus, rather than individual prowess, which has contributed to the rise in Japan's competitiveness. The solution rests with leadership at a number of levels, from both sides of the them-and-us divide, though greater awareness of the damage wrought by such problems might help.

What makes progress in this direction all the more pressing is that British industrial relations are on the threshold of a new challenge. The first, now almost surmounted, was the challenge of restoring appropriate manning levels. Yet in view of arguments presented in this study Britain now would seem to face the dual problem of achieving international standards of flexible working practices just as, even in the context of a slightly more buoyant labour market, management nevertheless needs to strive to hold down real wage pressure. Britain will need leadership, both from management and from trade union organisations, and some longer-term vision of industrial relations, if it is not to brook the fence and this second, essential, yet even more challenging revolution is to take place; it is only to be hoped that the cancellation of Ford's new electronics plant at Dundee as a result of the TUC's somewhat ambivalent commitment does not portend the future.

Conclusion

The demise of Britain's competitiveness in the past has reflected a disregard for those key principles outlined in Figure 7.1 and an overly generalist approach to policy issues in the realms of both economic and business management. At a business level, the concept of competitiveness put forward in this chapter should act as a reminder that success hinges not on unbalanced approaches to strategy, whether it be undue financial or marketing orientation, but on a proportionate appreciation of all the main policy issues, together with a much more penetrating analysis of more specific contextually determined issues in areas such as operations and technology. The final less tangible ingredients depends on some renewed sense of entrepreneurial vision and leadership, the latter of course being intricately tied up with the people side of business. Only then will we arrive at a positive strategy for fully restoring Britain's longer-term competitiveness.

Whilst the position has improved in recent years, Britain's progress in terms relative to its major rivals looks more questionable, but things at last are starting to change. Armed with greater understanding of the realities of modern business competition, the financial and human costs, Britain must surely seek to learn from lessons so painfully wrought, so as to escape the myopia which has contributed to decline over the best part of a century, and thereby to ensure that the country is now set on a more positive path for the future.

Bibliography

ABA Research (1984) *The Automotive Report*, ABA Research, Newport, Essex.

ARMC (Automotive Research and Management Consultants) (1984), 'Current relationships between vehicle manufacturers and component suppliers', *International Automotive Review*, 3rd Quarter.

Abell, D.F. and Hammond, J.S. (1979) *Strategic Market Planning: Problems and Analytical Approaches*, Prentice Hall, Englewood, NJ.

Abernathy, W.J. (1978) *The Productivity Dilemma: Roadblock to Innovation in the Automobile Industry*, John Hopkins University Press, Baltimore.

Abernathy, W.J., Clark K.B. and Kantrow A.M. (1981) 'The new industrial competition', *Harvard Business Review*, 59 (5), 68-82.

Abernathy, W.J., Clark, K.B. and Kantrow, A.M. (1983) *Industrial Renaissance : Producing a Competitive Future for America*, Basic Books, New York.

Abernathy, W.J. and Wayne, K. (1974) 'Limits of the learning curve', *Harvard Business Review*, Sept/Oct 1974, 109.

Ackoff, R.L. (1970) *A Concept of Corporate Planning*, Wiley, New York.

Ackoff, R.L. (1981) *Creating the Corporate Future: plan or be planned for*, Wiley, New York.

Adachi, F., Ono, K. and Odaka, K. (1982) *Ancilliary Firm Development in the Japanese Automobile Industry: selected case studies II*, Institute of Economic Research Discussion Paper 42, Jan 1982, Hitotsubashi University, Japan. (See also Ono and Odaka, 1979).

Adair, J. (1985) *Management Decision Making*, Gower, Aldershot, UK.

Allen, G.C. (1979) *The British Disease: A Short Essay on the Nature and Causes of the Nation's Lagging Wealth*, Hobart Paper 67, Institute of Economic Affairs.

Allen, G.C. (1980) *Japan's Economic Policy*, Macmillan, London.

Allison, G.T. (1971) *Essence of Decision Making : Explaining the Cuban Missile Crisis*, Little, Brown, Boston.

Bibliography

Altshuler, A., Anderson, M., Jones, D., Roos, D. and Womack, J. (1984) *The Future of the Automobile: The Report of MIT's International Automobile Program*, George Allen and Unwin, London.

Anderson, M.L. (1981) *The strategic organisation of the Japanese Automobile Groups*, mimeo, Cambridge, Mass, USA.

Andrews, K.R. (1971) *The Concept of Corporate Strategy*, Dow Jones-Irwin, Illinois, USA.

Andrews, K.R. (1984) 'Corporate strategy: the essential intangibles', *McKinsey Quarterly*, Autumn 43-50.

Ansoff, H.I. (1968) *Corporate Strategy: an analytical approach to business policy*, Penguin, London.

Ansoff, H.I (1972) *Twenty Years of Acquisitive Behaviour in America: a comparative study of mergers and acquisitions of US manufacturing firms 1946-1965*, Associated Business Programs.

Appleby, C. (1981) 'The economics of the UK motor car industry and the future of the West Midlands region', *Journal of Industrial Affairs*, vol 9, no. 1, Autummn 1981.

Argenti, J. (1976a) *Systematic Corporate Planning*, Nelson.

Argenti, J. (1976b) *Corporate Collapse: the Causes and the Symptoms*, McGraw Hill, New York.

Argenti, J. (1980) *Practical Corporate Planning*, Allen and Unwin, London.

Ashworth, M.H., Kay, J.A. and Sharpe, T.A.E. (1982) *Differentials between Car Prices in the Unitied Kingdom and Belgium*, Institute of Fiscal Studies Report Series, No. 2.

Bacon, R.W. and Eltis, W.H. (1978) *Britain's Economic Problem: Too Few Producers*, Macmillan, London.

Baden-Fuller, C. and Stopford, J. (1987) 'Global or national? An examination of strategy choice and performance in the European white goods industry', Centre for Business Strategy, London Business School, October 1987.

Bailey, P. and Farmer, D. (1981) *Purchasing Principles and Management*, Pitman, London.

Bank of England (1982) 'British Industry in a Competitive World', *Bank of England Quarterly Bulletin*, Sept 1982, 366-368.

Bannock, G. (1983) 'Does the components industry need radically restructuring', paper presented at Financial Times Conference *The Outlook for Motor Components*, 1-2 June 1983, 35-43.

Barbier, J. P. (1983) *The Automotive Components Industry Study*, WZB Papers, The Science Centre, Berlin. May 1982.

Barclays Review (1983) 'UK Trade in Manufactured Goods', *Barclays Review*, November 1983.

Barnard, C.I. (1972) *The Functions of the Executive*, Harvard University Press.

Barnett, C. (1986) *The Audit of War : The Illusion and Reality of Britain as a Great Nation*, Macmillan, London.

Barnett, C. (1986) 'The truth of British decline', *Management Today*, April 1986.

Beckerman, W. (Ed) (1979) *Slow Growth in Britain: Causes and Consequences*, Oxford University Press, Oxford.

Begg, I. and Rhodes, J. (1982) 'Will British Industry Recover', *Cambridge Economic Policy Review, 8 (1), 18-26.*

Bessant, J., Jones, D.T., Lamming, R.L. and Pollard, A. (1984) *The West Midlands Automobile Components Industry: Recent Changes and Future Prospects*, West Midlands County Council Economic and Development Unit Sector Report No 4, West Midlands County Council.

Beynon, H. (1984) *Working for Ford*, Penguin, London.

Bhaskar, K. (1979) *Future of the UK Motor Industry*, Kogan Page, London.

Bhaskar, K. (1980) *Future of the World Motor Industry*, Kogan Page, London.

Bhaskar, K (1984) *The UK and European Motor Industry*, vols 1 and 2, R. Sewell, Bath, UK.

Bibeault, D.B. (1981) *Corporate Turnaround*, McGraw-Hill, New York.

Blackaby, F.T. (Ed) (1979) *De-Industrialisation*, National Institute for Economic and Social Research - Proceedings, Heinemann, London.

Boston Consulting Group (1968) *Perspectives on Experience*, BCG.

Boston Consulting Group, (1975) *Strategy Alternatives for the British Motorcycle Industry*, HMSO, London.

British Automotive Parts Council (1980) *The Threat to the United Kingdom Motor Vehicle Components Industry*, British Automotive Parts Council, Nottingham.

British Institute of Management (1986) *Managing Manufacturing Operations in the UK, 1975-1985*, BIM

Brittan, S. (1984a) 'The "be more competitive" fallacy', *Financial Times*, 23 Feb.

Brittan, S. (1984b) 'The problem of competitiveness', *Financial Times*, 12 Jan., 23.

Brooke, M.Z. and Remmers, H.L. (Eds) (1977) *The International Firm. A study of management across frontiers - trade and investment*, Pitman, London.

Brown, C.J.F. and Sherriff, T.D. (1978) *De-Industrialisation in the U.K. : background statistics*, NIESR Discussion Paper No 23.

Brown, W. (1977) 'Britain's design gap' *Management Today*, Dec.

Buchele, R.B. (1962) 'How to Evaluate a Firm', *California Management Review*, Autumn, 5.

Burns, T. and Stalker, G.M. (1966) *The Management of Innovation*, Tavistock, London.

Buzzell, R.D., Gale, B.T. and Sultan, R.G.M. (1975) 'Market share: key to profitability', *Harvard Business Review*, Jan/Feb.

Cadbury, A. (1981) 'Big business must devolve to a human scale to survive', *Guardian*, 9 Sept.

Carr, C.H. (1982) *A Comparison of British and German Companies Producing Components for the Automotive Industry*, unpublished paper, Lord Rootes Fund research, University of Warwick.

Carr, C.H. (1985) *The Competitiveness of UK Vehicle Component Manufacturers*, unpublished doctoral thesis, University of Warwick

Carr, C.H. (1988) 'Strategy alternatives for vehicle component manufacturers', *Long Range Planning*, 21(4), 86-97.

Caves, R.E. and Krause, L.B. (1980) *Britain's Economic Performance*, The Brookings Institute.

Central Policy Review Staff (1975) *The Future of the British Car Industry*, HMSO, London.

Chandler, A.D. (1962) *Strategy and Structure: Chapters in the History of the American Industrial Enterprise*, MIT Press, Cambridge, Mass.

Channon, D.F. (1971) *Norcros Ltd*, Manchester Business School case study no. MBS/BP/4. Manchester Business School.

Channon, D.F. (1973) *The Strategy and Structure of British Enterprise*, Macmillan, USA.

Chew, E. (1984) 'The future of international specialisation in the automotive industry' *Policy Studies*, 5 (1).

Coate, M.B. (1983) 'Pitfalls in portfolio planning', *Long Range Planning*, 16 (3), 47-56.

Coates, D. and Millard, J. (Eds) (1986) *Economic Decline of Modern Britain : The Debate Between Left and Right*, Harvester.

Connell, D. (1979) *The UK's Performance in Export Markets: Some Empirical Data from International Trade Data*, NEDO, London.

Constable, J. (1986) 'Diversification as a factor in UK industrial policy', *Long Range Planning*, 19 (1), 52-60.

Cox, A. (1984) 'Managing for stable productivity', paper presented at Coventry Polytechnic/BIM supper conference, Coventry 22 May 1984.

Crosby, P (1979) *Quality is Free*, McGraw Hill, New York.

DRI Europe (1987) *World Automotive Forecast Report*, London, DRI International Automotive Services, Nov.

Dahrendorf, R. (1982) *On Britain*, BBC, London.

Daly, A., Hitchens, D.M.W.N. and Wagner, K. (1985) 'Productivity, machinery and skills in a sample of British and German manufacturing plants' *National Institute Economic Review*, Feb.

Davidson, W.H. and Haspeslaugh, P. (1982) 'Shaping a global product organisation', *Harvard Business Review*, 60 (4), 125-133.

Davies, S.W. and Caves, R.E. (1987) *Britain's Productivity Gap*, Cambridge University Press, Cambridge.

Department of Industry (1976) *The British Motor Industry*, Cmnd 6377, Jan 1976, HMSO, London.

Department of Trade and Industry (1987) *Identifying Areas of Strength and Excellence in UK Technology*, DTI, London.

Dodwell Marketing Consultants (1983) *The Structure of the Japanese Auto Parts Industry*, Dodwell, Tokyo.

Donaldson and Lorsch (1984) *Decision Making at the Top*, Basic Books, New York.

Dornbusch and Fischer (1980) 'Sterling and the external balance', in R.E. Caves and L.B. Krause (Eds) *Britain's Economic Performance*, The Brookings Institute.

Doyle, P. (1986) 'Marketing and Britain's Industrial Competitiveness,' inaugural lecture given at the University of Warwick, 9 Dec, Coventry.

Doyle, P., Saunders, J. and Wong, V. (1985) *A Comparative Investigation of Japanese Marketing Strategies in the British Market*, University of Bradford, Bradford.

Doz, Y. (1985) 'Automobiles: shifts in international competitiveness' in Hochmuth, M. and Davidson, W. (Eds) *Revitalizing American Industry*, Ballinger.

Drucker, P. (1968) *The Practice of Management*, Pan, London.

Dunnet, P. (1980) *The Decline of the British Motor Industry. The Effects of Government Policy 1945-1979*, Croom Helm, London.

Dyas, G.P. and Thanheiser, H.T. (1976) *The Emerging European Enterprise: Strategy and Structure in French and German Industry*, Macmillan, London.

EIU *Motor Business*, Economist Intelligence Unit, London.

EIU/Kearney Consultants (1982) *The Automotive Industry of the 1980's: Strategy for Revival*, Proceedings of a conference held in Birmingham, 21 Oct.

Eatwell, J. (1982) *Whatever Happened to Britain*, BBC, Duckworth.

Edwardes, M. (1983) *Back from the Brink*, Collins, London.

Ellsworth, R.R. (1983) 'Subordinate financial policy to corporate strategy', *Harvard Business Review*, 61 (6), 170-183.

Engineering Council (1983) *Appraising the Technical and Commercial Aspects of a Manufacturing Company*, The Engineering Council, London.

Eurofinance *The Components Industry in the UK*, S.Straw.

Euromonitor (1984) 'Car replacement parts', *Market Research Great Britain*, Sept 1984.

European Management Forum (1980) *Report on the Competitiveness of European Industry*, Geneva, European Management Forum.

Expenditure Committee (1975) *The Motor Vehicle Industry*, 14th Report Session 1974/75, vols 1,2 and 3, House of Commons, HMSO, London.

Financial Times Conferences (1983) *The Outlook for Motor Components*, Geneva 1-2 June 1983.

Financial Times Conferences (1984) *The World Automotive Aftermarket Conference*, London 5 March 1984.

Financial Times (1985) 'False dawn in the new world of manufacturing', 14 May.

Financial Times (1986a) 'UK science and industry : a dangerously deep divide', 18 Dec.

Financial Times (1986b) 'Flexible marriage of old and new', 30 May.

Financial Times (1986c) 'Japan's overseas assets increased 7.4% last year', 28 May.

Financial Times (1986d) 'UK shipbuilding. The seeds of decline', Correlli Barnet, 28 May.

Financial Times (1986e) 'Merchant fleet set to dwindle away by 1990s', 30 May.

Financial Times (1986f) 'Japanese regain lead in table of competitiveness', 18 Aug.

Financial Times (1987a) 'Manufacturing output growing at an annual 6.5%', 16 Dec.

Financial Times (1987b) 'The need to bolster confidence', 30 Nov.

Financial Times (1987c) 'Why British Steel looks on itself as a sunburst industry', 8 July.

Financial Times (1987d) 'Production machine makers battle for a return to the big league', 25 Nov.

Financial Times (1987e) 'German kitchens wipe the floor', 19 Nov.

Financial Times (1987f) 'Now the heat is on in the kitchen', 20 Nov.

Financial Times (1987g) 'BT productivity among the lowest in the West', 19 Oct.

Financial Times (1987h) 'Flying but maybe not high enough', 8 April.

Financial Times (1987i) 'Healthier but the scars still show', 1 April.

Financial Times (1987j) 'Why research is in the driving seat', 2 June.

Financial Times (1987k) 'Scram and scramble - the Japanese style', 19 June.

Financial Times (1987l) 'The ideas machine which drives Japan' 29 May.

Financial Times (1987n) 'TI selling Raleigh for £18m to US led consortium', 22 Jan.

Financial Times (1987o) 'Electrolux burdens of a global viewpoint', 14 April.

Financial Times (1987p) 'UK domestic appliance industry. Dilemmas of the final cycle', 22 May.

Financial Times (1987q) 'Electronics sector shows plenty of profit but not enough growth', 24 Nov.

Financial Times (1987r) 'A program of shake-up and shake-out', 30 Dec.

Financial Times (1987s) 'Why Scandinavians are classic exporters', 14 Jan.

Financial Times (1987t) 'Huge potential for overseas sales', 14 Jan.

Financial Times (1988a) 'UK industrial prospects', Survey, 4 Jan.

Financial Times (1988b) 'Spending on US acquisitions "doubled"', 13 Jan.

Financial Times (1988c) 'Maggie Urry shows how UK mills can give producers a valuable foothold in the EEC', 13 Jan.

Financial Times (1988d) 'Japanese lead in the chips market', 4 Jan.

Finlay, P. (1981) 'Overmanning: Germany v. Britain' *Management Today*, Aug, 43-47.

Follett, M.P. (1973) *Dynamic Administration. The Collected Papers of Mary Parker Follett*, Fox, E.M. and Urwick, L. (Eds), Pitman, London.

Fores, M., Sorge, A. and Lawrence, P. (1978) 'Why Germany produces better' *Management Today*, Nov.

Foster, G (1984) 'Turner and Newall's tough turnabout' *Management Today*, July, 58-65.

Franks, J.R., Broyles, J.E. and Hecht, M.J. (1977) 'An industrial study of the profitability of mergers in the UK', *Journal of Finance*, 32, 1513-1525.

Fujimoto, T. (1983) *Technology Systems: a comparison of the US and Japanese Automobile Industries*, unpublished paper, Mitsubishi Research Institute, Tokyo. March.

Garvin, D.A. (1983) 'Quality on the line', *Harvard Business Review*, 61 (5), 64-76.

Ghemawat, P. (1985) 'Building strategy on the experience curve', *Harvard Business Review* March-April, 143-149.

Gill, R.W.T. and Lockyer, K.G. (1979) *The Career Development of the Production Manager in British Industry*, British Institute of Management.

Glaser, B.G. and Strauss, A.L. (1967) *The Discovery of Grounded Theory: Strategies for Qualitative Research*, Aldine Publishing Co, Chicago.

Glyn, A.J and Harrison, J. (1980) *The British Economic Disaster*. Pluto Press, London.

Goldsmith, W. and Clutterbuck, R. (1984) *The Winning Streak. Britain's Top Companies Reveal their Formulas for Success*, Weidenfeld and Nicholson, London.

Goold, M. and Campbell, A. (1987a) 'Managing diversity: strategy and control in diversified British companies', *Long Range Planning*, 20 (5), 42-52.

Goold, M. and Campbell, A. (1987b) *Strategies and Styles: The Role of the Centre in Managing Diversified Corporations*, Basil Blackwell, Oxford.

Grant, R.M. (1985) 'Adjusting to low-cost import competition : business strategy and firm performance in the UK cutlery industry', Centre for Business Strategy, London Business School, *Working Paper Series*, Dec.

Hague, D. and Wilkinson, G. (1983) *The IRC - An Experiment in Industrial Intervention*, George Allen and Unwin, London.

Hall, W.H. (1980) 'Survival strategies in a hostile environment', *Harvard Business Review*, Sept-Oct, 75-85.

Hamel, G. and Prahalad, C.K. (1985) 'Do you really have a global strategy?' *Harvard Business Review*, July-August, 139-148.

Hamermesh, R.G. and White, R.E. (1984) 'Manage beyond portfolio analysis', *Harvard Business Review*, 64 (1), 103-109.

Hampden-Turner, C. (1983) *Gentlemen and Tradesmen : The Values of Economic Catastrophe*, Routledge and Kegan Paul, London.

Hannah, L. (1983) *The Rise of the Corporate Economy*, Methuen, London.

Harrigan, K.R. (1980) *Strategies for Declining Businesses*, Lexington.

Harrigan, K.R. and Porter, M.E. (1983) 'End-game strategies for declining industries', *Harvard Business Review*, 61 (4), 111-121.

Hartley, J. (1980) 'Home truths to knock the myth that Japan's industry is unbeatable', *Engineer*, 20 Nov.

Hartley, J. (1985) *Fighting the Recession in Manufacturing*, IFS.

Harvey-Jones, J. (1988) *Making It Happen*, Collins, London.

Haspeslaugh, P. (1982) 'Portfolio planning: uses and limits', *Harvard Business Review*, 60 (1), 58-74.

Hawkins, C. (1983) *Britain's Economic Future: An Immediate Programme for Revival*, Wheatsheaf Books.

Hayes, R.H. (1981) 'Why Japanese factories work', *Harvard Business Review*, 59 (4), 56-67.

Hayes, R.H. and Abernathy, W.J. (1980) 'Managing our way to economic decline', *Harvard Business Review*, July.

Hayes, R.H. and Garvin, D.A. (1982) 'Managing as if tomorrow mattered', *Harvard Business Review*, 60 (3), 70-80.

Hayes, R.H. and Wheelwright, S.C. (1985) 'Competing through manufacturing', *Harvard Business Review*, 85 (1), 99-109.

Hedley, B. (1976) 'A Fundamental Approach to Strategy Development', *Long Range Planning*, Dec., 2-11.

Hedley, B. (1977) 'Strategy and the Business Portfolio', *Long Range Planning*, 10 (1), 9-16.

Heller, R (1987) *The State of Industry. Can Britain Make it?* BBC Books, London.

Hill, T. (1983) *Production / Operations Management*, Prentice Hall International, Englewood, NJ.

Hofstede, G. (1984) *Culture's Consequences : International Differences in Work-Related Values*, Sage Publications, London.

Hogarty, T.F. (1970) 'The profitability of corporate mergers', *Journal of Business*, 43, 317-325.

Horngren, C.T. (1984) *Introduction to Financial Accounting*, Prentice-Hall, Englewood, NJ.

Houlden, B.T. (1985) 'Audit your company's strategic management capability' *Management Today*, Autumn.

House of Commons (1987) *'The UK Components Industry', Third Report from the Trade and Industry Committee Session 1986-87. Report, Proceedings of the Committee, Minutes of Evidence and Appendices.*

House of Lords (1985) 'Report from the Select Committee on Overseas Trade Vol. I-III', HMSO, London.

Hout, T., Porter, M.E. and Rudden, E. (1982) 'How global companies win out', *Harvard Business Review*, 60 (5), 98- 109.

Hutber, P. (Ed) (1978) *What's Wrong With Britain?*, Sphere Books, London.

Hutton, S.P and Lawrence, P.A. (1978) *Production Managers in Britain and Germany*, Interim Report September 1978, University of Southampton.

Hutton, S.P. and Lawrence, P.A. (1979) *The Work of Production Managers: Case Studies at Manufacturing Companies in West Germany*, Interim Report October 1979, University of Southampton.

Hutton, S.P. and Lawrence, P.A. (1981) *German Engineers. The Anatomy of a Profession*, Oxford University Press, Oxford.

Industrial Society (1987) *Quality Circles : a Survey on Quality Circles in the UK*, Industrial Society New Series No 5.

Institution of Mechanical Engineers (1981) *Third International Conference on Automotive Electronics*, London, 20-23 Oct 1981, Conference Publications 1981 · 10, Mechanical Engineering Publications.

Inter Company Comparisons (annual) *Business Ratio Report: Drop Forgers*, ICC, London.

Inter Company Comparisons (annual) *Business Ratio Report: Motor Components*, ICC, London.

Inter Company Comparisons (1981) *Motor Components Industry in Europe (E,F,G)*, ICC, London.

Jacobs, J. (1961) *The Death and Life of Great American Cities*, Random House, USA.

JAPIA/JETRO (1979) *A Review of the Japanese Automotive Parts Industry*, JAPIA/JETRO, Tokyo.

Jauch, L.R. and Wilson, H.K. (1979) 'A strategic perspective for make or buy', *Long Range Planning*, 12 (6), 56-62.

Johnson, C. (1982) *MITI and the Japanese Miracle. The Growth of Industrial Policy 1925-1975*, Stanford University Press, Stanford.

Johnson, G. and Scholes, K. (1984) *Exploring Corporate Strategy*, Prentice Hall, Englewood, NJ.

Johnson, J. (1987) *Strategic Change and the Management Process*, Blackwell , Oxford.

Jones, D.T. (1981) *Maturity and Crisis in the European Car Industry*, Sussex European Papers No 8, Brighton, European Research Centre, University of Sussex.

Jones, D.T. (1983) 'Technology and the UK automobile industry', *Lloyds Bank Review*, No148, April, 14-27.

Jones, D.T. (1985a) 'How cars came back', *Management Today*, April, 71ff.

Jones, D.T. (1985b) *The import threat to the UK car industry*, Science Policy Research Unit, University of Sussex.

Kaldor, N. (1966) *Causes of the Slow Rate of Economic Growth in the United Kingdom*, Cambridge University Press, Cambridge.

Kanter, R.M. (1984) *The Change Masters*, Allen and Unwin, London.

Kantrow, A.M. (Ed) (1983) *Survival Strategies for American Industry*, Harvard Business Review, USA, John Wiley and Sons, New York.

Kaplan, R.S. (1984) 'Yesterday's accounting undermines production', *Harvard Business Review*, 62 (4), 95-102.

Kearney/EIU (1984) *World Automotive Conference: Productivity and Opportunity*, proceedings of conference held in Birmingham, 18 Oct.

Keegan, W. (1984) *Mrs Thatcher's Economic Experiment*, Allen Lane, London.

Kendrick, R. (1983) 'What is competitiveness?: a framework for further development', paper prepared for the ESRC workshop on *Competitiveness and Regeneration of British Industry*, London, 18-19 Nov.

Kennedy, P. (1981) *The Realities behind Diplomacy. Background influences on British External Policy 1865 - 1980*, Fontana Paperbacks.

Keynes, J.M. (1936) *The General Theory of Employment, Interest and Money*,Macmillan Papermac, London.

Kiechel, W III (1981) 'The decline of the experience curve', *Fortune*, 5 Oct., 139ff.

Killing, J.P. (1982) 'How to make a global joint venture work', *Harvard Business Review*, 60 (3), 120-128.

Kitching, J. (1967) 'Why do mergers miscarry?', *Harvard Business Review*, 45 (6), 84-101.

Knapp, R. (former MD, Timken Europe) (1984) 'Why industry must not let itself be talked into decline', *Engineer*, 8 Nov., 22-24.

Knibb, B. (1982) 'OE supplier prospects in Western Europe during the 1980's', in EIU/Kearney *The Automotive Industry of the 1980's: Strategy for Revival*.

Knibb, B. (1983) 'What component manufacturers will be required to do in order to survive to 1990', paper presented to Financial Times Conference *The Outlook for Motor Components*, 1-2 June, 121-130.

Kono, T. (1982) 'Japanese management philosophy: can it be exported?', *Long Range Planning*, 15 (3), 90-103.

Koshiro, K. (1983) *Personnel Planning, Technological Changes, And Outsourcing in the Japanese Automobile Industry*, Discussion Paper 83-3, Center for International Trade Studies, Yokahama National University, Yokahama, Japan.

Laing, S. and Rahn, R. (1983) *Foreign Outsourcing by US Auto Manufacturers*, Special Report No. 151, EIU.

Lamming, R. (1986) 'For Better or Worse' - Technical Change and Buyer-Supplier Relationships in the UK Automotive Components Industry, in C. Voss (Ed.), IFS, *Managing Advanced Manufacturing Technology*.

Layard, R. (1986) *How to Beat Unemployment*, Oxford University Press, Oxford.

Leibenstein, H. (1966) 'Allocative Efficiency vs 'X- Efficiency'', *American Economic review*, LVI (3), 392-415.

Lethbridge, D.G. (Ed) (1976) *Government and Industry Relationships*, The Lubbock Memorial Lectures, 1974/1975, Pergamon, Oxford.

Levitt, T. (1965) 'Exploit the product life cycle', *Harvard Business Review*, Nov-Dec, 81-94.

Levitt, T. (1965) 'Marketing Myopia', *Harvard Business Review*, July.

Levitt, T. (1983) 'The globalisation of markets', *Harvard Business Review*, 61 (3), 92-103.

Levitt, T. (1983) *The Marketing Imagination*, Collier Macmillan, London.

Limprecht, J.A. and Hayes, R.H. (1982) 'Germany's world class manufacturers', *Harvard Business Review*, 60 (6), 137-146.

Lorenz, C. (1986) *The Design Dimension*, Basil Blackwell, Oxford.

Lowry, A.T. (1986) 'A financial appraisal of the West European motor industry', *Automotive Special Report* No. 4, EIU, Economist Publications.

Lowry, T. (1987) 'The South Korean motor industry : A rerun of Japan?', *Economist Intelligence Unit*

Lubatkin, M. (1983) 'Mergers and the performance of the acquiring firm', *Academy of Management Review*, 8 (2), 218.

Luffman, G. and Reed, R. (1985) 'The giant company comeback', *Management Today*, June.

Luffman, G.A. and Reed, R. (1984) *Strategy and Performance of British Industry 1970-80*, Macmillan, London.

McArdle, J and Jones, D.T. (1984) *The Japanese Automobile Challenge. Competitive Strategies for the 1980's in Europe and the United States*, James McArdle and Associates.

McGregor, D. (1960) *The Human Side of Enterprise*, McGraw-Hill, New York.

Mace, M.L. and Montgomery, G.C. (1969) 'The chief executive's role in acquisition planning', in Harvey, J.L. and Newgarden, A. (Eds) *Management Guides to Mergers and Acquisitions*, Wiley-Interscience, New York, 6.

Magaziner, I.C. and Hout, T.M. (1980) *Japanese Industrial Policy*, No 585, Policy Studies Institute.

Mant, A. (1979) *The Rise and Fall of the British Manager*, Pan, London.

Marfels, C. (1983) *Concentration, competition and competitiveness in the automobile industries and in the automotive components industries of the European Community*, Commission of the European Communities, Luxembourg.

Market Studies International (undated) *UK Trade Development Survey of Motor Components*, Inter Company Comparisons Ltd.

Mathias, P. (1969) *The First Industrial Nation*, Methuen, London.

Meeks, G. (1977) *Disappointing Marriage: A Study of Gains from Merger*, Occasional Paper 51, Cambridge University Press, London.

Melrose-Woodman, J. (1978) *Profile of the British Manager*, Management Survery Report No 38, British Institute of Management.

Middleton, P. (1984) 'In praise of life cycles', *Financial Times*, 12 Nov., 12.

Miles, R.E. and Snow, C.C. (1978) *Organizational Strategy, Structure and Process*, McGraw-Hill, New York.

Millman, A.F. (1983) 'Improving the international competitiveness of the UK by licensing product technology from overseas', *Institute of*

Marketing Professional Papers, No.6, December.

Mintzberg, H. (1973) *The Nature of Managerial Work*, Harper and Row, New York.

Mintzberg, H. (1979) *The Structuring of Organisations*, Prentice Hall, Englewood, NJ.

Monks Publications (1987) *Monks Guide to Board and Senior Management Remuneration in Companies with* £1m-£20m Turnover, Saffron Walden

Monopolies Commission (1967) *Guest Keen and Nettlefolds Ltd and Birfield Ltd: a report on the merger*, Cmnd 3186, HMSO, London.

Moritani, M. (1982) *Japanese Technology. Getting the Best for the Least*, Simul Press, Tokyo.

Motor Industry Research Unit (In Association with University of East Anglia) (1988) *A Single European Market - An Automotive Perspective*

Motoring Which? (1978) 'A survey of prices of car spare parts', April.

NADFS (1980) *Buyers Guide to the Drop Forgings Industry*, National Association of Drop Forgers and Stampers

NADFS *Economic and Statistical Review*, National Association of Drop Forgers and Stampers NEDO (1978) *Telecommunications: annual progress report by the SWP*, NEDO, HMSO, London.

NEDO (1981) *Toolmaking: A comparison of UK and West German companies*, HMSO, London.

NEDO (1984) *Competence and Competition: Training and education in the Federal Republic of Germany, the United States and Japan*, HMSO, London.

NEDO (1984) *Crisis facing UK information technology*, HMSO, London.

NEDO (1985) *Quality and Value for Money*, HMSO, London.

NEDO (1987a) *British Industrial Performance and International Competitiveness Over Recent Years*, HMSO, London.

NEDO (1987b) *The Making of Managers: A report on management, education, training and development in the United States, West Germany, France, Japan and the UK*, HMSO, London.

New, C. (1976) *Managing Manufacturing Operations*, Management Survey Report No 35, British Institute of Management.

Newbould, G.D. and Luffman, G.A. (1978) *Successful Business Strategies*, Gower Press, Aldershot.

Newton, J.K. (1983) 'Market share - key to higher profitability?', *Long Range Planning*, 16 (1), 37-41.

Nind, P. (1985) 'British Industry and the anti-intellectual tradition', *Royal Society for the Encouragement of the Arts, Manufactures and Commerce*, April, No.5345, vol. cxxxiii.

O'Callaghan, J.M. (1986) *Managerial Characteristics and Financial Performance of Construction Companies*, Construction Study Unit Project 86/13, Brunel University, MSc Dissertation, Dec.

OECD (1983) *Long term Outlook for the World Automobile Industry*, OECD, Paris.

Ohlin, B. (1933) *Interregional International Trade*, Harvard University Press, Cambridge, MA.

Ohmae, K. (1982) *The Mind of the Strategist: The Art of Japanese Business*, McGraw-Hill, New York.

Ono, K. and Odaka, K. (1979) *Ancilliary Firm Development in the Japanese Automobile Industry - selected case studies I*, Institute of Economic Research Discussion Paper No. 24, Dec 1979, Hitotsubashi University, Japan. (See also Adachi, F., Ono, K. and Odaka, K.).

Oxford Economic Research Associates (1982) *Productivity: is there a new realism?*, Oxford Economic Research Associates, Oxford.

Panic, M. and Rahjan, A.H (1971) *Product Changes in Industrial Countries' Trade 1955-68*, NEDO Monograph no. 2, NEDO, London.

Paribus Quilter Securities (1987) *The French Engineering Industry*, London.

Parker, R.C. (1985) *Going for Growth : Technological Innovation in Manufacturing Industries*, Wiley, London.

Pascale, R.T. and Athos, A.G. (1982) *The Art of Japanese Management*, Penguin, London.

Patel, P. and Pavitt, K. (1987) 'The elements of Britain's technological competitiveness', *National Economic Review*, November, 72-82.

Pavitt, K. (Ed.) (1980) *Technical Change and British Economic Performance*, Science Policy Research Unit, Sussex University, Macmillan Press, London.

Pears, G. (1982) *Automotive Products: strategy for survival*, lecture given at Coventry Polytechnic, 18 May.

Peters, T.J. and Waterman, R.H. (1984) *In Search of Excellence: Lessons from America's Best-Run Companies*, Harper and Row, New York.

Pettigrew, A. (1985) *The Awakening Giant: Continuity and Change in ICI*, Blackwell, Oxford.

Pettigrew, A., Whipp, R. and Rosenfeld, R. (1986) 'Competitiveness and the management of strategic change processes : a research agenda', *Conference on Competitiveness of European Industry : Country Policies and Company Strategies*, European Institute for Advanced Studies in Management, Brussels, Feb.

Phillips, R. and Way, A. (1979) *The West European Automotive Industry: Where now in the 1980's?*, Special Report No. 77, EIU.

Piore, M.J. and Sabel, C.F. (1984) *The Second Industrial Divide*, Basic Books, New York.

Planning and Research Systems (1987) *World Engine Study*, London

Pollard, S. (1982) *The Wasting of the British Economy*, Croom Helm, London.

Porter, M.E. (1980) *Competitive Strategy: Techniques for Analysing Industries and Competitors*, Free Press, New York.

Porter, M.E. (1985) *Competitive Advantage: Creating and Sustaining Superior Performance*, Collier Macmillan/Free Press, New York.

Porter, M.E. (Ed.) (1986) *Competition in Global Industries*, Harvard Business School Press, Boston, Mass.

Porter, M.E. (1987) 'From competitive advantage to corporate strategy', *Harvard Business Review*, May-June.

Prais, S.J. (Ed.) (1981) *Productivity and Industrial Structure*, NIESR, Cambridge University Press, Cambridge.

Pratten, C.F. (1976a) *A Comparison of the Performance of Swedish and UK Companies*, Occasional Paper 47, Cambridge University Press, Cambridge.

Pratten, C.F. (1976b) *Labour Productivity Differentials within International Companies*, Occasional Paper 50, Cambridge University Press,

Cambridge.

Price Commission (1979) *Prices, Costs and Margins in the Manufacture and Distribution of Car Parts*, HMSO, London.

Prior, P.J. (1977) *Leadership is Not a Bowler Hat*, David and Charles, London.

Quinn, J.B. (1980) *Strategies for Change: Logical Incrementalism*, Irwin, Illinois, USA.

Rafferty, J. (1987) 'Exit barriers and strategic position in declining markets' *Long Range Planning*, 20 (2), 86-91.

Redden, D.A. (1975) *West Midlands Automotive Component Industry*, Small Business Centre, University of Aston.

Rhys, D.G. (1972) *The Motor Industry: an Economic Survey*, Butterworth, London.

Rhys, D.G. (1977) 'The position and behaviour of smaller firms in the motor industry', *Management Decision*, November.

Robinson, S.J.Q. (1986) 'Strategies for declining industrial markets', *Long Range Planning*, 19 (2), 72-78.

Robinson, S.J.Q., Hichens, R.E. and Wade, D.P. (1978) 'The directional policy matrix - tool for strategic planning', *Long Range Planning*, 11 (3), 8-16.

Rothberg, R.R. (Ed) (1981) *Corporate Strategy and Product Innovation*, Free Press, New York.

Rugman, A.M. (1987) 'Strategies for national competitiveness', *Long Range Planning*, 20 (3), 92-97.

Rumelt, R.P. (1974) *Strategy, Structure and Economic Performance*, Harvard University Press, Cambridge, MA.

Ryder Report (1975) *British Leyland: The Next Decade*, 1974- 75, HMSO, London.

SMMT *Monthly Statistical Review*

SMMT *Motor Industry of Great Britain*, Society of Motor Manufacturers and Traders, London.

Sainsbury, D. (1981) *Government and Industry: A New Partnership*, Fabian Society, London.

Saunders, G. (1984) *The Committed Organisation: How to Develop Companies to Compete Successfully in the 1990's*, Gower Press, Aldershot.

Schoeffler, S., Buzzell, R.D. and Heany, D.F. (1974) 'Impact of strategic planning on profit performance', *Harvard Business Review*, March-April, 137-145.

Schonberger, R.T. (1983) *Japanese Manufacturing Techniques: Nine Hidden Lessons in Simplicity*, Collier Macmillan, London.

Scott, B. and Lodge, B. (1985) *U.S. Competitiveness in the World Economy*, Harvard Business School Press, Boston.

Scott Ward, J. (1981) *The Changing Face of the UK Automotive Components Industry*, Special Report No. 91, EIU.

Scott Ward, J. and Way, A. (1987) *The UK Passenger Car Market*, Economist Intelligence Unit, London.

Scott, W.E (1966) 'Activation theory and task design', *Organisational Behaviour and Human Performance*, September, 3-30.

Select Committee Inquiry (1975) *Future of the British Car Industry*, House of Commons, London.

Shimokawa, K. (1982a) 'Development of the supplier relationship in Japan - its innovation and production flexibility', paper presented at

International Policy Forum of the MIT Future of the Automobile Program, 16- 20 May, Hakone, Japan.

Shimokawa, K. (1982b) 'Entrepreneurship and the social environment change in the Japanese automobile industry: on the key elements of high productivity and innovation', *Social Science Information*, 21, 2.

Shimokawa, K. (1982c) 'The structure of the Japanese auto parts industry and its contribution to automotive process innovation', paper presented at *International Policy Forum of the MIT Future of the Automobile Program*, 16-20 May, Hakone, Japan.

Shingo, S. (1981) *Study of Toyota Production System from Industrial Engineering Viewpoint*, Japanese Management Association, Tokyo.

Singh, A.(1972) *Takeovers*, University of Cambridge Department of Applied Economics, Monograph 19, Cambridge University Press, Cambridge.

Singh, A. (1977) 'UK industry and the world economy: a case of deindustrialisation', *Cambridge Journal of Economics*, 1 (2), 113-36.

Skinner, W.G. (1978) *Manufacturing in the Corporate Strategy*, Wiley, London.

Skinner, W.G. (1985) *Manufacturing: the formidable competitive weapon*, Wiley, London.

Slatter, S. (1984) *Corporate Recovery: Successful Turnaround Strategies and their Implementation*, Penguin, London.

Sleigh, P.A.L. (1988) *The UK Automotive Components Industry : An Assessment of its Structure, Changes, Foreign Participation, Product Aeas, Sales and Performance Prospects*, Economist Intelligence Unit.

Smith, A. (1970) *Adam Smith. The Wealth of Nations. Books I - III*, A. Skinner (Ed.), Penguin, London.

Smith, K. (1984) *The British Economic Crisis. Its Past and Future*, Penguin, London.

Spurrell, D.J. (1980) 'Business strategy in the United Kingdom - the challenge from abroad', *National Westminster Bank Quarterly Review*, August.

Stopford, J. and Turner, L. (1985) *Britain and the Multinationals*, Wiley, London.

Stout, D.K. (1977) *International Price Competitiveness, Non- Price Factors and Export Performance*, NEDO, London.

Stuart Jones, C. (1982) *Successful Management of Acquisitions*, Derek Beatie, London.

Sunday Times (1986a) 'France works wonders in bricks and mortars', 25 May.

Sunday Times (1986b) 'That ole-style boss just keeps bungling along', 1 June.

Sunday Times (1987) 'Self taught bosses reluctant to learn', Keith Lockyer, 27 Oct.

Sunday Times (1988) 'Outrunning the recession', 3 Jan.

Symonds, J. and Newell, A. (1985) *Wages and Employment in the OECD Countries*, London School of Economics, Centre for Labour Economics, Disscussion Paper 219.

Terry, P.T. (1979) *An Investigation of Some Cultural Determinants of English Organisational Behaviour*, unpublished dissertation, University of Bath, Bath.

The Times (1983) 'Britain overtakes West German steel productivity', 4 July.

Thirwell, A.P. (1982) 'De-industrialisation in the UK', *Lloyd's Bank Review*, 144, 22-37.

Thomas, R.E. (1981) *The Government of Business*, 2nd edn, Philip Allan, Oxford.

Toyne, B., Arpan, J.S., Ricks, D.A., Shimp, D.A., Barnett, A. (1984) *The Global Textile Industry*, World Industry Studies 2, I. Walter (Ed.), George Allen and Unwin, London.

Toyota (undated) *Japan's high labor productivity and its causes as seen in Toyota*, Fact Series No.II, Sheet No.1, Toyota.

Tugendat, C. (1978) *The Multinationals*, Penguin, London.

Turner, G. (1984) 'How GKN plans now', *Long Range Planning*, 17 (5), 12-17.

Twiss, B.C. (1980) *Managing Technological Innovation*, 3rd ed, Longman, London.

United States General Accounting Office, Comptroller General (1982) *Industrial Policy: Japan's Flexible Approach*, US General Accounting Office, Gaithersbury, 23 June.

Uttal, B. (1982) 'Texas Instruments regroups', *Fortune*, 9 Aug, 40-45.

Van de Vliet, A. (1987) 'Britain's biggest fall behind', *Management Today*, Feb.

Van Rossum, R. (1984) 'Is the theory of life cycles pure humbug?', *Financial Times*, 23 Aug, 14.

Voss, C.A. (1983) 'Japanese manufacturing management practices in the UK', *International Journal of Operations Management*, 4,2.

Wagstaff, I. (1986) *The UK market for replacement parts : Automotive Special Report No. 5*, Economist Intellience Unit.

Walton, R.E. (1985) 'From control to commitment in the workplace', *Harvard Business Review*, March-April 1985, no.2, 77-84.

Ward, D. (1982) 'Why plastics will not be taking a back seat', *Engineer*, 3 June, 21-29.

Way, A. (1978) *The UK Automotive Components Industry*, Special Report No. 58, EIU.

Webb, S. and Webb, B. (1932) *Methods of Social Study*, Longmans, London.

Weber, H. (1982) *Problems when introducing Kanban in UK*, paper presented at Technology Transfer TTI (UK) Ltd conference, London, 8 June.

Weiss, A. (1984) 'Simple truths of Japanese manufacturing', *Harvard Business Review*, 62 (4), 119-126.

Wells, S.J. (1964) *British Export Performance*, Cambridge University Press, Cambridge.

Whipp, R. and Clark, P. (1986) *Innovation and the Auto Industry*, Frances Pinter, London.

Wheelwright, S.C. (1981) 'Japan - where operations really are strategic', *Harvard Business Review*, 59 (4), 67-75.

Whitbread, C. (1983) *The Car of the Future in Western Europe*, Special Report No. 155, EIU.

White, M. and Trevor, M. (1983) *Under Japanese Management: the Experience of British Workers*, Heinemann/Gower, London.

Whittington, G. (1980) 'The profitability and size of United Kingdom companies 1960-1974', *Journal of Industrial Economics*, xxviii (4), June.

Whyte, W.F. (1943) *Street Corner Society*, University of Chicago Press, Chicago.

Wickens, P. (1987) *The Road to Nissan*, Macmillan, London.

Wiener, M.J. (1981) *English Culture and the Decline of the Industrial Spirit 1850 - 1980*, Cambridge University Press, Cambridge.

Williams, K., Williams, J. and Haslam, C. (1987) *The Breakdown of Austin Rover: a Case Study in the Failure of Business Strategy and Industrial Policy*, Berg Publishers, London.

Williams, K., Williams, J. and Thomas, D. (1983) *Why are the British Bad at Manufacturing?*, Routledge & Kegan Paul, London.

Woo, C.Y. (1984) 'Market share leadership - not always so good', *Harvard Business Review*, 62 (1), 50-56.

Woo, C.Y. and Cooper, A.C. (1982) 'The surprising case for low market share', *Harvard Business Review*, 60 (6), 106- 114.

Yin, R.K. (1984) *Case Study Research : Design and Methods*, Sage, Beverley Hills.

Index